Aida Slavic & Maria Inês Cordeiro (eds.)

Classification & Authority Control
Expanding Resource Discovery

Classification & Authority Control

Expanding Resource Discovery

Proceedings of the International UDC Seminar
29-30 October 2015
Lisbon, Portugal

Organized by
UDC Consortium, The Hague

Edited by
Aida Slavic & Maria Inês Cordeiro

ERGON VERLAG

Bibliographic information published by the Deutsche Nationalbibliothek
The Deutsche Nationalbibliothek lists this publication in the
Deutsche Nationalbibliografie; detailed bibliographic data are available in the
Internet at http://dnb.d-nb.de.

www.ergon-verlag.de

ISBN 978-3-95650-124-1

Contents

Posters - Short papers

Preface

These proceedings record most of the talks and posters presented at the International UDC Seminar 2015 "*Classification & Authority Control: Expanding Resource Discovery*" that took place on 29-30 October in Lisbon (Portugal). The programme of the Seminar comprised nineteen talks and six poster presentations. The proceedings contain thirteen full papers and four short poster papers which are presented in the sequence in which they appear in the programme. Some of the invited talks were not accompanied with a full paper and they are presented in this volume with abstracts and short biographies of the speakers.

"*Classification & Authority Control: Expanding Resource Discovery*" is the fifth in a series of International UDC Seminars organized by the UDC Consortium. This Seminar is hosted by the National Library of Portugal, in Lisbon. The last seminar entitled "*Classification & Visualization: Interfaces to Knowledge*" took place on 24-25 October 2013 in the National Library of the Netherlands, in The Hague. Earlier seminars, also in The Hague, were "*Classification & Ontology: Formal Approaches & Access to Knowledge*", 19-20 September 2011, "*Classification at a Crossroads*", 29-30 October 2009 and *Information Access for the Global Community*", 4-5 June 2007. The UDC Consortium which organizes these conferences is a consortium of publishers that owns and manages the Universal Decimal Classification (UDC). The goal of the UDC Seminars is to advance research into bibliographic classifications and enable communication between developers and classification users, UDC in particular. In addition, these international meetings aim to promote interaction between the domain of bibliographic control and other information fields in which knowledge classifications may be used.

The theme of this year's Seminar is focused on the issues and prospects of leveraging library authority data, in particular classification data, towards achieving better integration in the information environment. If we look into the local level of a particular system, this integration is taking place through the improved complementarity between different kinds of subject metadata by interrelating them in a more systemic approach that can improve retrieval systems' dynamics, coherence and productivity. Integration in the global information landscape calls for disclosing of subject library authority data to the wider data space in such a way as to facilitate its understanding and reuse for enhancing network resource discovery.

We can see the perspectives at these two levels as convergent in principles and equally enabled by the current technological trends, especially through linked data. Conceptual and technical aspects underlying linked data translate fully the systemic principles of the global information environment: open vs. closed systems, mixed vs. separate use of metadata schema, explicit vs. implicit meaning, actionable vs. static information relationships. These principles should guide the evolution of our authority controlled vocabularies within a system and beyond.

Putting together a conference programme on subject authority control was not without its challenges. In principle, authority control addresses very practical and technical issues within bibliographic control which rarely draws the attention of researchers or academics. Due to its close dependence on the architecture and inner workings of bibliographic databases the topic of authority control has usually been dealt with in the background or was assumed to have been dealt with within library system design and supporting bibliographic standards. For cataloguers the principles of controlling vocabularies are basic, well understood and well established. Designers of library systems often see the topic of authority control reduced to relational database design. It seems as if the issue of subject authority control somehow fell through the gap between specialised interests and the experts within and outside of bibliographic control failed to connect or embrace the bigger picture.

Our previous UDC Seminars showed that the value of classifications in information and knowledge organization has been recognized and appreciated outside the domain of bibliographic control. However, when it comes to the topic of classification authority control, until the idea of the Semantic Web started to unfold through open linked data, researchers outside the bibliographic domain showed little interest in subject authorities and the work undertaken in this area in libraries.

The challenges and opportunities for authority data held in library systems, including classification systems, are twofold. Firstly, there should be better interoperation between different vocabularies internally and within the library domain, to avoid redundancies and inconsistency in information representation and processing. Secondly, interoperation should scale across the linked data environment, expanding the potential of subject authority control data as shared knowledge structures.

The main objective of this conference was to explore such opportunities and potential with an international audience. We thank the contributions from all experts in authority control, classification schemes and linked data, who provided their views of current issues, analysis of and experiences with classification data management and exploitation.

In preparing these proceedings we were privileged to collaborate with many specialists and we endeavoured to produce the most accurate record of the original manuscripts while maintaining the consistency in the presentation of the entire volume. Minor changes in the text were made with regards to standardising the spelling to British English. All the web addresses provided were checked prior to publication. A short subject alphabetical index and the list of the authors with general information about the conference organization can be found at the end of the book.

We would like to use this opportunity to thank all authors for their contribution and their help with the editing process. Our heartfelt thanks also go to the conference programme committee listed at the end of the book whose help was essential in paper selection and the paper review process. Finally, we are grateful to the National Library of Portugal for its warm hospitality in hosting this conference.

Editors:
Aida Slavic
Maria Inês Cordeiro

The Hague, July, 2015

Classification, links and contexts

Keynote Address

Michael K. Buckland
University of California, Berkeley, USA

Abstract: Links commonly refer to models developed for the World Wide Web Consortium, but these are a special case within the wider field of links and references used in resource discovery, including subject indexes to classifications, relationships used in vocabulary control, and search term recommender services. There is a tension between standardised relationships (symbolized by Paul Otlet's modernist universalism and the Semantic Web) and the particular, subjective situations in which individuals try to make sense (symbolized by Ludwik Fleck's emphasis on the influence of local cultural contexts). A subject index to a classification is a collection of links, sometimes qualified by context. Different domains (specialties) have their own cultural contexts and benefit from differently tailored links even when searching within the same resources. Making links is a descriptive, language activity. Probabilistic methods can create links from familiar to unfamiliar vocabularies economically. Links commonly use a limited set of relationships, mainly equivalence, inclusion, and inheritance. A far wider range of relationships would help resource discovery. Extending resource discovery requires not only same-facet links to reach additional resources but also links across different facets to provide explanatory context.

Keywords: links; references; facets; contexts; Ludwik Fleck

1. Introduction

The title of this Seminar is "Classification & Authority Control: Expanding Resource Discovery" and the selected theme is the use of linked data to open new possibilities in exploiting controlled vocabularies to improve resource discovery and to extend it from the local perspective to the global environment. We are invited to find new ways of sharing knowledge structures across the linked data environment. The theme is well-chosen for two reasons: it focuses on promising technical developments in professional practice and it also invites attention to some basic questions in our field. Other speakers and seminar participants are very expert in these technical developments. I have been asked to consider these issues within a wider context.

We are here to improve resource discovery in the spirit of Paul Otlet's grand vision of universal access for all media, for all topics, and for all people. This dream lives on in the Semantic Web and in this Seminar's agenda. It is our vision and we should remember why: our purpose is to empower people to learn, to know more, and to understand better than before.

I will emphasize the following points:

1. Learning, knowing, and understanding constitute how we view the world and how we live, so Documentation, by whatever name, is

ultimately a kind of cultural engagement and language is central in what we do (Buckland, 2012b).

2. Our systems have links of many kinds, including subject indexes, syndetic structures, and search term recommender services as well as "linked data" in the narrow sense.

3. There is a tension between logic and language. Our machinery, whether cards or computers, use logic, which is stable but has limited expressive power. Natural language is endlessly expressive and dynamic. So much so that the struggle to "control" vocabulary is a central concern in Documentation.

4. Probabilistic approaches are useful in this complex and unstable world.

5. The challenge is to embrace the full expressive power of language and to acknowledge the cultural complexity of our environment.

2. Paul Otlet and Ludwik Fleck

At a UDC seminar it is proper to pay homage to Paul Otlet and his concern with building a universal resource discovery system based on standards, compatibility, systems, and machinery (Buckland, 2007). His first paper on this topic in 1892 is a good start. Entitled "Un peu de bibliographie" (Something about bibliography), it is a plea for collective action in analysing, cataloguing, and classifying facts for "the creation of a kind of artificial brain by means of cards containing actual information or simply notes of references" and, relevant to this Seminar, he includes a plea for vocabulary control through:

> " . . . a careful arrangement of its nomenclature . . because of its conciseness and the influence it would have on the creation of a scientific language *ne varietur* of which the social sciences are particularly in need. This nomenclature, which usage would soon shape and stabilise, could also be used for the classification cards in the catalogue. It would thus permit the creation of very practical links . . ." (Otlet, 1892/1990:19).

Otlet was introduced very well at the last Seminar by Boyd Rayward (2013) and I think that we might understand Otlet better if paid more attention to his contemporaries (Buckland, 2012a). So, for this year's Seminar theme, I draw attention to Ludwik Fleck (1896-1961). Fleck, a Polish microbiologist, was younger than Otlet, but his key work, *Genesis and development of a scientific fact*, was published in 1935, just one year after Otlet's *Traité de documentation* and the same year as Otlet's other summation, *Monde* (Fleck, 1935/1979; Otlet, 1934, 1935; Sady, 2012).

Fleck's insistence that cultural context is important for sense and understanding is subversive of Otlet's modernist, global vision. The tension between Fleck and Otlet, between the local and the global, is fundamental to our seminar theme of classification, authority control, and links for expanding resource discovery from a local perspective to the global environment.

In a narrow interpretation, linked data uses standards and practices (URI, RDF, OWL) that allow machine operations within the Semantic Web vision of a World Wide Web of data in which machines could process independently of humans. A broader view of linked data would include all forms of links likely to be useful in documentation systems including authority control and mapping between different vocabularies. The next sections consider context, vocabulary and relations.

3. Context

Fleck argued that a text has to be understood in relation to three entities: the writer, the text, and the cultural habits and cultural context of the writer (*Denkstil, Denkkollectiv*). And when a text is read it is necessarily read with the cultural habits and cultural context of the reader. So there is, in effect, a double Fleck effect: Not only the writer, the text, and the writer's cultural context, but also the reader, the text, and the reader's cultural context. Difficulties arise from differences between the two cultural contexts. We understand ancient, medieval, and renaissance authors with difficulty because the writers' knowledge and ways of thinking are so different from ours. And those writers would have difficulties understand our current writings. Context matters!

For similar reasons, Fleck was critical of factual encyclopaedias which were central to Otlet's vision, shared with Wilhelm Ostwald and H. G. Wells, for a universal encyclopaedia with many small factual entries ("monographs") linked together to constitute a "World Brain." Fleck's view was that brief factual entries in a reference work were necessarily unsatisfactory because the reduction to brief facts removed the explanatory context necessary to make sense adequately.

3.1. Meaning, sense and context

The ability to make sense is what enables living organisms to survive. Documentation exists to help us to find evidence that will help us to make better sense.

Communication between individuals and/or machines is through language and meaning. Here I distinguish between meaning and sense. A sentence can be meaningful yet not make sense. "A mouse swallowed the elephant" is a meaningful statement, but it does not make sense in any realistic context, although it could in cartoons or other fictional contexts. Also, we commonly make sense when there is uncertain or incomplete meaning, such as abstract art or Rohrschach images.

In documentation we make sense of documents in order to describe them so that searchers will be able to find and make sense of them. Assigning a class number, a subject heading, or other metadata is an act of description, a language act and a traditional term for metadata vocabularies is "documentary languages." Making links is a descriptive, language act and links, being language acts, express meaning not sense.

Fleck's insistence that context is important for making sense is subversive of resource discovery tools because it means that convenient, formal relationships are not as reliable as one would like. Machines operate and communicate mechanically, using algorithms. The economic advantage of using machinery is compelling, but their effectiveness in performance is reduced by the limitations of formal (algorithmic, mechanical) procedures, as is seen in artificial intelligence, information retrieval, and machine translation, areas in which sense matters. There are useful compromises to reduce these inadequacies by restricting the scope to a smaller, more homogeneous field (i.e. with less difference in cultural context), by moving from deterministic rules to probabilistic results, and by accepting imperfect results as a useful, worthwhile, and cost-effective compromise.

3.2. Links and context

A link, by definition, leads from one point to another point elsewhere. So, necessarily, *a link leads from one context to another*. Otlet, the enthusiast, would see links as making a connection, a positive achievement. But Fleck, I believe, would remind us that moving from one context to another is problematic for meaning and sense.

4. Vocabulary and context

4.1. Vocabulary and links

We can start with a simple example from the subject index to the first edition of the Dewey's decimal classification, in 1876:

Railroads 385

where this "See" reference implies equivalence. "The number after it is its class number and refers to the place where the topic will be found," explained Dewey (1899: [405]). It is a link between terms in two different languages. Such a mapping is necessary whenever an artificial language is used. Starting with a classification, then adding natural languages avoids the usual problems of vocabulary control. We might now call Dewey's "relative" index a search term recommender. We can mention some elaborations:

(1) Dependence on context. The sixth edition of Dewey's *Decimal Classification and Relativ Index for Libraries, Clippings, Notes, etc.*, of 1899, used Railroad to illustrate that the best link may vary according to the context ("in different connections" (Dewey, 1899: 10)):

Railroad	architecture	725
	corporations	385
	engineering	625
	law	385
	travel	614.863

(2) Mapping between more than two vocabularies. The multiple subject indexes in different natural languages to the Universal Decimal Classification all link to the same set of class numbers, so, although it was not the purpose, terms in one natural language can lead (via the class number) to corresponding terms in another natural language using the classification number as a "pivot" or switching language (also known as intermediate lexicon) to map presumed synonyms across multiple languages to each other through a star network. See http://www.udcc.org/udcsummary/php/index.php.

(3) Unfamiliar documentary languages. The link Railroads 385 leads from a familiar term to an unfamiliar term. Experienced searchers know that familiarity with a classification or indexing vocabulary improves both effectiveness and efficiency in searching. People search less effectively and less efficiently when using documentary languages that are not familiar to them. The expanding range of the Internet is like getting access to a much larger reference library, with two consequences: A greatly increased range of resources becomes available, but these additional resources are likely to have different, less familiar documentary languages. The number of accessible resources has increased, but, also, the proportion of available resources with unfamiliar metadata and so more difficult to search effectively or efficiently also increases. Examples are easy to find. How many people know that proper search terms for automobiles include:

- PASS MOT VEH, SPARK IGN ENG (US Federal Import/Export statistics)
- TL 205 (Library of Congress Classification)
- 180/280 (US Patent classification)
- 3711 (Standard Industrial Classification)

The use of standardised indexing languages can be recommended but not mandated and might not always be entirely desirable. So helping searchers to use unfamiliar vocabularies by providing links in the form Railroads 385 becomes increasingly needed. The Unified Medical Language System (http://www.nlm.nih.gov/research/umls/,UMLS) is an outstanding example of direct mapping between many health and biomedical vocabularies and standards to support interoperability. Creation of such mappings by humans is difficult and expensive and more so as the subject scope and number of languages increase. And the results are necessarily obsolescent as time passes because knowledge and word usage (both part of Fleck's cultural context) evolve (Buckland, 2007, 2011).

4.2. Probabilistic mapping

Fortunately, probabilistic methods can help as we found in a series of studies at Berkeley based on the important work by Ray Larson on "classification clustering." Terminology varies in different subject areas and Larson showed that a sample of catalogue records could be used as a training set to estimate how individual Library of Congress Classification (LCC) numbers were statistically associated with words found in titles and in Library of Congress Subject Headings. From that he was able to predict with some reliability from the words in a book's title what LCC number would be assigned (Larson, 1991, 1992).

A system that can predict assigned classification numbers can also be used as an economical automatic classifier or as a human classifier's aid. Equally the same capability could be used as a search term recommender for anyone wanting to know suitable LCC numbers for any given topic. Further, this methodology is good for the probabilistic mapping of any two vocabularies (whether natural language words or classification numbers) if a suitable training set can be found. This versatile and economical method for creating "see" references like Railroads 385 from familiar vocabularies to unfamiliar ones can be frequently regenerated using more up-to-date training sets to reduce the effects of obsolescence. A series of studies exploring these issues was undertaking at Berkeley. Buckland, et al. (1999) is a concise summary. Petras (2006) provides a detailed explanation. This approach is now also called "instance-based matching" (e.g., OAEI, 2014).

4.3. Collection vocabulary and domain discourse

Any large collection (database, catalogue, bibliography) usually covers a range of subject matter and includes many specialized subdomains, each with its specialized word usage. Anyone interested in a subdomain needs the specialized concepts and vocabulary of that subdomain, so there should be advantages in having a suitably specialized index that would improve resource discovery in that subdomain. This can be done by using training sets drawn only from that subdomain (Buckland, et al., 2000).

4.3.1. "Galileo" in different contexts

In our first experiment with subdomain vocabulary mapping, we used the INSPEC database and in addition to a general search term recommender (based on an unbiased, collection-wide sample), we also picked a separate sample for each of three specialized subdomains: Information Science, Biotechnology, and Water Resources to create three different search term recommenders. The first query posed was "Galileo" and the differently-derived search term recommenders yielded different search term recommendations:

- The collection-wide index: "*Jupiter*" then "*Planetary sciences*"
- The Information Science index: "*Reservation computer systems*" then "*Travel industry*"
- The Biotechnology index: "*History*"
- The Water Resources index: "*Planetary atmospheres*"

On inspection we found that the first arose from the space probe named Galileo then seeking evidence of water on the planet Jupiter and its moons. The second derived from the Galileo online ticketing system then used by the travel industry. The third recognized an historical name, Galileo Galilei. The fourth also was derived from the Galileo space probe. Each was valid in its context!

4.3.2. "Cardiac arrest" in different specialties

Imagine three doctors -- an anaesthesiologist, a drug therapy specialist, and a geriatrician – who each wanted recent literature on cardiac arrest (i.e. heart attack). Cardiac arrest itself is not a MeSH (Medical Subject Headings) heading, so what would be most effective MeSH headings to use? The three doctors are specialists. They do not have the same kind of interest in cardiac arrests. Each inhabits a different medical micro-culture. Each would not be interested in (and might not understand) the specialized literature of interest to the others. Suitably biased training sets can generate specialized search term recommendations for each. See Table 1.

Table 1: *Medical specialty search term recommender results* (Petras, 2006)

Recommended MeSH Headings for query "Cardiac arrest" for three specialties		
Anaesthesiology	Drug therapy	Geriatrics
1. Heart arrest	1. Heart	1. Coronary disease
2. Heart surgery	2. Purkinje fibers	2. Heart diseases
3. Cardiac output	3. Myocardium	3. Crime
4. Respiratory insufficiency	4. Anti-arrhythmia agents	4. Heart
5. Heart attack, induced	5. Arrhythmia	5. Cardiovascular agents
6. Heart	6. Heart conduction system	6. Mitral valve insufficiency
7. Heart diseases	7. Cardiac output	7. Cardiomyopathy, hypertrophic
8. Resuscitation	8. Myocardial contraction	8. Aortic valve insufficiency
9. Coronary artery bypass	9. Anilides	9. Up-regulation (Physiology)
10. Hyperkalemia	10. Heart arrest	10. Pindolol

Each column can be interpreted as follows: In the context of anaesthesiology, recommended search terms for documents relating to "cardiac arrest" are 1. Heart arrest, 2. Heart surgery, etc. Each ranked list appears reasonable for its specialty, but they are remarkably different from each other and they lead, quite properly, to different documents.

More generally, context-specific training sets significantly improve retrieval performance within a subdomain compared with an "unbiased" (collection-wide) training set. They also severely decrease performance if the wrong specialty recommender is used. The more the training set is specific to the context (the specialty) the better the improvement in resource discovery within that specialty and the worse the results if the wrong specialty index if used. There are several ways to define context-based training sets. Using a classification, when available, allows a specialty to be defined efficiently and effectively by choosing classes of interest.

4.3. Personalized contexts

Commercial advertising has become more targeted within data-rich environments with the ideal being the "market of one." So perhaps for resource discovery the ideal would be entirely individual, personalized indexes: *In the context of your own personal knowledge*, for A see B. An expert reference librarian would try to do this. It is a logical consequence of shifting attention from Otlet to Fleck and it is completely different from the traditional practice of one single, collection-based index for all users which was the only affordable method before digital technology.

The ideal of unique personalized indexes might be difficult to implement, in part because what one knows is uniquely personal. It reflects our personal cultural context and is more than and different from an isolated topical specialty. Nevertheless, the idea is worth considering, especially given the general failure in library and information science to act on the basic principle that what a person already knows is highly relevant to what resource discovery would be most helpful (Konrad, 2007: 517-593, esp. 526).

4.4. Synonyms in different natural languages

Consider *Alcoholism* (English), *Alkoholismus* (German), and *Alcoholismo* (Spanish). These three words would ordinarily be considered synonyms, but when used as search terms the situation is less simple. They will, of course, find English, German and Spanish language texts respectively, but the discourses found are liable to have different concerns and emphases. Predictably they tend to focus, explicitly or implicitly, on different geographical areas based on their language area or country of publication.

Differences in cultural context may be associated with different aspects of alcoholism and these can be inferred from the additional subject headings assigned, which indicate interest in drug abuse and ethyl alcohol in English language discourse, in employment issues and women alcoholics in German language discourse, and in youth and drunkenness as a criminal offense in Spanish language discourse. Spanish and, especially, German books seem to emphasize social and psychological aspects of alcoholism and the English-language books give more attention to medical and psychiatric issues.

To the extent that *Alcoholism*, *Alkoholismus*, and *Alcoholismo* are associated with different discourses in their different cultural contexts, they are not equivalent *as search terms*.

5. Relations

Links are seen as logical relations that could be operationalized algorithmically in a Semantic Web sense, but many links express relationships that are vague or unspecified or difficult to use algorithmically. I suggest that all links and mappings are in some sense descriptive and could, therefore, be regarded as language acts in a very broad sense and only a subset are recognizable as logical relations. In this view, logical links are a subset of language links.

Much attention is given to semantic links based on semantic similarity, inclusion/exclusion, and inheritance: vocabulary control (syndetic structure within a documentary language); authority control (links to preferred forms); and mappings between terms in different vocabularies (categories, classifications, ontologies, subject headings, thesauri). However, a broad view of links would include all forms of reference and citation, including the link between a query and a retrieved set. Selection systems work algorithmically, so the internal logic of retrieval systems can also be considered a link: a given query always responds with (links to) the same retrieved set (also known as system relevance) in any stable situation.

5.1. Link relations

In linked data, links are commonly in the form of A <sameAs> B. We know that, strictly speaking, this is always incorrect because no two different entities items can ever be the same, as Patrick Hayes explained in the 2011 Seminar (Hayes, 2011). "Same" is commonly used to mean similar enough for the present purpose (in English, when different alternative options are equally acceptable, one might say, "it is all the same to me"). Thesauri and ontologies use some additional relationships of inclusion, ancestry and hierarchy, but in practice the repertoire is small and limited to relationships suited to logical (inference) relations.

5.2. Functional relations

Some links reveal functional rather than semantic relationships. Consider *Pig manure, Water hyacinths*, and *Biogas*. These three differ greatly in their nature, appearance, and smell. They are semantically distant. In operational systems these three are likely to be only distantly connected, if at all. The Library of Congress Subject Headings has two headings, *Biogas* and *Biogas Industry,* with almost no related headings. However, pig manure and water hyacinths are major ingredients for biogas, so anybody interested in one should be made aware of the other two. Such non-semantic relationships are easily identified by examining frequently co-occurring headings within a retrieved set.

5.3. Biographical records

Biographical records provide interesting examples. There are unlimited ways in which humans can relate to each other, but in practice databases about persons are largely limited to a small set of familial relations: parent / child; spouse; and sibling. Some prosopographies have an expanded range of relationships. For example, the *Standards for Networking Ancient Prosopographies: Data and Relations in Greco-Roman Names* (SNAP:DRGN) (Standards, 2015) project has fifty-six classes of interpersonal relationships, including <FreedmanOf> and <ExtendedHouseholdOf>. Similarly *AgRelOn*, an Agent Relationship Ontology, has an enlarged range of familial, quasi-familial, and a few other relationships (e.g., murderer, muse, physician) (Deutsche Nationalbibliothek, 2011). Nevertheless, these expanded repertories are only a small selection of all possible relations. One could not write a biography with such a limited set of relationships. One explanation is that prosopographies are about persons not lives. Perhaps they were limited by design to relationships that lend themselves to logical inference.

We can illustrate this limitation by considering a biographical record in the style of the Who's Who genre for another pioneer from the period of Otlet and Fleck, Emanuel Goldberg, who developed an early search engine.

> Emanuel Goldberg, b. Moscow, 1881; son of Grigorii Goldberg; Univ. of Moscow, 1900-04; Ph.D w. Robert Luther, Leipzig Univ., 1906; m. Sonja Posniak, 1907; Assistant, Adolf Miethe, TU Charlottenburg, 1906-07; Prof, Akad. f. graphische Künste, Leipzig, 1907-17; ICA, Zeiss Ikon, Dresden, 1917-1933; Kinamo cine camera, 1921; microdots, 1925; search engine, 1927; Contax 35 mm camera 1932; kidnapped by Nazi SA; refugee in Paris, 1933-37; Laboratory, Palestine, Israel, 1937; d. 1970.

What sense a reader might make of such a record depends on the reader's prior knowledge. The more you know about doctoral study in Leipzig in 1906 or "Nazi SA" the more fully one would understand Goldberg's experience. Which explanatory resources would be most helpful will be situational, depending the knowledge, language skills, and cultural context of the reader.

Here there are many proper names that are easily linked to authority files for resource discovery. But even this brief example includes non-familial relations: <studied at> <studied with>, <assistant to>, <kidnapped by>, <taught at>, <invented>, and <became refugee in>. If we are to be serious about using links for expanding resource discovery then starting with the richness of the human experience is more attractive than a limited set of logical relationships.

In the case of biographical narratives we have experimented with decomposing a life into a series of events, each of which appears to form 4-tuples of values for persons, action/status, place, and time (Buckland & Ramos, 2010). Whether or not that design would prove adequate and robust is less important than recognizing that if we are to understand a person's life it is necessary to understand the contexts (cultural as well as spatio-temporal) and also the full range of what individuals do during their lives. In reality, the list of interpersonal relationships is very long: friend, fellow-student, critic, plagiarist, admirer, co-worker, committee colleague, military comrade, and so on. And people have many relationships to objects (designer, maker, owner, collector, repairer, ...) and performances (witness, instigator, victim, chronicler, ...).

5.4. Using relations

While <sameAs> and its variants are clearly useful for purposes of identity and disambiguation, our seminar agenda of expanding resource discovery should include using descriptive links for the full range of relationships. Maybe the only way to do that is to use natural language or a very versatile universal artificial one, such as the UDC (see American Library Association, 1997).

We could use natural language A <English: co-worker> B. We could use a classification, maybe A <UDC: 622.33> B, for A was a coal miner with B. Then algorithmic processing could do operations on such statements. This implies use of complex inference using probabilistic methods, natural language processing, and/or network analysis after an initial resource discovery to select statements. I suppose ontologies could in theory have unlimited relations. But how? Use of the syntax and relationships of synthetic classification systems could replace the limited logical relations currently in use. If all relations that a computer might encounter and not recognize were defaulted to a generic <is related to>, little has been lost and something may have been gained.

6. Facets, links, and contexts

Facets, the most fundamental divisions, are central in classification and knowledge organization. Because linked data normally have a <sameAs> or similar relationship mappings are ordinarily within the same facet. Likewise, in a library reference collection, the reference works are arranged by facet-specific genres: biography is separate from geography (maps and place name gazetteers) which is separate from history (and chronologies), and so on.

But when we look beyond the main heading in a knowledge organization system (or at the body of an entry in a reference work) we find no such limit to a single facet. Instead we find any or all other facets.

- A library subject headings will have a main heading, but then commonly a geographic subdivision, a chronological subdivision, or a form designation, and, sometimes, a personal name.
- A place name gazetteer will have a place name as a main heading, but then a geographical feature type, and spatial markers for latitude and longitude. It could have a note of when that name was in use and/or mention of an especially significant associated person or historical event.
- A time period directory would have a period name as heading, qualified by what kind of period or event it was, time markers (calendar time), and where that period or event occurred.
- A biographical dictionary will be arranged by personal name, but, as in the Goldberg example above, followed by multiple instances of activity, date, other persons, and locations (e.g. "b. Moscow, 1881; son of Grigorii Goldberg", etc.).

Instances will vary greatly. The important point is that any main heading in a bibliography or catalogue and any entry in any facet-limited reference work is likely to have qualifiers or explanations using any or all other facets. So same-facet links can be made across different facet genres. Diagram 1 shows what one might expect, with lines connecting instances from different facets: When, Where, Who, and What. We see the same effect in complex pre-coordinate systems such as LCSH and UDC.

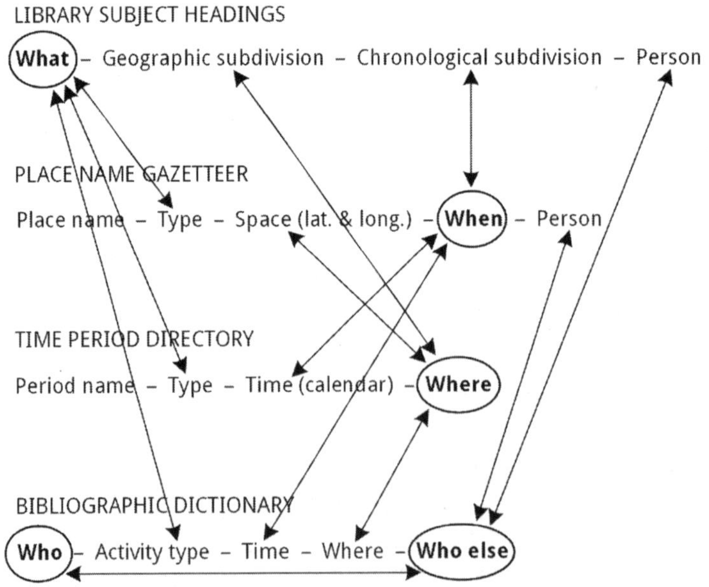

Figure 1: *Same-facet links across different facet genres.*

There may be reasons for the sequence of the facets in each row, but if, for the purposes of discussion, we rearrange the elements in each row such that the facets align vertically we get Figure 2.

Facet genres with with facets realigned

	What	Where	When	Who
WHAT (LCSH)	X	X	X	X
WHERE (Place name list)	X	X	X	-
WHEN (Time period dir.)	X	X	X	-
WHO (biographical dict.)	X	X	X	X

Vertical mappings extend semantic links to new vocabularies
Horizontal links provide additional links

Figure 2: *Realignment of Figure 1 by facet, with examples of links.*

Present practice in linked data is dominated by within-facet links, which would be represented by vertical arrows in Figure 2. But if we are to understand how anything fits into its context we must also have links between different facets. For example the subject heading "Lighthouses" in a library catalogue could quite easily link to the geographical feature type "Lthse (Lighthouse)" in a place name gazetteer. The catalogue subject heading will lead to literature about lighthouses and the place name gazetteer will lead to the locations of actual lighthouses, a nice example of expanded resource discovery.

7. Conclusions

Our seminar agenda is to explore how classifications, vocabulary control and links can expand resource discovery. The prospect of combining methods developed for World Wide Web with our own existing techniques is very promising. There is, however, a tension between standardised relationships, symbolized by Otlet's modernistic universalism and the Semantic Web, and the particular, subjective situations in which individuals try to make sense, reflected in Ludwik Fleck's emphasis on the role of local, temporary cultural contexts. This is important because Documentation exists to promote knowing and is, therefore, a form of cultural engagement.

Our systems already have descriptive links of many kinds but the repertoire of relations has remained limited.

Natural language is endlessly expressive and adaptive. Logic, however, is not. Natural language is capable of reflecting well the uncertainties, ambiguities, and dynamic change with which we must deal. Formal systems are less so.

The challenge faced in this Seminar is to accept the full expressive power of language, to acknowledge the cultural complexity of our environment, *and* to find ways to use and improve the tools available to us. We can take pride in what we, Otlet's heirs, have achieved, but at the same time we need to take account of the insights of Ludwik Fleck as well as the vision of Paul Otlet.

Acknowledgements

I am grateful for the advice of Ron Day and Vivien Petras.

References

American Library Association. Subcommittee on Subject Relationships/Reference Structures. (1997). *Final report to the ALCTS/CCS Subject Analysis Committee.* Available at: http://www.ala.org/alcts/mgrps/camms/cmtes/ats-ccssac/srrsreport.

Buckland, M. (2007). Naming in the library: marks, meaning and machines. In: *Nominalization, nomination and naming in texts.* Edited by C. Todenhagen, W. Thiele. Tübingen, Germany: Stauffenburg Verlag, pp. 249-260. Available at http://people.ischool.berkeley.edu/~buckland/naminglib.pdf.

Buckland, M. (2007). On the cultural and intellectual context of European documentation in the early twentieth century. In: *European modernism and the information society: informing the present, understanding the past.* Edited by W. B. Rayward. Aldershot, UK: Ashgate, pp 45-57.

Buckland, M. (2011). Obsolescence in subject description. *Journal of Documentation*, 68 (2), pp. 154-161.

Buckland, M. (2012a). Interrogating spatial analogies relating to knowledge organization: Paul Otlet and others. *Library Trends*, 61 (2), pp. 271-285.

Buckland, M. (2012b). What kind of science can Information Science be? *Journal of the American Society for information Science and Technology*, 63 (1), pp. 1-7.

Buckland, M. et al. (1999). Mapping entry vocabulary to unfamiliar metadata vocabularies. *D-Lib Magazine* 5 (1). Available at: http://www.dlib.org/dlib/january99/buckland/01buckland.html.

Buckland, M. et al. (2000). Variation by subdomain in indexes to knowledge organization systems. In: *Dynamism and stability in knowledge organization: Proceedings of the Sixth International ISKO Conference, 10-13 July 2000, Toronto, Canada.* Edited by C. Beghtol, L. C. Howarth, N. J. Williamson. Würzburg, Germany: Ergon Verlag, pp. 48-53.

Buckland, M.; Ramos, M. R. (2010). Events as a structuring device in biographical mark-up and metadata. *Bulletin of the American Society for Information Science and Technology* 36 (2), pp. 26-29. Available at: http://www.asis.org/Bulletin/Dec-09/Bulletin_DecJan10_Final.pdf.

Deutsche Nationalbibliothek. (2011). *AgRelOn, an Agent Relationship Ontology*. Available at: http://d-nb.info/standards/elementset/agrelon.owl#RelatedAgent.

Dewey, M. (1899). Dewey's *Decimal Classification and relativ index for libraries, clippings, notes, etc.* Boston: Library Bureau.

Fleck, L. (1935/1979). *Entstehung und Entwicklung einer wissenschaftlichen Tatsache: Einführung in die Lehre vom Denkstil und Denkkollectiv*. Basel: Schwabe, 1935. English ed.: *Genesis and development of a scientific fact*. Chicago: University of Chicago Press, 1979.

Hayes, P. (2011). On being the same as. Keynote address at the International *UDC Seminar 2011: Classification & Ontology: Formal Approaches and Access to Knowledge, The Hague (Netherlands) 19-20 September. Presentation* available at: http://www.udcds.com/seminar/2011/media/slides/UDCSeminar2011_PatrickHayes.pdf.

Konrad, A. (2007). *On inquiry: human concept formation and construction of meaning through library and information science intermediation*. Dissertation, University of California, Berkeley. Available at: http://escholarship.org/uc/item/1s76b6hp#page-1.

Larson, R. R. (1991). Classification clustering, probabilistic information retrieval, and the online catalog. *Library Quarter*ly, 61 (2), pp.133-173.

Larson, R. R. (1992). Experiments in automatic Library of Congress Classification. *Journal of the American Society for Information Science,* 43 (2), pp.130-148.

OAEI 2014: Instance Matching Track. (2014). Available at: http://islab.di.unimi.it/im_oaei_2014/index.html.

Otlet, P. (1934). *Traité de documentation*. Brussels: Editiones Mundaneum.

Otlet, P. (1935). *Monde: Essai d'Universalisme*. Brussels: Editiones Mundaneum.

Otlet, P. (1990). Something about bibliography. [Translation of "Un peu de bibliographie." Palais 1891/92: 254-271]. In: Otlet, P. 1990. *International Organisation and Dissemination*. Amsterdam: Elsevier, pp.11-24.

Petras, V. (2006). *Translating dialects in search: mapping between specialized languages of discourse and documentary languages*. Dissertation, University of California, Berkeley. Available at: http://www.sims.berkeley.edu/~vivienp/diss/vpetras-dissertation2006-official.pdf.

Rayward, W. B. (2013). From the index card to the World City: knowledge organization and visualization in the work and ideas of Paul Otlet. In: *Classification and visualization: interfaces to knowledge: International UDC Seminar 2015*. Edited by A. Slavic, A. Akdag Salah & S. Davies. Würzburg: Ergon Verlag, pp. 1-42. Presentation available at: http://seminar.udcc.org/2013/programme.php.

Sady, W. (2012). Ludwik Fleck. In: *The Stanford Encyclopedia of Philosophy* (Summer 2012 Ed.). Edited by E. N. Zalta. Available at: http://plato.stanford.edu/archives/sum2012/entries/fleck/.

Standards for Networking Ancient Prosopographies: Data and Relations in Greco-Roman Names. (SNAP:DRGN). (2015). Available at: http://snapdrgn.net/.

MICHAEL K. BUCKLAND is Emeritus Professor at the School of Information, University of California, Berkeley, USA and Co-Director of Electronic Cultural Atlas Initiative. Prof. Buckland was born and educated in England. He studied History and Librarianship then joined the University of Lancaster Library in 1965, where from 1967 to 1972 he worked in the Library Research Unit on studies of book usage and book availability. His PhD dissertation (Sheffield University, 1972) was published as *Book Availability and the Library User* (Pergamon, 1975). In 1972 he moved to the United States to Purdue University Libraries in Indiana as Assistant Director of Libraries for Technical Services, before becoming Dean of the School of Library and Information Studies at Berkeley, 1976-84. From 1983 to 1987 he was Assistant Vice President for Library Plans and Policies for the nine campuses of the University of California. He has been a visiting scholar in Austria and Australia, was President of the American Society for Information Science in 1998, and became emeritus professor in 2004. Professor Buckland has written widely on library services, bibliographical access, cultural heritages, and the history of documentation. His books include *Library Services in Theory and Context* (Pergamon, 1983; 2nd ed. 1988), *Information and Information Systems* (Praeger, 1991), *Redesigning Library Services* (American Library Association, 1992), and a biography, *Emanuel Goldberg and his Knowledge Machine* (Libraries Unlimited, 2006). His principal project currently is "Editorial Practices and the Web" which makes historians' working notes openly accessible at editorsnotes.org.

1. Past and future perspectives on subject data assets

Complementarity of perspectives for resource descriptions

Barbara B. Tillett
Retired, Library of Congress, Washington, D.C., USA

Abstract: Bibliographic data is used to describe resources held in the collections of libraries, archives and museums. That data is mostly available on the Web today and mostly as linked data. Also on the Web are the controlled vocabulary systems of name authority files, like the Virtual International Authority File (VIAF), classification systems, and subject terms. These systems offer their own linked data to potentially help users find the information they want - whether at their local library or anywhere in the world that is willing to make their resources available. We have found it beneficial to merge authority data for names on a global level, as the entities are relatively clear. That is not true for subject concepts and terminology that have categorisation systems developed according to varying principles and schemes and are in multiple languages. Rather than requiring everyone in the world to use the same categorisation/classification system in the same language, we know that the Web offers us the opportunity to add descriptors assigned around the world using multiple systems from multiple perspectives to identify our resources. Those descriptors add value to refine searches, help users worldwide and share globally what each library does locally.

Keywords: authority control; Virtual International Authority File (VIAF); subject terms; classification systems; bibliographic data

1. Bibliographic resources and bibliographic descriptions

As we know, information is communicated and shared in many ways. When information is documented and stored in libraries or made accessible for users through our libraries, it can be in many forms. For example, we have

- Manuscripts
- Books
- Maps
- Globes
- Musical scores
- Electronic texts and data

and much more. These are the containers or carriers for information - the "manifestation" perspective when we look through our *Functional Requirements for Bibliographic Records* (FRBR) glasses. The researcher or user of our collections is usually trying to get to the "work", that is, the intellectual or artistic content of those resources. What FRBR teaches us is that resources can be viewed from many perspectives, and for the sake of simplicity, FRBR uses 4 perspectives to describe resources: work, expression, manifestation, and item. Also very importantly, the FRBR conceptual model includes relationships among resources, and acknowledges the importance of subject relationships.

When we describe the resources in our collections we create a bibliographic description. Our bibliographic description is not the resource itself, but rather a substitute, a surrogate for the resource, a placeholder in the environment in which we look for and find information - just as with René Magritte's picture of a pipe, "Ceci n'est pas une pipe". Our bibliographic descriptions and the various access points we include provide a searchable surrogate for the resources we hold in our libraries, so we can assist users in finding what we have to offer. The description can serve not only as a locating device for users to find resources they want in our own collections, but also can be used to link to related resources they may find of interest through the Semantic Web.

2. Descriptors: self-describing elements and added descriptors

A bibliographic description can include data from the resource itself, so called "self-describing elements" and also added value data, such as the access points we include to increase access to the description.

The self-describing elements that we take from a resource itself are data such as titles, names of authors, publication information, series, and identifiers like ISBN. They also include data that can be objectively measured, like the extent (e.g., number of pages) and dimensions.

This is "objective" (vs. "subjective") data in that it does not require human interpretation. Perhaps in the future such data can be automatically provided by systems/machines. This would certainly reduce the costs of cataloguing. This self-describing data can be used in searching to improve the recall and, in turn, can be adjusted through relevance ranking and other algorithms of search engines to improve search results.

Then we have data that is added by human beings. This includes the various access points we add to bibliographic records. So, we have controlled vocabularies for names and subject terms, classification numbers and other categorisations of the resource, like genre/form determinations that humans assign. Some libraries even augment resource description with added images or sound bites, etc. Because humans, each coming from their own perspective, provide this type of data, it is "subjective" data.

Involving humans is expensive, but this added value data is extremely helpful to users and helps provide precision for searches. This data is even more important from an international perspective. When descriptions from many countries for a given resource are linked, we gain the global perspective of differing points of view from the various indexers and cataloguers who have created the descriptions. Those different perspectives provide access and offer users suggestions to continue their searches from various points of view, often in multiple languages that may be of interest to them.

3. Authority control and multiple perspectives

When we create a bibliographic description of a resource, we give our users information to find, identify, select, and obtain[1] resources that are of interest to them. The bibliographic data is augmented by data in authority records, which provides access to variant forms of names or terms, as well as links to related entities in our catalogues and in Web systems.

Each cataloguer or indexer creating bibliographic descriptions and authority records includes information from their own perspective. When we link bibliographic and authority records worldwide for the same entities, we benefit from the added perspectives of multiple cataloguers and indexers.

There are several philosophies about which is better for an international system: to map all the data into a single record or to link the multiple records for an entity. It just depends on what system is being used and the capabilities for searching and displaying the data to be clear to the users. It also may depend on the type of data being related. Over the years, we have seen that there is a difference between mapping name authority data versus subject authority data.

3.1. Name authorities

In the 1980s authority control started to get a lot of attention, as the first and second generation computer systems were being developed and refined. There had been several programmes, particularly in the United States, to share bibliographic data and authority data, but mostly the requirement in those shared programmes was for participating institutions to follow the same cataloguing rules and use the same classification and subject systems, to build a single union catalogue, name authority file or subject authority file. For example, In the United States, the Library of Congress established several cooperative projects over many decades, such as the National Union Catalog, which was essentially overtaken by OCLC during the 1970s, and also the authority control programmes NACO (Name Authority Cooperative) and SACO (Subject Authority Cooperative) projects which are now worldwide programmes. However, it was not until the 1990s that the idea of a "virtual" authority file came to fruition that linked the name authority files of the world rather than building a single authority file that everyone had to use.

3.1.1. VIAF (Virtual International Authority File)

From the start, it was agreed that VIAF would be for entities that could be internationally shared, that is, name authority data for persons, corporate bodies, families, geographic place names, and what are sometimes called

---

1 These are the FRBR "user tasks".

"uniform titles" for identifying works and expressions. VIAF also links to biographical data, some images of the entities described and includes links to other data on the Web.

I helped create VIAF with colleagues from the Deutsch Nationalbibliothek and, later, the Bibliothèque nationale de France along with the computer system experts at OCLC's Research Office. Today, VIAF has hundreds of members from around the world (see Figure 1) and has become a freely available service under the auspices of OCLC for everyone to use. You can access it online at viaf.org.

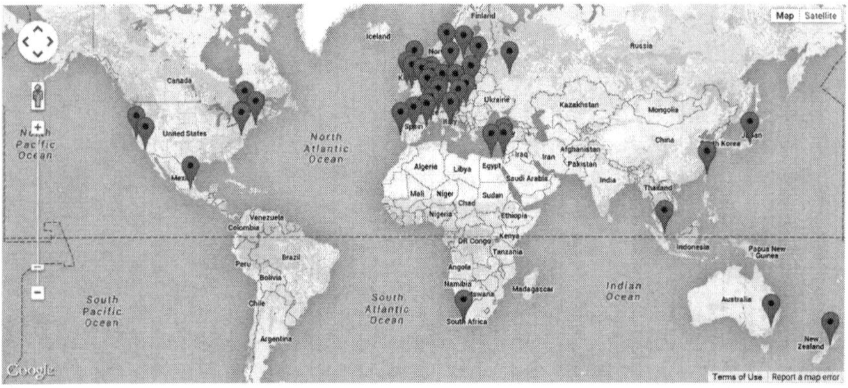

Figure 1: *VIAF (Virtual International Authority File) membership 2015*[2]

VIAF does not include subjects, at least for now. Lessons learned from several subject projects showed how difficult it is, if not impossible in many situations, to map terminology across languages and systems for concepts or topics. However, there are other solutions to linking subject vocabularies and classification systems, especially in the Semantic Web and Linked Open Data environment. I will come back to this in a moment.

3.2. Subject authority control

Currently, there is a wide range of subject systems and vocabularies from general vocabularies such as the Library of Congress Subject Headings (LCSH), to very specific vocabularies, like MeSH for Medical Subject Headings from the National Library of Medicine in the United States.

Some vocabularies or subject terminology systems may share the same basic principles and construction and scope, such as the sister systems of LCSH, RAMEAU (Répertoire d'autorité-matière encyclopédique et alphabétique unifié)

2 Image from The VIAF: The Virtual International Authority File webiste (http://www.viaf.org/) based on Google Maps/Google Earth (captured on 21 July 2015).

from the Bibliothèque nationale de France, and RVM (Répertoire de vedettes-matière) from the University of Laval, in Canada. You would think it would be easy for those systems to map their terms from one to another, but as with any multilingual effort, there are the usual issues of terms that do not translate directly from one language to another or even from one dialect of a language to another dialect of the same language, as with French and Canadian versions of French. We even found with LCSH that the contributors to SACO from non-US countries had issues with terminology that was very different in their dialects of English - such as football and soccer. However, other subject terminology systems, such as MeSH (Medical Subject Headings), are based on completely different sets of principles and structures and levels of specificity.

Within a given system, authority control is provided for the terms. Typically, the authorized term is given along with synonyms and related terms, as well as notes and links. Some classification systems also do the same for their represented topics.

Many subject terminologies include terms for concepts or topics along with terms for events, historical periods, and more. Some also embody links to classification numbers. You all are already familiar with the systems used for classification numbers: systems such as UDC (Universal Decimal Classification), LCC (Library of Congress Classification), and DDC (Dewey Decimal Classification) available in print, online, and as linked data on the Web for most of them. And you are also familiar with the links provided between classification systems and some subject vocabularies, like the links between LCSH and the Library of Congress Classification numbers. The classification is paired with words that in turn can be linked in many cases with a subject vocabulary.

From an international perspective, the beauty of classification systems is that classification numbers are usually independent of language. I say usually, because even those classification systems based on numbers may display numbers according a specific script that may not be universally used.

Over the years we have learned many lessons about trying to map terminologies across languages with multilingual thesauri. Basically, we have found that trying to map different classification systems or different subject terminologies cannot be totally successful - especially when the systems are based on different foundations and principles and with different scopes - but even just because different languages may have different terminology for given concepts.

I helped create IFLA's MulDiCat (Multilingual Dictionary for Cataloguing Terms and Concepts) to provide a mapping of terms used in the *International Cataloguing Principles* and the various FRBR family of conceptual models. We found it sometimes impossible to provide a one-to-one mapping of terms across all the languages that were included. They were originally around 25 languages and more now.

Whether just in the same language (such as UK versus US, Canadian, or Australian English) or across languages, when we compare words in one language with words in another for the same concepts, we find the usual situations. We may find that a single term translates or "maps" nicely to another single term in the other language with a one-to-one relationship, for example, for English to Italian:

> Mathematics→Matematica
> Algebra→Algebra.

Or, we may have a one-to-many relationship where a single term in one language translates to multiple words in another language, for example for German to English:

> Sontagsrückfahrkarte→weekend ticket.

Or, we may have a one-to-none relationship, such as when something new is discovered and one language gives it a name, and there is no equivalent in the other language. Often, the other language over time may just incorporate the term from the original language into its own language, such as for *geyser* from Icelandic or *tsunami* from Japanese. Or there may be ambiguity as to which meaning for a term is intended, for example, the term "Football". Do we mean "Soccer" or "American football"? You will get different answers from an English-speaking person in the United States than you will from one in England.

When I worked at the Library of Congress, I was involved with experiments to map the subject vocabularies of LCSH, RAMEAU, and RVM. Even with these three systems, based on the same conceptual structure, principles and scope, we noticed that the language variations, even for the same French language, was sometimes without a one-to-one match of terms for topical concepts. We could not provide a complete mapping of all the terms. This effort was in parallel with the MACS project (Multilingual Access to Subjects) that linked LCSH, RAMEAU, and SWD (*Schlagwortnormdatei*). But during this effort we noticed an interesting fact. The terms assigned in bibliographic records from the multiple language systems provided useful suggestions for users to explore concepts. When viewed together in bibliographic records, they could be seen as complementary ways of viewing the resource that was being described.

I have already mentioned differences coming from the scope and level of specificity across vocabularies, such as the general LCSH versus the more specific medical subject headings found in MeSH. Systems can compensate for these variations to help guide a user of a multilingual system to navigate to information they are looking for. There often are notes to explain how to search in the alternate system or language, or qualifiers to lessen the ambiguity and several other techniques, but that work takes a lot of time and human effort.

Complete mappings are very costly and, in fact, may not be necessary. We may be able to help users get information they want in other ways than authority control of terms or classification numbers across the world. In addition to the complementarity of having multiple classification numbers and multiple subject descriptors in the same bibliographic record or linked bibliographic records for a resource, there is also the ability to use natural language from the resource itself. In 1982, Robert Fugmann wrote an article "*The complementarity of natural and indexing languages*" to remind us that it is beneficial to include controlled vocabularies and classification data along with natural language for better recall and precision of searches.

4. Perspectives and systems

The Web offers us the opportunity to take advantage of descriptors assigned around the world to bibliographic descriptions for the same resource, using multiple systems from multiple perspectives to identify our resources along with the natural language from the resources themselves. Those descriptors add value to refine searches and help users worldwide. They provide complementary perspectives to each other and to the natural language in the resource itself.

There is a famous Japanese film, called *Rashomon*, that tells a story from four different perspectives of people who observed an event and tell their tales (Figure 2). Each perspective offers a different individual view of the event, and they may each be correct, but each is very different.

I bring this up as an analogy to global cataloguing of the same resource. Each cataloguer or indexer may see a resource in a different way. When they document their bibliographic description, including the chosen classification number, subject terms and other access points, they record their point of view, their perspective. And when we examine their bibliographic description along with those of other cataloguers worldwide who may also have catalogued the same resource, we get an increased number of access points to connect users with the resources we have in our collections.

Different perspectives or points of view come from cataloguers having different academic backgrounds and different training in applying cataloguing rules, classification schemes and subject terminology. The bibliographic descriptions they create can complement those created by other cataloguers and could be very beneficial to users.

I found an interesting book by Marcia Ascher called *Ethnomathematics: a multicultural view of mathematical ideas*. It is fascinating to me to see that different cultures have different ways of counting and measuring things and none are "wrong". Similarly, no one has the *only* "correct" perspective for cataloguing a resource. We do not need to force everyone in the world to use the same language or point of view about how the bibliographic universe is to be organized or classified or described by subject terms. We can let different communities use their own terms and link those descriptors to increase the perspectives about the resources.

Figure 2: *Rashomon cover art*[3]

In the Web environment, it is even easier to provide complementary perspectives to access resources. Once a resource is described locally, we can share that descriptive data and add local or regional perspectives to enhance access for users internationally. We may find the local or regional information is of great value to researchers across the world who "speak the same language" either literally or figuratively.

Subject terminology and classification numbers do not need to be mapped across languages or systems. Just by being in the bibliographic records for the same resource, they are associated and can be seen by the user as complementary ways to access desired information. All of the descriptors from the various perspectives can all be together in a description or linked descriptions. The terminology and classification numbers assigned in a bibliographic description become associated by virtue of being in the same

3 Cover art image for the DVD of *Rashomon*, courtesy of Criterion Collection (https://www.criterion.com/).

description or linked descriptions of a resource. What this means for classification schemes and subject thesauri and systems is that it is not essential to *a priori* map concepts across the systems and schemes. They can be associated when the bibliographic records are displayed to the user.

As we well know, many libraries are typically limited to providing a single classification number to be used for shelving the resource in a collection. However, in the Web environment, multiple numbers can be assigned. Having multiple numbers in bibliographic records or linked records for the same resource offers users additional data to use in their searches. We do not have to be limited to the budgetary decisions of a single institution that may limit a cataloguer to providing one or no subject access points. We can take advantage of the multiple perspectives and multiple bibliographic records that have been created to offer our users pathways to resources they may find helpful. The complementarity of providing multiple perspectives helps users.

Enabling systems to share the multiple descriptions worldwide would reduce costs worldwide. When we share the descriptions, we share the work. OCLC's WorldCat has certainly shown how effective this can be, but OCLC requires membership and fees that the Semantic Web does not. We really need better search systems that take advantage of linked data on the Web and make information freely accessible.

Obviously, libraries choose a cataloguing system for the predominant local needs of its users, but they can also take advantage of the descriptions, descriptors, and classification numbers assigned for that work/manifestation (resource) worldwide to increase access for their researchers and other users. With the Web, we could let all the descriptors of a resource serve as access, providing multiple perspectives. We do not need to rely on just one perspective when we work on a global scale. Our local work can provide helpful perspectives when we share globally.

5. Linked data and the future

Libraries will continue to evolve, just as ways to communicate information and ways of making information accessible continue to evolve. We have moved from clay tablets in cuneiform that inventoried collections, through book catalogues to card catalogues. And once we had computers, we moved to online catalogues and then Web catalogues. Our bibliographic data may be limited to our one collection (or consortia) of resources or be shared by a homogenous community from a shared perspective that is meaningful to them. Or we can globally share our bibliographic data and authority data to facilitate finding information users need from anywhere in the world at anytime they wish to look for it.

The Web, now the Semantic Web, enables global sharing of our data. For those resources that can be used by different communities, providing the bibliographic descriptions from the perspectives of different cataloguers and

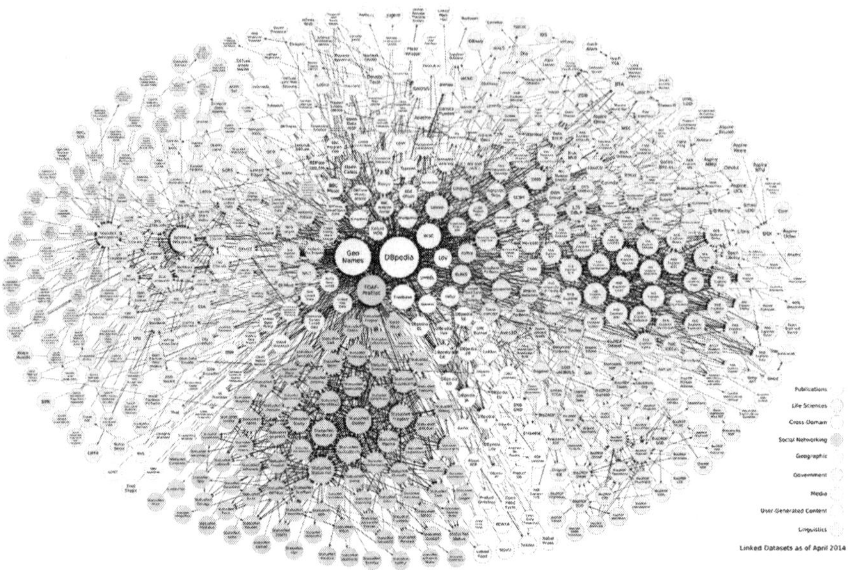

Figure 3: *Linked Open Data cloud diagram*[4]

indexers worldwide increases the access opportunities by displaying alternative terms that may be used to following pathways to further information on the Web.

Linked Open Data and the Semantic Web offer us opportunities to link the bibliographic descriptions with authority data and sounds and images that are connected to the resources our institutions provide. Figure 3 is the 2014 view of the Semantic Web of Linked Open Data showing VIAF and various other authority files, like LCSH, and systems.

Bibliographic data and digital resources are on the Web now, and we have added controlled vocabularies to help identify resources; other elements on the Web can be used to present displays and show pathways to related resources. By linking and providing creative displays of the linked data from all the available systems on the Web, we could offer our users multiple classification numbers and multiple subject terms in multiple languages they may find helpful to continue their searches or expand the scope of their research to related information that is available to them on a global scale.

Is it not, indeed, time to share globally what each library does locally?

4 Linking Open Data cloud diagram (2014). By Max Schmachtenberg, Christian Bizer, Anja Jentzsch and Richard Cyganiak. Available at: http://lod-cloud.net/.

This conference will surely explore different projects currently underway or new initiatives and hopefully many of you in the audience will go away with great ideas for the future.

Where will you take us?

Acknowledgements

I would like to thank Ronald Murray for sharing his books about ethnomathematics and the communication of objective and subjective perspectives.

Credits

(Figure 1) 21 July 2015 image captured from viaf.org, based on Google Maps/ Google Earth.

(Figure 2) Thanks to the Criterion Collection for permission to use their cover art image for the DVD of Rashomon.

(Figure 3) Linking Open Data cloud diagram (2014). By Max Schmachtenberg, Christian Bizer, Anja Jentzsch and Richard Cyganiak. Available at: http://lod-cloud.net/.

References and suggested readings

Ascher, M. (1994). *Ethnomathematics: a multicultural view of mathematical ideas*. Boca Raton: Chapman & Hall. ISBN: 0-412-98941-7.

Daston, L.; Galison, P. (2010). *Objectivity*. New York: Zone Books.

Fugmann, R. (1982). The complementarity of natural and indexing languages. *International Classification*, 9 (3), pp. 140-144.

Functional requirements for authority data: a conceptual model. (2009). Ed. by Glenn E. Patton. IFLA Working Group on Functional Requirements and Numbering of Authority Records (FRANAR), final report, December 2008. Approved by the Standing Committees of the IFLA Cataloguing Section and IFLA Classification and Indexing Section, March 2009. München: K.G. Saur. (IFLA Series on Bibliographic Control, v. 34). ISBN: 978-3-598-24382-3.

Functional requirements for bibliographic records: final report. (1998). IFLA Study Group on the Functional Requirements for Bibliographic records (FRBR), approved by the Standing Committee of the IFLA Section on Cataloguing. München: K. G. Saur.

Functional requirements for subject authority data (FRSAD): a conceptual model. (2011). Edited by M. Lei Zeng, M. Žumer and A. Salaba. IFLA Working Group on the Functional Requirements for Subject Authority Records (FRSAR). München: De Gruyter Saur.

Harper, C. A.; Tillett, B. B. (2006). Library of Congress controlled vocabularies and their application to the Semantic Web. *Cataloging & Classification Quarterly*, 43 (3/4), pp. 47-68. [Best paper of *CCQ*, 2007 award]. Available at: https://scholarsbank.uoregon.edu/dspace/bitstream/1794/3269/1/ccq_sem_web.pdf.

Schmachtenberg, C. B.; Jentzsch, A.; Cyganiak, R. (2014). *Linking Open Data cloud diagram*. Available at: http://lod-cloud.net/.

Theory of subject analysis: a sourcebook. (1985). Edited by L. M. Chan, P. A. Richmond, E. Svenonius. Littleton, Colo.: Libraries Unlimited.

BARBARA B. TILLETT served as a professional librarian from 1970-2013. From 1994-2012, she was Chief of the Cataloging Policy & Support Office, later renamed the Policy & Standards Division, of the Library of Congress. As Chief, she was responsible for the *Library of Congress Classification Schedules* and *Library of Congress Subject Headings*, as well as cataloguing rule interpretations, Library of Congress name authority files and LC's database integrity. From 1998-2012, she was the co-founder and leader of the Virtual International Authority File and its VIAF Council, which is now operated under OCLC. During the 1990's, she was a consultant to the International Federation of Library Associations and Institutions in the development of the theoretical, conceptual model of the bibliographic universe, known as FRBR, Functional Requirements for Bibliographic Records, and served on the IFLA Working Group that developed the follow-on conceptual model, FRAD, Functional Requirements for Authority Data. From 2002-2007, she was Chair, IFLA Planning Committee for the IFLA Meetings of Experts on an International Cataloguing Code, organizing and leading regional meetings worldwide successfully to agree on the new International Cataloguing Principles. She received an IFLA Certificate in 2009 in recognition for her leadership in international bibliographic control. From 1994-2012, she served as the Library of Congress representative on the Joint Steering Committee for Revision of AACR and then the Joint Steering Committee for Development of RDA and was the JSC Chair, 2011-2013. She continues to serve on several editorial boards and has written many publications, given lectures and Webinars in several languages, and taught classes on authority control, bibliographic relationships, cataloguing principles and codes, and library systems.

Libraries, classifications and the network: bridging past and future

Maria Inês Cordeiro
National Library of Portugal, Lisbon, Portugal

Abstract: The history of controlled vocabularies in libraries has long carried the promise of improved retrieval systems based on common goals and shared efforts. This is especially true of subject vocabularies whose data have been managed at two levels. Firstly, in management systems of their own, from which vocabulary products are derived, as in the case of the most commonly used subject heading languages, thesauri and classification schemes. Secondly, in the so called library authority files, that may apply such vocabularies or be used to develop local ones, to control subject access to a given library or bibliographic collection. This two-levelled model of building and sharing subject vocabularies' data is about to change. For many decades the concept of 'intellectual sharing' has been prevalent in such activities, underpinning re-use by adoption and/or collaboration in the management of shared subject systems. Although the Internet has enabled the exposure of centrally managed subject systems and library authority files it has done little to alleviate the significant efforts needed for a full deployment of network shared vocabularies. In particular, the use of classification systems did not advance much. While in theory their potential for subject interoperability across domains and languages is recognized, classifications remain poorly used in practice. They still lack intelligent means to effectively connect and communicate data throughout the network, in a synchronic and non-redundant way. More recently, the development of web technologies has leveraged the concepts of connection, communication and sharing of data to a new level, through linked data. What changes will this bring to the architecture of library subject authority data? Will classification systems live to see the age of their full and easy deployment?

Keywords: controlled vocabularies; library systems; authority control; bibliographic control; subject interoperability; classification schemes; library linked data

Invited talk, paper not submitted.
Presentation materials are available on the conference website: http://seminar.udcc.org/2015.

MARIA INÊS CORDEIRO is Director-General of the National Library of Portugal. She holds a PhD in Library and Information Studies from University College London and degrees in History and Librarianship from the universities of Lisbon and Coimbra. Her professional career includes several management positions at the National Library of Portugal and at the Art Library of the Calouste Gulbenkian Foundation, where she was Head of Library Information Systems and Innovation Projects. Previously UDC Editor-in-chief, she is currently the Chair of the UDC Consortium. Inês has been a member of several IFLA standing committees (Classification and Indexing, Information Technology, Audiovisual and Multimedia and ICADS) and working groups, such as the Working Group on Principles Underlying Subject Heading Languages. She currently serves as Director of the IFLA UNIMARC Strategic Programme. Her research interests include knowledge organization and representation systems, information systems and library technologies.

Linking library data: contributions and role of subject data

Nuno Freire
The European Library, The Hague, Netherlands

Abstract: Linking and sharing data across organizations has been practiced by libraries for many decades, and can be observed in some of the most common data resources from libraries, such as union catalogues, authority files, and controlled vocabularies. In the new global data space, the benefits of library linked data (LLD) have been widely recognized within the library community. LLD practice emerged as a new approach to data sharing within and beyond the library environment, transforming the old models of distribution and reuse of subject library data. There are several parallel on-going activities towards establishing standards and best practices for the creation and publishing of LLD to meet the growing prospects of a more data-oriented global information space. In this context, the opportunities for libraries are twofold: not only do LLD initiatives bring librarians' data management expertise into the limelight, they also extend the value and reach of library data resources which become widely and easily reusable across domains. Libraries are already contributing open linked datasets which are being re-used by many different communities and for a variety of purposes. Some success cases already exist, such as library controlled vocabularies becoming linkable major reference sources for certain types of entities, or fundamental data service infrastructures based on, or derived from, library authority files. An additional field for LLD use is emerging within the new research data e-infrastructures, which provides new opportunities for the application of library classification and subject authority control expertise and resources in research data management.

Keywords: library linked data; controlled vocabularies; subject access; data services; e-infrastructures

Invited talk, paper not submitted.
Presentation materials are available on the conference website: http://seminar.udcc.org/2015.

NUNO FREIRE is currently the Chief Data Officer at The European Library. He holds a PhD in Information Systems and Computer Engineering from the Instituto Superior Técnico (Lisbon). His research interests include information systems, information retrieval, information extraction, data quality, and knowledge representation - particularly in their application to digital libraries and bibliographic data. Nuno has been working in data oriented projects in the area of digital libraries. In his recent work, at The European Library, he conducted the governance and utilisation of aggregated data from European national bibliographies and special library collections via data integration, processing, analysis, and data mining. He has also been a member of the programme committees of major international conferences in the area: JCDL (Joint Conference on Digital Libraries) and TPDL (Theory and Practice in Digital Libraries).

2. Data models and semantic structures

Application of FRBR and FRSAD to classification systems

Maja Žumer
University of Ljubljana, Ljubljana, Slovenia

Marcia Lei Zeng
Kent State University, Kent, Ohio, USA

Abstract: The Functional Requirements for Subject Authority Data (FRSAD) conceptual model defines entities, attributes and relationships as they relate to subject authority data. FRSAD includes two main entities, thema (any entity used as the subject of a work) and nomen (any sign or arrangement of signs that a thema is known by, referred to, or addressed as). In a given controlled vocabulary and within a domain, a nomen is the appellation of only one thema. The authors consider the question: can the FRSAD conceptual model be extended beyond controlled vocabularies (its original focus) to model classification data? Models that are developed based on the structures and functions of controlled vocabularies (such as thesauri and subject heading systems) often need to be adjusted or extended to accommodate classification systems that have been developed with different focused functions, structures and fundamental theories. The Dewey Decimal Classification (DDC) system and Universal Decimal Classification (UDC) are used as a case study to test applicability of the FRSAD model for classification data and the applicability of the Functional Requirements for Bibliographic Records (FRBR) for modelling versions, such as different adaptations and different language editions.

Keywords: FRBR; FRSAD; conceptual models; classification data modelling; Dewey Decimal Classification; DDC; Universal Decimal Classification; UDC

Invited talk, paper not submitted.
Presentation materials are available on the conference website: http://seminar.udcc.org/2015.

MAJA ŽUMER is Professor of Information Science at the University of Ljubljana (Slovenia). Her research interests include the design and evaluation of information retrieval systems, end-user interfaces and conceptual modelling. She has been involved in several IFLA working groups, NISO committees and several EU projects. She has received several international and national research grants. She was a member of the IFLA FRBR Review Group and the co-chair of IFLA Working Group on the Functional Requirements for Subject Authority Records (FRSAR).

MARCIA LEI ZENG is professor at Kent State University. She has been involved in the development and research of knowledge organization systems (KOS) for over 20 years and has been contributing to related standards including NISO Z39.19 and ISO 25964 for controlled vocabularies. She was the chair of IFLA Working Group that developed the model of Functional Requirements for Subject Authority Data (FRSAD) and an Invited Expert on the W3C Library Linked Data Incubator Group. She also served as the Executive Board member of the International Society for Knowledge Organization (ISKO), Director-at-large of the American Society for Information Science and Technology (ASIS&T) and Chair of the Advisory Board of Dublin Core Metadata

Initiative (DCMI). Her major research interests include knowledge organization structures and systems, Linked Data, metadata and mark-up languages, database quality control, multilingual and multicultural information processing and digital humanities.

Relational aspects of subject authority control: the contributions of classificatory structure[1]

Rebecca Green
OCLC, Inc., Dublin, Ohio, USA

Abstract: The structure of a classification system contributes in a variety of ways to representing semantic relationships between its topics in the context of subject authority control. We explore this claim using the Dewey Decimal Classification (DDC) system as a case study. The DDC links its classes into a notational hierarchy, supplemented by a network of relationships between topics, expressed in class descriptions and in the Relative Index (RI). Topics/subjects are expressed both by the natural language text of the caption and notes (including Manual notes) in a class description and by the controlled vocabulary of the RI's alphabetic index, which shows where topics are treated in the classificatory structure. The expression of relationships between topics depends on paradigmatic and syntagmatic relationships between natural language terms in captions, notes, and RI terms; on the meaning of specific note types; and on references recorded between RI terms. The specific means used in the DDC for capturing hierarchical (including disciplinary), equivalence and associative relationships are surveyed.

Keywords: Dewey Decimal Classification; DDC; relationships; subject authority control; classification system structure

1. Subject authority control and classification schemes

> "The purpose of authority control is to ensure consistency in representing a value - a name of a person, a place name, or a term or code representing a subject - in the elements used as access points in information retrieval. . . . In addition to ensuring consistency in subject representation, a subject authority system may also record established semantic relationships among subject concepts and/or their labels" (FRSAD, 2011: 8).

The FRSAD (2011) model sets forth three groups of entities as potential bibliographic subjects. Group 1 entities - work, expression, manifestation, item - are the intellectual or artistic products described by bibliographic records. Group 2 entities - person, corporate body, family - are responsible for the content, production, dissemination or custodianship of Group 1 entities. Group 3 includes all other subject entities: concept, object, event and place. From the perspective of subject authority control, entities in Groups 1 and 2 rely on the same fundamentals that govern (non-subject-oriented) authority control over them. Authority control over two of the Group 3 entities - events and places - are addressed in part in authority control over corporate bodies. This leaves authority control over concepts and objects within the unique scope of subject authority control.

---

1 DDC, Dewey and Dewey Decimal Classification are registered trademarks of OCLC Online Computer Library Center, Inc.

In this paper we explore the contributions of classificatory structure to semantic relationships in the context of subject authority control, using the Dewey Decimal Classification (DDC) system as a case study. We focus our attention on subject authority control over Group 3 entities, which we collectively refer to as *topics*, especially concepts and objects.

Discussions of subject authority control typically focus on thesauri, featuring atomic concepts and their corresponding post-coordinate terms. But classification systems differ from thesauri in significant ways; these differences have profound effects on the semantic relationships operative in the system. The most significant difference is that the central unit of a classification is a class, designated by a notation or code, rather than a concept, designated by a term (alternatively, a class may be designated by its hierarchically-contextualised caption). By definition, a class is a set. Alternatively, we may say that the essential nature of classes is to group (presumably like) things together. From an extensional perspective, the members of the classes in a bibliographic classification system are the bibliographic resources assigned to them. But from an intensional perspective (which is our perspective here), the members of the classes in a bibliographic classification system are topics.

The classes of the DDC have been described as "topic neighborhoods" (Green & Panzer, 2010) or "conceptual [spaces] in which topics are located" (Green et al., 2013). The classificatory structure of the DDC links its classes into a notational hierarchy, supplemented by a network of relationships between topics, expressed in class descriptions and in the Relative Index (RI). That is, topics are expressed both by the (semi-)natural language text of the caption and notes (including Manual notes) given for a class and by the controlled vocabulary of the alphabetic index that shows where topics are treated in the classificatory structure.[2] The expression of relationships between topics depends on paradigmatic and syntagmatic relationships between natural language terms in captions, notes, and RI terms; on the meaning of specific note types; and on references recorded between RI terms. The interrelationships among the components of the DDC are shown in Figure 1.

2. DDC classificatory structure and paradigmatic relationships

While classification systems differ from thesauri in significant ways, the two types of knowledge organization systems also have major similarities, especially with respect to the types of semantic relationships they convey. Indeed, we find the same paradigmatic relationships in both: hierarchical relationships, equivalence relationships, and associative relationships.

---

2 Even though the topics in bibliographic classification systems are often complex (pre-coordinate) concepts, thesaurus-like features are not absent from them.

These semantic relationships hold between topics. Due to their conceptual nature, we often refer to topics symbolically, using words as our default symbol system. As a result, lexical relationships commonly parallel the semantic relationships of interest to us. In the discussion below, we take advantage of this parallelism between semantic and lexical relationships, avoiding the risk of being overly pedantic by not being too careful to distinguish between them. But

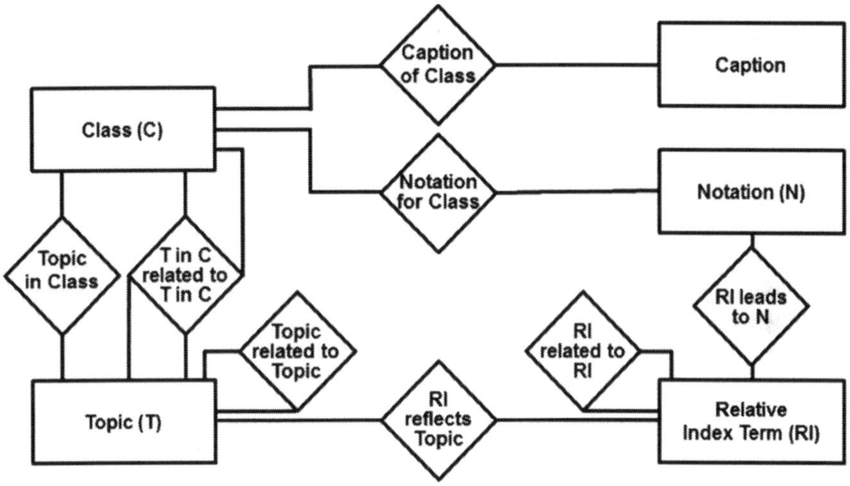

Figure 1: *Topic-oriented data model of DDC*[3]

where it matters, we will refer to topic X and use quotation marks around lexical items.

2.1 DDC classificatory structure and hierarchical relationships

Hierarchical relationships are expressed in the DDC through its structural hierarchy, which consists of both its notational hierarchy (where the decimal notation is expressive in that the relative specificity of hierarchically-related classes tends to correlate with the length of their corresponding notations) and the additional relationships defined through see references. A study of the relationships underlying the DDC notational hierarchy (Green & Panzer, 2011) identified specialization (FRSAD's generic relationship), instantiation (FRSAD's instance relationship), and whole-part relationships. For example, the relationship between 005.75 *Specific types of data files and databases* and 005.758 *Distributed data files and databases* is one of specialization: all distributed-data-files-and-databases are specific-data-files-and-databases, but only some specific-data-files-and-databases are distributed-data-files-and-

3 Figure previously published in Green et al., 2013, p. 179.

databases. The relationship between 224 *Prophetic books of Old Testament* and 224.8 *Amos* is one of instantiation, the book of Amos being a named instance of the class of prophetic books of the Old Testament. Various whole-part relationships are also found: T2—57 *Siberia (Asiatic Russia)* is a portion of T2—5 *Asia*; within public administration, 352.4 *Financial administration and budgets* has as one of its components 352.46 *Public expenditures*; and 340.55 *Medieval European law* is an element of the 340.55-340.59 *Medieval, modern, religious systems of law* collection. While the notational hierarchy ostensibly identifies relationships between classes, the ability to differentiate between types of hierarchical relationships relies wholly on the topical character of the classes.

The DDC's notational hierarchy defines a monohierarchical tree structure. Its structural hierarchy accommodates polyhierarchy through see references. The DDC's see references ostensibly lead from one class (the source class) to another class (the target class) by virtue of a topic in the target class; the fuller picture is that a see reference is dependent on topics in both source and target classes. Consider, for example, the following class description, which contains three see references:

170 Ethics (Moral philosophy)

Class here conscience, good and evil; ethics of specific subjects, interdisciplinary works on social ethics

For religious ethics, see 205; for social ethics as a method of social control, see 303.372. For ethics of a specific religion, see the religion, e.g., Christian ethics 241

This class is the interdisciplinary number for ethics (a statement confirmed by the Relative Index entry for *Ethics*, with no subheading, which points to this class), and the ethics of several specific subjects (e.g., political ethics, medical ethics, legal ethics) are set out in its subdivisions. We would therefore expect to find religious ethics here as well. But the first see reference tells us that works on this particular specialization of ethics / on the ethics of this specific subject are to be classed elsewhere, in 205 *Religious ethics* (the third see reference tells us, however, that ethics of specific religions are not classed in 205 *Religious ethics*, but in classes specific to each religion). On the basis of the first see reference, the topic religious ethics is hierarchically subordinate to both 170 *Ethics* and 201–209 *Specific aspects of religion*. Although the topics are interrelated, it is not the presence of "conscience" or of "good and evil" in the class-here note at 170 that motivates this see reference; it is the presence of "ethics of specific subjects". Thus, while only the topic in the target class is named in a see reference, the topic in the source class (although often named in the class description) must be inferred. In the case of scatter see references, of which the third see reference is an example, the see reference leads to a set of target classes; the topic in each target class must be instantiated separately. Thus, "ethics of a specific religion" refers in turn to Christian ethics, Buddhist ethics, Hindu ethics, Jewish ethics, Islamic ethics, and so forth.

2.2. DDC classificatory structure and equivalence relationships

FRSAD (2011) treats the equivalence relationship only as a lexical relationship between words and not as a semantic relationship between topics. That is, FRSAD may be said to posit the unity of any given topic (FRSAD's *thema*), to which multiple lexical items (FRSAD's *nomens*), within a single language or across multiple languages, may refer. An equivalence relationship holds between the various lexical items that refer to the same topic.

Is it possible for two topics to be equivalent? In some contexts it has been argued that two concepts are equivalent if their extension is the same, that is, if they apply to the same set of items. But we really are more concerned with equivalent intension/meaning. We resolve the quandary only pragmatically by positing semantic relationships among the topics in class descriptions and restricting lexical relationships to the Relative Index.

Equivalence relationships have several modes of expression in the DDC (Mitchell, 2001), including caption qualifiers, variant name notes, and former name notes. Consider, for example, the following class descriptions:

612.115 Coagulation (Clotting)

Including role of fibrin, fibrinoplastin, plasma, thrombin in clotting

796.356 64 Rink hockey

Variant names: hardball hockey, quad roller hockey

324.294 04 The Nationals

Former names: Australian Country Party, National Country Party, National Party of Australia

The caption qualifier at 612.115 *Coagulation (Clotting)* indicates that coagulation and clotting are the same phenomenon. The variant names note at 796.35664 *Rink hockey* similarly indicates that rink hockey, hardball hockey, and quad roller hockey are all the same game, while the former names note at 324.29404 *The Nationals* indicates that Australian Country Party, National Country Party, and National Party of Australia all refer to the same political party.

Of the topics belonging to a class, some (e.g., those in class-here notes) are said to approximate the whole of the class. For some internal purposes (e.g., number building), all topics that approximate the whole of a class might be said to be equivalent. Independent semantic analysis, however, may or may not support such a characterization. An equivalence relationship holds between the topics named in the class-here note at 005.74015113 *Mathematical logic* - logic databases and deductive databases, but often, a different type of relationship (perhaps most often an associative relationship) holds between the multiple topics named in a class-here note. In the class-here note at 512.92 *Algebraic operations*, we have sibling relationships among the specific algebraic operations; in the class-here note at 808.5 *Rhetoric of speech*, it is difficult to identify which, if indeed any, particular relationship holds.

005.740 151 13 Mathematical logic

Class here logic databases, deductive databases

512.92 Algebraic operations

Class here addition, subtraction, multiplication, division

808.5 Rhetoric of speech

Class here voice, expression, gesture

2.3. DDC classificatory structure and associative relationships

Associative relationships are generally understood as the varied set of semantic relationships that are not accounted for by hierarchical or equivalence relationships. Optimally, specific types of associative relationships can be identified, since without such specification, associative relationships cannot be used for much besides bringing the user's attention to another, potentially relevant, topic.

FRSAD (2011) mentions a number of specific associative relationship types, including Cause/Effect, Process/Agent, Action / Product of action, Raw material / Product, and so forth. Here is a context where the difference between the granularity of their basic units - a concept in a thesaurus vs. a class in a classification system - makes a real difference. The design of a bibliographic classification could easily incorporate topics interconnected by associative relationships into the same class. For example, at 730.92 *Biography*, the class-here note gathers together "description and critical appraisal of sculptors or plastic artists and their works", alongside biographical material (the parallel situation occurs for other, but not all, arts in the 700s). But in 641 Food *and drink*, separate developments exist for 641.3 *Food* and 641.5 *Cooking*.

Associative relationships in the DDC are typically expressed through either class-elsewhere notes or see-also references. Like see references, such relationships are topical relationships, with the topic in the target class specified explicitly in the note/reference, while the topic in the source class must be inferred.

Giving the location of interrelated topics is only one of several functions of class-elsewhere notes. Other roles include "[showing] preference order among topics, [leading] to broader or narrower topics in the same notational hierarchy, [overriding] the first-of-two rule, [and leading] to the comprehensive or interdisciplinary number for the topic" (Chan & Mitchell, 2003: 25).

962.054 Administration of Anwar Sadat, 1970-1981
Class Israel-Arab War, 1973, in 956.048

415.92 Word formation
Including affixes (infixes, prefixes, suffixes), clitics; formation of compound words

Class here derivational morphology

Class etymology in 412

Numbers for historical periods in the span for 930-990 *History of specific continents, countries, localities; extraterrestrial worlds* are formed using notation from Table 2 for geographic area and area-specific notation for the period. The periods may be defined by political administrations (as is the case with 962.054 *Administration of Anwar Sadat, 1970-1981*), by periods of foreign rule / political alignments, of war, etc. The number 962.054 lies within the development for the history of Egypt and covers a span of 11 years, from October 1970 to October 1981. The Israel-Arab War, 1973 (also known as Yom Kippur War) falls entirely within this time frame. The class-elsewhere note found at 962.054 is also found at 956.91042 *Period of Republic, 1945-*, where 956.91 introduces the development for the history of Syria, and at 956.94053 1967-1974, where 956.94 introduces the development for the history of Palestine/Israel.

In all three cases, the class-elsewhere note takes us to 956.048, where we find the following upward hierarchy:

956 Middle East (Near East)

956.04 1945–1980

956.048 Israel-Arab War, 1973 (Yom Kippur War)

Thus, for the Israel-Arab War, 1973, these class-elsewhere notes lead from historical period numbers for the principal countries involved in the war (Egypt, Syria, and Israel) to a number for an historical period for the wider region. The relationship between the war and any historical period is associative.

The class at 415.92 *Word formation* contains a class-elsewhere note that sends works on etymology away, to their own class. Unlike the example just examined, the relationship between word formation and etymology does not fit a regular pattern. Word formation refers to the process of forming new words through derivation or compounding, while etymology refers to the history of words and their origins. Thus, word formation stands at the beginning of a process that etymology stands at the end of; word formation may be part of the history of a word that etymology examines.

A systematic study of the semantic relationships expressed by class-elsewhere notes in the DDC has yet to be conducted. We anticipate identifying some productive associative relationships, but suspect that the associative relationships in many class-elsewhere notes will be of a relatively unique nature.

See-also references are said to "point to topics that are [only] tangentially related to the topic where the note is given" (Chan & Mitchell, 2003: 28). A study of see-also references in the DDC (Green, 2011) found relationships established on the basis of lexical similarity, complementarity, facet difference, and relational configuration difference, as evident in the following examples:

T2—764 252 Austin County

See also—76431 for Austin (city)

641.865 4 Cookies

Variant name: biscuits

See also . . . 641.8157 for biscuits (quick breads)

190 Modern western and other noneastern philosophy

See also 181 for eastern philosophy

621.91 Planing and milling tools

See also 671.35 for machining metal

616.075 Diagnosis and prognosis

616.075 61 Blood analysis

See also 616.15075 for diagnosis of diseases of blood

616.15 Diseases of blood

See also 616.07561 for use of blood analysis in diagnosis of diseases in general

616.150 75 Diseases of blood—diagnosis and prognosis

See-also references based on lexical similarity depend on the presence of two lexical items (words or phrases) that could be mistaken for each other. For example, the see-also reference at T2—764252 serves to differentiate between a county and a city in Texas with the same name (Austin); the reference is especially needed because the city is *not* located in the county of the same name. At 641.8654, the see-also reference has its basis in the homonymy between the meanings of the word "biscuit" in American cooking and British cooking.

Complementary topics exhaust the universe with respect to some property. For instance, the scope of the development at 190 is noneastern philosophy; the see-also reference points to the complementary topic (eastern philosophy). See-also relationships are also used for topics that represent different facets of a subject. At 621.91, the emphasis is on the tools used for milling; at 671.35 the emphasis is on the object that is milled.

Finally, we also find see-also relationships linking complex topics that include the same topical components, but relate them in different ways. The end result is that the relationships among the topical components form different configurations. In the nearly reciprocal see-also relationships between 616.07561 and 616.15075, the relationships distinguish between diagnosis based on analysis of blood at 616.07561 and diagnosis used to identify diseases of blood at 616.15075.

Additional see-also references were based on real-world knowledge; their relationships did not appear to be generalizable.

2.4 DDC classificatory structure through the Relative Index

We have previously noted the role played by the DDC's Relative Index in giving access to the DDC's classified arrangement of classes through an alphabetically ordered set of terms. Access to the classification is achieved through Figure 1's Relative-Index-Term-<reflects>-Topic relationship. Given this overarching relationship, we would expect to find essentially the same kinds of relationships / a parallel set of relationships in the Relative Index as we find in the classification itself, only now we consider the relationships from a lexical perspective.

The MARC authority format, which is used to store Relative Index data, provides for the capture of relationships between Relative Index terms. In this format, hierarchical and equivalence relationships between topics may be expressed using explicitly coded references between corresponding RI headings. Although only a small number of hierarchical and equivalence relationships have been coded at present in the DDC, many others can be identified automatically (Green, 2014). To some extent, this depends on the process of matching topics expressed by RI headings to topics expressed in class descriptions, which is not entirely straightforward (Green, 2008). For example, if RI terms can be matched to topics expressed in class descriptions, equivalence relationships expressed using caption qualifiers, variant name notes, and former name notes can be detected by virtue of those phenomena in class descriptions, as discussed in section 2.2.

Other equivalence relationships can be detected by comparing each pair of Relative Index terms that index the same number. One comparison looks for the replacement of a hyphen with a space (thus identifying the equivalence of "Full-text indexing" and "Fulltext indexing" at 025.486). Another comparison examines whether single word terms could be acronyms (thus identifying the equivalence of PRECIS indexing and Preserved Context Indexing System at 025.47).

The identification of yet other equivalence relationships among Relative Index terms takes advantage of matches between (a) RI terms and (b) Library of Congress Subject Headings (LCSHs) or variant access points. Processing such matches ferrets out Bliss Bibliographic Classification and Bliss Classification as equivalent terms at 025.434. Other equivalence relationships can be identified on the basis of matching RI terms with lexical entries in WordNet[4], a lexical database of English word senses, and of membership in the same WordNet "synset" (where a synset is a set of synonymous word senses). Processing these matches supports the equivalence of Bigfoot and Sasquatch at 001.944 and of Annuals and Yearbooks at 050.

The automatic identification of hierarchical relationships similarly can rely solely on internal data or can take advantage of connections with relationships in external data. In English, the phrase X A (in which X is likely to

4 Available online at http://wordnet.princeton.edu/.

be an adjective modifying A) is typically more specific than A, especially if X A indexes a class that is subordinate to a class indexed by A. This heuristic supports the following relationship:

- Small-scale systems (003.7) BT Systems (003)
- Analytical bibliography (010.42) BT Bibliography (010)
- Pictorial journalism (070.49) BT Journalism (070.4)

Some hierarchical relationships between Relative Index terms are of the form A—X BT A, but others are of the form A—X BT X. We have identified some number of patterns that operate in one fashion or the other. On the basis of these patterns, we identify the following hierarchical relationships:

- Art metalwork—to 4000 B.C. (739.09012) BT Art metalwork (739)
- Museums—Washington (D.C.) (069.09753) BT Museums (069)
- Finance—library operations (025.11) BT Finance (332)
- Computer graphics—dictionaries (006.603) BT Dictionaries (413)
- Adolescents—libraries for (027.626) BT Libraries (027)
- Union catalogs—library cooperation (021.642) BT Library cooperation (021.64)

An important subset of hierarchical relationships is that in which A—X BT A and X names a discipline. Consider, for example, the RI Gambling—law. We can assert Gambling—law BT Gambling in that 306.482, the number indexed by Gambling, is its interdisciplinary number. That interdisciplinary number is broader than Gambling in the context of any specific discipline. Additional cross-disciplinary relationships are addressed in Gnoli, De Santis & Pusterla (2015).

Other hierarchical relationships can be identified on the basis of LCSH and WordNet data. For example, LCSH data supports the identification of a hierarchical relationship between the broader RI term Special libraries, which indexes 026, and the RI term Technical libraries, which indexes 026.6. WordNet data supports the identification of a hierarchical relationship between the broader RI term Computer networks, which indexes 004.6, and Internet, which indexes 004.678.

Automatic identification of associative relationships has not been attempted.

3. DDC classificatory structure and syntagmatic relationships

Although the DDC is not a fully faceted classification scheme, faceting underlies the development of portions of the system and is visible in many of its add instructions. Inter-facet relationships, which are syntagmatic in nature, have already been noted among the associative relationships in see-also references. Inter-facet relationships are also expressed with some degree of systematicity in the complex structure of many RI headings. Consider, for example, the number 787.871642, which is built with the following components:

787.87 Guitars

(784-788:)1 General principles, musical forms, instruments

(781.)642 Country music

and is indexed with the RI Guitars – music – country music. It is not necessarily the case that all components (main heading + subheadings) of a Relative Index term will match up on a one-to-one basis with the components of a built number, but often there is partial alignment. In such cases it is often possible to see syntagmatic relationships expressed systematically across a set of Relative Index headings, as is the case in Table 1.

4. Conclusions

If thesauri provide the prototypical pattern for subject authority control, it is because of the simplicity and clarity with which they express relationships. The basic pattern used is the assertion of a hierarchical, equivalence, or associative relationship between terms, each of which expresses a concept. Possible extensions to this pattern are the specification of type of hierarchical relationship (e.g., instance, whole-part) and expression of concepts through the conjunction (ANDing) or disjunction (ORing) of terms.

Table 1: *Correspondence between built number and Relative Index term components*

Base number	Component 1	Component 2	Relative Index term
787.87 Guitars	(784-788:)1 General principles, musical forms, instruments	(781.)642 Country music	Guitars – music – country music
787.87 Guitars	(784-788:)1 General principles, musical forms, instruments	(781.)643 Blues	Guitars – music – blues
787.87 Guitars	(784-788:)1 General principles, musical forms, instruments	(781.)644 Soul	Guitars – music – soul
787.87 Guitars	(784-788:)1 General principles, musical forms, instruments	(781.)65 Jazz	Guitars – music – jazz
787.87 Guitars	(784-788:)1 General principles, musical forms, instruments	(781.)654 Mainstream jazz ("including swing")	Guitars – music – swing
787.87 Guitars	(784-788:)1 General principles, musical forms, instruments	(781.)66 Rock (Rock 'n' roll)	Guitars – music – rock

Subject authority control is, of necessity, more complicated in a classification system like the DDC. We add another basic unit, a class, to the mix. On the one hand, this means having to take the inherent nature of classes as a gathering place for like items into account. In the context of a bibliographic classification that "likeness" often encompasses a variety of relationship types, including associative relationships (and we have seen that the expression of associative relationships in the context of the DDC needs further investigation). On the other hand, the relationship between the topics that are part of the class and the Relative Index terms that index the class also needs accounting for. Doing so will require (1) establishing relationships between natural language expressions in class descriptions and Relative Index terms; and (2) recognizing the roles played by specific note types and other features in the system. Direct relationships between Relative Index terms follow the thesaural pattern more closely than other aspects of the DDC, but the complex, pre-coordinate, nature of many RI terms adds further complexity to the situation.

Why does the relational side of subject authority control in a classification system like the DDC matter? The importance lies in the user tasks supported by these relationships, with the users including, minimally, developers of the classification system, persons providing crosswalks between knowledge organization systems, classifiers, and last, but not least, end-users. FRSAD (2011: 34) sets forth three generic user tasks supported in part by relationships within a subject authority control system: finding subjects (and/or their appellations), identifying subjects (and/or their appellations), and exploring relationships between subjects (and/or their appellations). Practically speaking, a strong set of relationships is required in a subject authority control system for these purposes:

- to help developers maintain the system without introducing confusion,
- to support the establishment of crosswalks between systems that can assist in knowledge discovery when an end-user searches with entry vocabulary from one system against bibliographic records to which subject appellations from other systems have been assigned,
- to help classifiers assign most appropriate subject appellations to bibliographic records, and
- to help end-users find the most appropriate resources for their needs.

References

Functional requirements for subject authority data, a conceptual model (FRSAD). (2011). IFLA Working Group on Functional Requirements for Subject Authority Records (FRSAR). Edited by M. L. Zeng, M. Žumer, A. Salaba. Berlin/München: De Gruyter Saur. Available at: http://www.ifla.org/files/assets/classification-and-indexing/functional-requirements-for-subject-authority-data/frsad-final-report.pdf.

Chan, L. M.; Mitchell, J. S. (2003). *Dewey Decimal Classification: principles and application.* Dublin, Ohio: OCLC Online Computer Library Center.

Gnoli, C.; De Santis, R.; Pusterla, L. (2015). Commerce, see also Rhetoric: cross-discipline relationships as authority data for enhanced retrieval. In: *Classification & authority control: expanding resource discovery: proceedings of the International UDC Seminar, 29-30 October 2015, Lisbon, Portugal.* Edited by A. Slavic, M. I. Cordeiro. Würzburg: Ergon Verlag, pp. 151-161.

Green, R. (2008). Making visible hidden relationships in the Dewey Decimal Classification: how Relative Index terms relate to DDC classes. In: *Culture and identity in knowledge organization: proceedings of the Tenth International ISKO Conference, 5-8 August 2008, Montréal, Canada.* Edited by C. Arsenault, J. T. Tennis. Würzburg: Ergon, pp. 8-14.

Green, R. (2011). See-also relationships in the Dewey Decimal Classification. *Knowledge Organization*, 38, pp. 335-341. Available at: http://journals.lib.washington.edu/index.php/nasko/article/view/12789.

Green, R. (2014). *Moving towards a topic-based DDC.* Presented at 25th Annual SIG/CR Classification Research Workshop, Universal Classification in the 21st Century, in conjunction with ASIS&T 2014 Annual Meeting, Seattle, November 1, 2014.

Green, R.; Panzer, M. (2010). The ontological character of classes in the Dewey Decimal Classification. In: *Paradigms and conceptual systems in knowledge organization: proceedings of the Eleventh International ISKO Conference, 23-26 February 2010, Rome, Italy.* Edited by C. Gnoli, F. Mazzocchi. Würzburg: Ergon, pp. 171-179.

Green, R.; Panzer, M. (2011). Relationships in the notational hierarchy of the Dewey Decimal Classification. In: *Classification & ontology: formal approaches and access to knowledge: proceedings of the International UDC Seminar, 19-20 September 2011, The Hague, The Netherlands.* Edited by A. Slavic, E. Civallero, 161-176. Würzburg: Ergon Verlag.

Green, R. et al. (2013). From modelling to visualization of topic relationships in classification schemes. In: *Classification & visualization: interfaces to knowledge: proceedings of the International UDC Seminar, 24-25 October 2013, The Hague, The Netherlands.* Edited by A. Slavic, A. Akdag Salah, S. Davies, 177-190. Würzburg: Ergon Verlag.

Mitchell, J. S. (2001). Relationships in the Dewey Decimal Classification system. In: *Relationships in the organization of knowledge.* Edited by C. A. Bean, R. Green. Dordrecht: Kluwer Academic, pp. 211-226.

REBECCA GREEN is an assistant editor of the DDC, with specific responsibilities related to DDC training modules and investigation of relationships in the DDC, with a long-term goal of developing a topic-based version of the system to support automated applications. Other research interests include the ontological characterization of classes in classification systems, extension of the FRSAD model to accommodate a topic-centred view of the DDC, and automated methods for identifying the facet structure of a subject. Prior to joining OCLC, Rebecca was an associate professor in the College of Information Studies at the University of Maryland.

Distributed person data: using Semantic Web compliant data in subject name headings

Violeta Ilik
Galter Health Sciences Library, Feinberg School of Medicine, Northwestern University, Chicago, IL, USA

Abstract: Providing efficient access to information is a crucial library mission. Subject classification is one of the major pillars that guarantees the accessibility of records in libraries. In this paper we discuss the need to associate person IDs and URIs with subjects when a named person happens to be the subject of the document. This is often the case with biographies, schools of thought in philosophy, politics, art, and literary criticism. Using Semantic Web compliant data in subject name headings enhances the ability to collocate topics about a person. Also, in retrieval, books about a person would be easily linked to works by that same person. In the context of the Semantic Web, it is expected that, as the available information grows, one would be more effective in the task of information retrieval. Information about a person or, as in the case of this paper, about a researcher exist in various databases, which can be discipline specific or publishers' databases, and in such cases they have an assigned identifier. They also exist in institutional directory databases. We argue that these various databases can be leveraged to support improved discoverability and retrieval of research output for individual authors and institutions, as well as works about those authors.

Keywords: subject name headings; name authorities; non-MARC name authority records; VIVO; URI; RDF

1. Introduction

The library community currently does not make a full use of the rich information about persons that is available from various data sources. Most academic researchers publish only academic articles; therefore they do not exist in the Library of Congress Name Authority File (LCNAF)[1]. They do however exist in other data sources such as their respective institutional directory databases, discipline specific repositories and publisher databases, to name a few. In this paper we propose leveraging the data available in non-traditional library systems to support improved discoverability and retrieval of information about persons. To utilise these data sources, the library specific bibliographic databases such as the Online Computer Library Center (OCLC)[2] and SkyRiver[3] need to support the integration of data coming from non-traditional library sources. Currently OCLC supports "Control Heading" from the LCNAF. We think

1 The Library of Congress Name Authority File (NAF). Library of Congress. Available at: http://id.loc.gov/authorities/names.html.
2 OCLC Online Computer Library Center Inc. Available at: http://www.oclc.org/.
3 SkyRiver by Innovative Interfaces Inc. Available at: http://www.iii.com/products/skyriver.

the time is right to expand the available sources for controlled headings to other data sources.

In this paper we will give general background information about the use of distributed person data in subject name headings. We state the problem and the ideal solution, we discuss the current crowded landscape of person data, then, in the absence of ideal solutions, we discuss what currently can be done to enhance bibliographic records with non-traditional library data. We focus on one specific source of person data – VIVO, a semantic web application and we make the case why using URIs in bibliographic records is important.

1.1. Background

The Subject Authority Cooperative Program (SACO) document *Name Headings as Subjects H 430* states: "most RDA and AACR2 name headings are usable not only as main or added entries, but also as subject headings." (2013: 1). The document points out that there are some situations where a valid name heading may not be assigned as a subject heading and it is the cataloguers responsibility to be aware of and to be able to identify such situations. The SACO document *Subject Usage Information in Name Authority Records H 432* states "Information applicable to the usage of a name heading in subject cataloging may appear in a 667 field in the name authority record. Because the 667 field is also used for descriptive cataloging information, there may be more than one such field in a given NAR." (2014: 1). The following is not allowed as a subject heading:

> 110 1# $a United States. $b President (1801-1809 : Jefferson)
> 667 ## $a SUBJECT USAGE: This heading is not valid for use as a subject.
> Works about this person are entered under Jefferson, Thomas, 1743-1826.

The note in 667 points the cataloguer toward using the name authority record for Jefferson, Thomas, 1743-1826 which is the actual name authority record (NAR) for President Jefferson. This NAR has the following Unique Resource Identifier (URI) assigned from the LCNAF: id.loc.gov/authorities/names/n79089957.

The URIs, clearly, represent the most important piece of the puzzle in the current environment. As Verborgh & De Rose (2015) note, the Web has become the world's largest source of knowledge not just for people but for machines too. The Web has evolved and now it offers something more powerful: linked data, which represents each piece of data as a link between two objects. These links, or URIs, enable data mining programs to derive knowledge that is human-specific.

Harper & Tillett (2006) point out that the benefits of authority control apply to metadata about the creators of resources as well as to subject access. These benefits include search precision, powerful navigation, collocation and linking between various tools and resources. It is well known that libraries have been dealing with identification, disambiguation and collocation of the names of content creators since the beginning of cataloguing and at the same time with collocation of works about those same authors. Harper & Tillett (2006) mention the Friend of a Friend (FOAF) project[4] and the need to find ways to integrate similar initiatives with existing mechanisms for name authority control in libraries, which will in turn help bring library catalogues into the mix of tools available on the Web. They also point out that the availability of library authority data in a more Web-friendly format has the potential to positively influence the organization of the broad spectrum of Web content already available. The development of a Virtual International Authority File (VIAF) has been a key idea moving forward this initiative.

Rebecca Dean (2004) states that the rapid growth of the World Wide Web and the emergence of numerous metadata schemas have spurred a re-examination of the way subject data are provided for Web resources. She points out the need for having simple and interoperable subject schema for metadata to ensure usability by non-cataloguers and to enable users to search across both discipline boundaries and across information retrieval and storage systems. OCLC adapted the Library of Congress Subject Headings (LCSH) to create FAST (Faceted Application of Subject Terminology) which represents a simplified syntax that retains the very rich vocabulary of LCSH and is easier to understand, apply, control and use. As Dean (2004) points out, FAST headings for personal and corporate names are very similar, and in most cases exact, to the established name heading in the LC authority file.

Tillett (2004: 28) noted that the "Web environment opens up new uses for authority records and new objectives to augment the traditional objectives." She argues that the cataloguing community is moving "from the stand-alone authority files of a single institution, or even from the shared online files towards a goal of sharing authority files among all communities" (ibid). Tillett further discusses how the existence of authority records for an entity opens up new possibilities for links to other resources, and she includes examples such as a home page for the entity described, links to biographical dictionaries and other reference sources on the Web. She mentions the possibility that the records would serve to control the various forms of names for an entity rather than having any single heading be the only authorized form. The Getty Institute in its Union List of Artists Names (ULAN)[5] provides a listing of the forms of name for an entity that have been found in various resources and brought together to use for searching and displays. The Getty Institute released its Union List of Artists Names as Linked Open Data on 30th of April 2015, which will provide for much better retrieval and will resolve the current issue of retrieving all variant forms of names that do not have a clear connection between them.

4 FOAF is available at: http://www.foaf-project.org/.

5 The Getty's Union List of Artist Names is available at: http://www.getty.edu/research/tools/vocabularies/ulan/.

The use of standard numbers has been mentioned as a way to enable collocation when there are several variant forms of a name used by an entity. The use of the language-neutral number for the entity in a bibliographic record was discussed decades ago as pointed out in the review of the feasibility of International Standard Authority Data Number (ISADN) by Tillett (2008). She reminds us that other options were also in place such as the use of an International Standard Authority Number (ISAN), as well as the ISO International Standard Text Code (ISTC to identify works and expressions).

1.2. The current landscape

The current landscape that represents various systems that capture data about researchers is crowded. The systems fall into ten categories or types, according to a report by the OCLC Research, Registering Researchers in Authority Files Task Group (2014):

1. Authority hubs that provide a centralized location of authority records for multiple institutions - LC/NACO Authority File; ResearcherID; Virtual International Authority File (VIAF) ;
2. Current Research Information System (CRIS), which stores and manages data about research conducted at an institution and integrates it with data from external sources: Symplectic;
3. Identifier hubs, providing a centralized registry of identifiers (2): International Standard Name Identifier (ISNI); Open Researcher and Contributor ID (ORCID) ;
4. National research portals, providing access to all research data stored in a nation's network of repositories;
5. Online encyclopaedia: Wikipedia;
6. Reference management, a system that helps scholars organize their research, collaborate with others, and discover the latest research: Mendeley;
7. Research and collaboration hub, a centralized portal where scholars in a particular discipline can work together: nanoHUB;
8. Researcher profile systems, networks that facilitate professional networking among scholars: VIVO, Google Scholar; LinkedIn;
9. Subject author identifier system, a registration service to link scholars with the records about the works they have written: AuthorClaim;
10. Subject repository such as arXiv hosted by Cornell Library.

The challenge of compiling scholarly output, measuring it, finding collaborators, disseminating research and tracking funded research is substantial. Especially if we take into consideration that each system creates identifiers for each author and co-author and those identifiers are valid and usable only in that particular system. Additional challenges include disambiguating researchers across institutions, preserving the institutional authority over researcher scholarly contributions, handling multiple names/transliteration, change of names, pseudonyms, multiple profiles, identifiers that are not linked and, most importantly, the various data standards that are not interoperable. One data source cannot solve all these problems and this is why one has to "think globally and act locally".

All of us working in all these various systems dealing with person data at the moment seem to have an open door to experiment and do something about solving the problem of uniquely identifying researchers within our systems, but also to think beyond individual systems in terms of global approaches that would connect and enable the exchange of information between all the systems. Producing and publishing data that is interoperable and/or reusable is the most important aspect of the problem.

1.3 Uniquely identifying a person

Everyone wants to uniquely identify a researcher: the researchers themselves, institutions, publishers, libraries, funding organizations and identity management systems. However, we also want to identify works that are about that individual researcher, works in which he/she is the actual subject. If there were a unique identifier for each researcher, all these tasks would be easier, but no such identifiers exist at the moment, and this is a source of considerable difficulty. We need to address these issues and aid researchers in compiling and disseminating their scholarly output and to identify works about those researchers. We need to be able to retrieve all the information about researchers from various databases and obtain the best possible aggregated data. Interoperability and reuse of data can be and should be addressed, since we live in an age that offers unique opportunities - we already have ways of publishing Semantic Web compliant data that can be interlinked and useful across databases.

Many of us are asking the same question: how to best utilise the various types of researcher identifiers to be able to accurately identify researchers and their scholarly outputs for better research outcomes and for better retrieval? Identifying published works about those same researchers and works where researchers are the subject is equally important, since data containing that information would be extremely valuable not only to researchers themselves, but also to other stakeholders. In order to be able to represent that information in structured form, such as RDF, we need to have appropriate classes and properties defined in existing ontologies.

2. The problem and the ideal solution

As stated above, most academic researchers do not exist in the LCNAF, since they primarily publish academic articles. Because of the fact that information about those researchers exists in other data sources such as discipline specific repositories (arXiv), publishers' databases (Scopus) and their respective institutional directory databases, to name a few, we propose that the library community opens up to the use of that data and moves towards the implementation of technologies that would make this possible. OCLC, the biggest provider of bibliographic records to libraries around the world, is an essential partner in accomplishing this ideal solution, since they would have to open their doors to working with data from the non-traditional library world and enable the use and distribution of that data to the whole community.

In an ideal scenario, when a cataloguer comes across a person name that does not have a NAR, it would make sense to attempt to control that name heading with a possibly established form of the name not only in the LCNAF but also in various other databases and systems, either library specific (other national libraries), discipline specific, or any other global data source. What this means is that a cataloguer should be able to control the name heading of a person even if it comes from ISNI, ORCID, the Getty ULAN Catalog, the Dutch Digital Author ID, the Brazilian Lattes Platform, etc. We need to see this happen, so that when we come across authors that have no authority record created in the traditional library authority hubs we should be able to use non-traditional headings when importing authority records in our bibliographic data. This is nothing new since similar proposals have been known to exist (Tillett, 2004). Today we actually have the means to do it because we live in the age of the Semantic Web where data is published and structured in Resource Description Framework (RDF) format.

However, the bibliographic utilities (OCLC and SkyRiver) and the vendor community which includes Integrated Library Systems (ILS), automated authority control vendors, contract cataloguing vendors and publishers, are not yet ready to offer a technical environment that enables us to control the name headings that come from linked data products and services.

2.1. What can we do now: proposed solution

The focus of this paper is the researcher profile system VIVO and the Semantic Web compliant data that can be leveraged in different systems. VIVO is a discovery tool that connects researchers across disciplines, institutions, geography and time. With this in mind, acknowledging that the ideal solution will not be available in the near future, we propose the use of alternative and non-traditional library data in NARs when used as subject headings – more specifically we propose enhancement of name authority records by adding trusted VIVO person URIs.

The non-traditional library data in this case is the URI assigned to a person/researcher in an existing VIVO site. Non-traditional data can also include the identifier (ID) or URI of the person in question that comes from ORCID[6], ISNI[7], arXiv[8] and various other databases and/or repositories. The process of authority control is much broader than the one that traditionally takes place in large

6 ORCID- Connecting Research and Researchers is available at http://orcid.org/.

7 ISNI - International Standard Name Identifier (ISO 27729) is available at http://www.isni.org/.

8 arXIV.org (e-prints in Physics, Mathematics, Computer Science, Quantitative Biology, Quantitative Finance and Statistics) is available at http://arxiv.org/.

libraries or bibliographic agencies since it covers not only the task of identification of the entity "person," but also the tasks of contextualisation.

2.2. What is VIVO?

VIVO was developed by Cornell University in 2003 and, with the help of an NIH grant in 2009, grew to become an open source project. VIVO is an open, shared platform for connecting scholars, research communities, campuses and countries using Linked Open Data. It links data from institutional and public sources to create web profiles populated with researcher interests, activities and accomplishments.

The data sources used in VIVO are authoritative data sources that include university, agencies, repositories and aggregators. Private and sensitive information is never used or imported in VIVO. The rich information in VIVO profiles can be repurposed and shared with other institutional web pages and consumers. Data is housed and maintained at the local institution, which provides for regular updates. VIVO provides search results in faceted way. Researcher profiles are created via automated data feeds, but can also be customized to better fit the needs of the individual. Information is open source and it is available for use and re-use in other applications.

VIVO works with Resource Description Framework (RDF, 2004) and the Web Ontology Language (OWL, 2004) standards because of their wide adoption and because of the increasingly rich and diverse set of associated tools available (cf. Börner et al., 2012: 16). VIVO can be searched by keyword, as well as browsed by name, organization, or research area. When discussing searching it is worth noting that providing efficient access to information can be approached in different ways, and almost always implies the use of an indexing language such as a taxonomy or an ontology. The VIVO Semantic Web application uses the VIVO-ISF ontology. As noted on the Dura Space (2014) VIVO wiki page "The Integrated Semantic Framework ontology modules for VIVO (the VIVO-ISF ontology) provide a set of types (classes) and relationships (properties) to represent researchers and the full context in which they work." The ISF ontology leverages a number of ontologies in a unified, semantic structure. As stated on the DuraSpace (2013) VIVO wiki page "many of these ontologies are part of the Open Biological and Biomedical Ontologies organization, known as the OBO Foundry." These source ontologies may be imported in their entirety or included selectively through the MIREOT (Minimum Information to Reference an External Ontology Term) approach.

2.3. Why URIs and the current solution

Semantic Web and linked data communities and their attempt to tackle the problem of the semantics of metadata by giving each concept a URI, so that the URI can be linked with other URIs by an equivalence or related by a relationship.

Brickley (2011) states that "the strength of a URI-based approach is that the same URI can be given different expressions, allowing semantically different forms to be mapped and rich connections to be made between content." The problem with such an approach is that governance is required to ensure that the stated relationships are valid and useful in the contexts that they are practically being used. As Fran points out:

> "in the context of knowing what an author has written, it is valid to assert that a book is the same as an e-book, whereas in the context of delivering a purchase to a customer, treating the two as the same is not valid." (Fran, 2012: 90)

In the context of the VIVO Semantic Web application, the possibility to express the relationship of a person with the book that he/she is the subject of is not clearly represented in the VIVO-ISF ontology. Currently, VIVO-ISF supports only the *featuredIn* property and it is not clear if this property is sufficient to express the fact that the person is the subject of the specific work. For example *featuredIn* is defined in VIVO-ISF ontology as "This relates a person to an information resource that contains a featured article on that person" (vivoweb.org/files/vivo-isf-public-1.6.owl). Extending the definition of what *featuredIn* means will be sufficient, but as currently defined this property leads us to believe that we can only use it in cases when a person is featured in an article. Experimentation we performed proved that this property can be successfully used to express the relationship a person has with any type of information resource (publication type) and not just an article. For example if we have a person that is represented in our VIVO instance with the following URI: http://vivo.northwestern.edu/individual/nbf813378 and we have an article featuring him in our VIVO instance the relationship is represented as in Figure 1.

One can also represent the *featuredIn* relationship between the person and a book, a biography, or any other publication type (Figure 2).

As mentioned above few potential confusing points may be that it is not clear from the definition of the *featuredIn* property that one can represent the relationship between a person as a subject with any publication types, not just articles, and another is that this property is not representing the aboutness in a sense as understood in the traditional library world. As a reminder, according to Žumer, Zeng & Salaba (2012: 5)

> "aboutness is a statement of what a work (an information resource) is about, what topic it covers. It usually is expressed with the relationship "work is about/covers/has subject x, y, and z." Information professionals when analysing the content of the resource through the process of identifying the topics discussed or otherwise represented in the resource, are trying to assess the user information needs that can be fulfilled by the resource at a future time. The user, on the other hand, when trying to fulfil an information need, wants to find the appropriate resources or verify whether the resource(s) obtained contain relevant information."

Figure 1: VIVO featuredIn property

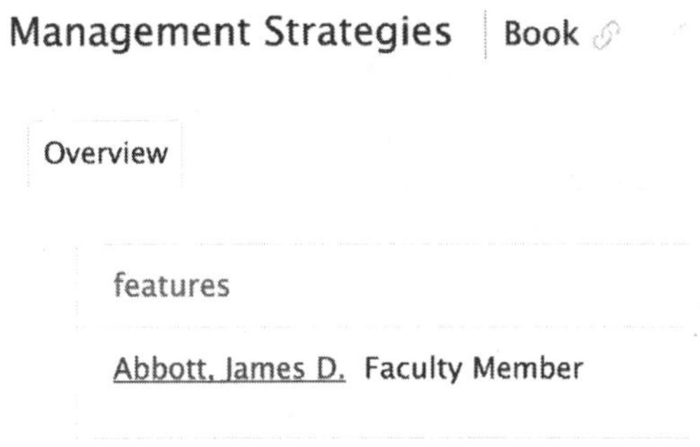

Figure 2: *Person as subject of a book*

One way to solve this problem is to possibly extend the VIVO-ISF ontology to represent the aboutness aspect in a clearer way since it is very important to know when a person is the subject of a work. The property will need to have *agent* in the range and needs to be defined in the domain of *information content entity (ICE)*.

As of now, the only way to capture non-traditional data in the form of IDs or URIs is to enhance the authority records with the VIVO URIs, or any other URIs, by adding the values in field 024, first indicator 7 with the value of the URI in subfield *a* as shown below:

024 7 # $a http://vivo.northwestern.edu/individual/nbf813378 $2 uri

In case the cataloguer is not at a NACO institution and cannot create the NAR for the person there should be the possibility to add the URI in field 600 - Subject Added Entry-Personal Name, in subfield $0 - Authority record control number or standard number, as shown below:

600 10$a Abbott, James D. $0(uri) http://vivo.northwestern.edu/individual/nbf813378

The authority record control numbers, such as the Library of Congress Control Numbers, can also be used as unique persistent identifiers. Lately we are seeing the trend of using the ORCID in authority records, more specifically in the 024, Other Standard Identifier field, with the value of ORCID entered in subfield 2. The same is true for the VIAF, ISNI, or the LCCN (see Figure 3).

010		‡a no2005043559
024	7	‡a 0000000043605828 ‡2 isni
024	7	‡a 0000-0002-7442-635X ‡2 orcid
024	7	‡a 36648407 ‡2 viaf

Figure 3: Use of person IDs in a NAR

Instead of using the value of ORCID, ISNI, or VIAF as a number string why not use the machine readable URI as already described by Agenjo, Hernández & Viedma (2012)? Using URIs in 024 field in authority records would enable the retrieval of relevant data about the person in real time. For example in the case of an individual by the name Michael Conlon whose ORCID is: orcid.org/0000-0002-1304-8447 and the VIVO URI that represents him is: vivo.ufl.edu/individual/n25562 we can add those values in 024. The problem with this specific individual is that he does not have his name established in the LCNAF, since he mostly publishes academic articles. For a large number of scholars and researchers this is the case. In our earlier papers and presentations we have argued for the need to leverage the existing data from databases, either sematic web or relational (Ilik, 2015). Not every person needs to exist in the LCNAF, but the information about that person that exists in other systems can still be leveraged by library specific databases like OCLC and SkyRiver. This brings us back to the problem presented in this paper and to its ideal solution, as indicated above.

3. VIVO and the ideal solution

We have discussed the possibility of moving towards creating persistent VIVO URIs that resolve at the central VIVO Registry, which represents a hub aggregation of all of the local deployments. Only at that point we would be able to introduce the VIVO Central Registry as a partner to OCLC, SkyRiver and the Program for Cooperative Cataloging (PCC), to name the widely known library specific bodies dealing with name authorities. This partnership means that cataloguers would be able to control the person name from not only LCNAF but also from other trusted data sources, VIVO being one example (Figure 4).

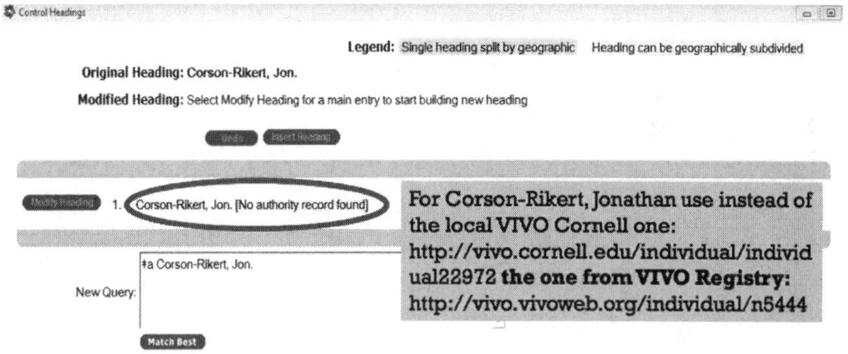

Figure 4: OCLC, VIVO and possible partnership

The goal is to work on asserting *rdfs:seeAlso* between local URIs and the central URIs. These URIs are RDF representations of a story or set of statements about that person that each institution makes. To assert relationships between external data sources and VIVO, like for example ORCID or ISNI, we need to assert the sameAs relationship. In order to support maximal data integration across sites and platforms, VIVO needs to support persistent VIVO person URIs that resolve to a central VIVO Registry, management of seeAlso assertions for person instances across various VIVO platforms and management of sameAs assertions for person instances across different data sources, which would lead to interoperability.

4. Conclusion

In this paper we discussed the need to associate person IDs and URIs with subjects when a person happens to be the subject of the document. Person can be a subject of documents and retrieval, as in the case of biographies, schools of thought in philosophy, politics, art and literary criticism. Authoritative information about researchers exist in various databases, which can be discipline specific, publisher's, or institutional. These various databases can be leveraged to support improved discoverability and retrieval of research output for individual authors and institutions, as well as works about those authors. We propose the use of alternative and non-traditional library data in NARs when used as subject headings – more specifically we propose enhancement of name authority records by adding trusted VIVO person URIs. URIs for VIVOs that commit to maintaining the historical data should be registered for on-going discoverability. VIVO has the capacity of recording the ORCID ID or the Scopus ID to aid in sameAs linking. Creating extensions to the core VIVO-ISF ontology would enable the recording of the ISNI, VIAF and many other IDs that originate in various databases and systems. We need to see this happen so that whenever we come across authors that have no authority record created in the traditional library authority hubs we would be able to use non-traditional headings in order to import authority records in our bibliographic data. Such headings would be utilised in the process of subject name authority control.

Acknowledgements

I would like to thank the whole VIVO open source community, especially the VIVO-ISF ontology lead, Dr. Melissa Haendel, Dr. Shahim Essaid, Brian Lowe, the VIVO Project Director, Dr. Michael Conlon, Dr. Kristi Holmes, and last but not least, Jonathan Corson-Rikert, for inspiring discussions and many hours of creative brainstorming.

References

Agenjo, X.; Hernández, F.; Viedma, A. (2012). Data aggregation and dissemination of authority records through linked open data in a European context. *Cataloging & Classification Quarterly*, 50 (8), pp. 803-829.

Börner, B. et al. (2012). *VIVO: a semantic approach to scholarly networking and discovery* Morgan & Claypool Publishers.*(Synthesis Lectures on the Semantic Web: Theory and Technology: Vol 2: no 1)*. Available at: http://www.morganclaypool.com/doi/pdf/10.2200/S00428ED1V01Y201207WBE002.

Brickley, D. (2011) Video linking: archives and encyclopedias (blog post). Available at: http://danbri.org/words/2011/02/01/658.

Dean, R. (2004). FAST: Development of simplified headings for metadata, *Cataloging & Classification Quarterly*, 39 (1-2), pp. 331-352.

DuraSpace, (2012). VIVO Glossary. Available at: https://wiki.duraspace.org/display/VIVO/VIVO+Glossary.

DuraSpace. (2014). VIVO-ISF Ontology. Available at: https://wiki.duraspace.org/display/VIVO/VIVO-ISF+Ontology.

DuraSpace. (2013). Source ontologies for VIVO. Available at: https://wiki.duraspace.org/display/VIVO/Source+ontologies+for+VIVO.

Fran, A. (2012). Building bridges: linking diverse classification schemes as part of a technology change project. *Business Information Review*, 29 (2), pp. 87-94. doi: 10.1177/0266382112446284.

Harper, C.; Tillett, B. (2007). Library of Congress controlled vocabularies and their application to the semantic web. *Cataloging & Classification Quarterly,* 43 (3-4). Available at: https://scholarsbank.uoregon.edu/dspace/handle/1794/3269.

Ilik, V. (2015), Cataloger makeover: creating non-MARC name authorities. *Cataloging & Classification Quarterly*, 53 (3/4), pp. 382-398.

Name Headings as Subjects H 430. (2013). The Subject Authority Cooperative Program (SACO). Available at: http://www.loc.gov/aba/publications/FreeSHM/H0430.pdf.

OWL. (2004) Web Ontology Language overview. World Wide Web Consortium (W3C) Recommendation 10 February 2004. Edited by D. L. McGuinness, F. van Harmelen. World Wide Web Consortium (W3C). Available at: http://www.w3.org/TR/owl-features/.

RDF. (2004) Resource Description Framework. World Wide Web Consortium (W3C), Resource Description Framework (RDF). Available at: http://www.w3.org/RDF/.

Smith-Yoshimura, K. et al. (2014). Registering researchers in authority files. Dublin, Ohio: OCLC Research. Available at: http://www.oclc.org/content/dam/research/publications/library/2014/oclcresearchregistering-researchers-2014-a4.pdf.

Subject usage information in name authority records H 432. (2014). The Subject Authority Cooperative Program (SACO). Available at: http://www.loc.gov/aba/publications/FreeSHM/H0432.pdf.

Tillett, B. (2004). Authority control : state of the art and new perspectives. *Cataloging & Classification Quarterly*, 38 (3/4), pp. 23-41. Available at: http://www.sba.unifi.it/ac/relazioni/tillett_eng.pdf .

Tillett, B. (2008). A review of the feasibility of an International Standard Authority Data Number (ISADN). Prepared for the IFLA Working Group on Functional Requirements and Numbering of Authority Records. Standing Committee of the IFLA Cataloguing Section. Available at: www.ifla.org/VII/d4/franar-numbering-paper.pdf.

Verborgh, R.; De Roo, J. (2015). Drawing conclusions from linked data on the Web, IEEE Software, 32 (5), pp. 23-17. Available at: http://online.qmags.com/ISW0515?cid=3244717&eid=19361#pg25.

Verify and control headings in bibliographic records. (2013). OCLC. Available at: http://www.oclc.org/content/dam/support/connexion/documentation/browser/authorities/apply_ac_bib_records/apply_ac_bib_records_pdf.pdf.

Žumer, M.; Salaba, A.; Zeng, M. L. (2012). *FRSAD : conceptual modeling of aboutness.* Santa Barbara, CA: ABC-CLIO, LLC.

VIOLETA ILIK is the Head of Digital Systems and Collection Services Department at Galter Health Sciences Library at Northwestern University's Feinberg School of Medicine. Violeta has experience in managing content creation and dissemination of print and digital resources, supporting scholars' online identity with researcher management systems, and providing support for faculty, students, and staff on scholarly communication issues. She has experience in managing VIVO Implementation at two different institutions and has helped various other institutions across the world with creating VIVO Semantic Web compliant data. Violeta experimented with creating non-MARC Name Authority Records in order to represent researchers who mainly publish academic articles. Through the VIVO-ISF Ontology Working Group she has advocated for creating a central VIVO platform that can manage a registry of URIs for people as persistent identifiers.

3. Authority control design and classification

Organization authority database design with classification principles

Dagobert Soergel
University at Buffalo, Buffalo, NY, USA

Denisa Popescu
World Bank Group, Washington, DC, USA

Abstract: We illustrate the principle of unified treatment of all authority data for any kind of entities, subjects/topics, places, events, persons, organizations, etc. through the design and implementation of an enriched authority database for organizations, maintained as an integral part of an authority database that also includes subject authority control / classification data, using the same structures for data and common modules for processing and display of data. Organization-related data are stored in information systems of many companies. We specifically examine the case of the World Bank Group (WBG) according to organization role: suppliers, partners, customers, competitors, authors, publishers, or subjects of documents, loan recipients, suppliers for WBG-funded projects and subunits of the organization itself. A central organization authority where each organization is identified by a URI, represented by several names and linked to other organizations through hierarchical and other relationships serves to link data from these disparate information systems. Designing the conceptual structure of a unified authority database requires integrating SKOS, the W3C Organization Ontology and other schemes into one comprehensive ontology. To populate the authority database with organizations, we import data from external sources (e.g., DBpedia and Library of Congress authorities) and internal sources (e.g., the lists of organizations from multiple WBG information systems).

Keywords: organization authority; organization metadata; unified authority data; linking data; comprehensive conceptual data schema; data import; World Bank Group

1. Introduction

This paper introduces the principle of unified treatment of all authority data for any kind of entities: subjects/topics, places, events, persons, organizations, etc. To illustrate this principle we present the design of an enriched authority database for organizations that very much parallels the structure of a database for classification and thesaurus data. Organizations play a key role in the information system of a large company or other organization and in storing and linking information in databases and on the Web. For these purposes it is essential that within a given context - the information system of a large company, the Web at large - organizations have unique URIs that in turn link to identifiers used in individual databases/systems and a preferred name and many variant names in multiple languages.

2. The use case

In a company, external organizations are of interest as suppliers, partners, customers, competitors (competitive intelligence), authors or subjects of documents (possibly in several systems that manage internal and external documents); in addition, the sub-units of the organization are themselves organizations about which information must be maintained. In complex organizations, such as the World Bank Group, there are even more roles, including loan recipients and suppliers or potential suppliers for projects funded by the WBG. Organizations in each of these roles (which may have overlap) are of importance to different departments in a company. One department may deal with suppliers, another with customers. The library deals with organizations as document creators or publishers and as document subjects. Each of these departments may have its own IT system with its own authority list of organization names and its own system of organization identifiers. Organizational units of the organization and their identifiers may be handled by a special administrative unit or by the human resources system, but they are also important as creators or publishers of internal documents. Furthermore, users in the organization may have information needs that require searching for texts that mention an organization, or any of a group of organizations; such texts may be internal documents, including email messages, or external documents, including news items, blog posts, social media posts and other kinds of documents on the Web.

In an environment as described above, it would be very hard to find everything about or connected with an organization in the company's data systems or in other information systems, including the Web. Solving this problem requires a central organization authority database (OAD) as shown in Figure 1. The environment described is an example of the problem of information silos that KOS system designers, including ontologists, try to address in areas such as health care through establishing standards for the classification of diseases, medical tests and treatments, etc. Following that example, we are developing for the World Bank Group a pilot for a proposed central Organization Authority Database with a unique URI for each organization.

Introducing such a database would have the following efficiencies and usage advantages:

1. Designing and implementing a single system for maintaining and serving organization data;
2. Acquiring data about organizations from external sources, resulting in savings in internal maintenance effort and a more complete database;
3. Accessing all data about an organization held in internal systems through the unique URI which links to system-specific identifiers;
4. Accessing data about an organization external sources, including the Web;
5. Providing superior support for searching.

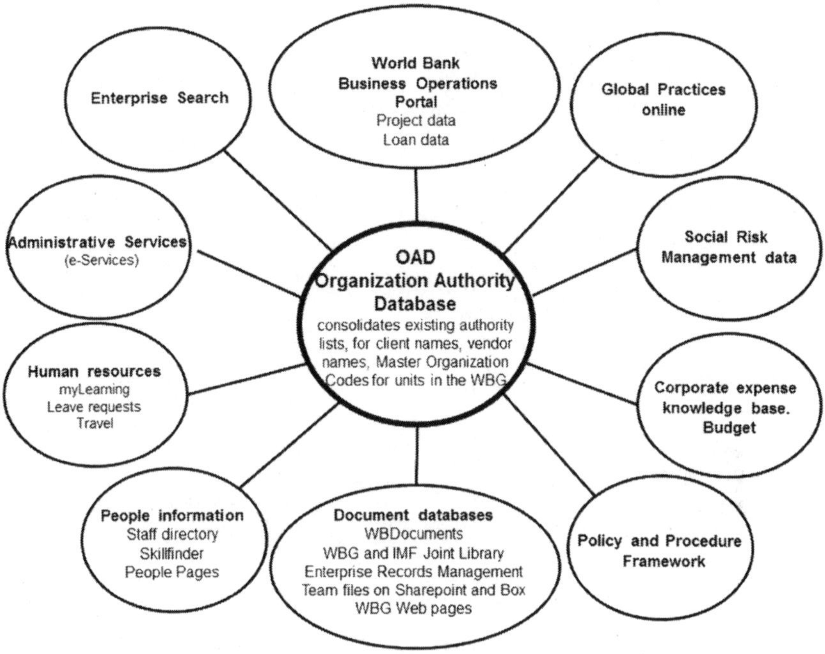

Figure 1: *A central organization authority database*

As an example, in such a system one could link organizations mentioned in a newspaper report about corruption with organizations serving as suppliers. More systematically, one could set up a monitoring service that tracks newspaper stories about corruption, makes a list of organizations suspected of corruption and checks the supplier and the loan recipient data systems for organizations on the list or related to an organization on the list - the power of authority control.

3. Design

In formal structure, user interaction and use to support search, an organization authority database has much in common with a hierarchically structured thesaurus. Organizations form a hierarchy. Organizations may have several names. Both the hierarchy and the multiple names can be used for query term expansion.

3.1. Data structure: beginnings of the conceptual data schema

A conceptual data schema is shown in Figure 2. We developed this schema based on the needs of the World Bank Group, consulting the W3C recommendation The Organization Ontology, SKOS (2009) and other standards such as the MARC 21 Formats for Authority Data and for Classification Data

Note 1. This ontology includes multiway relationships where this is more appropriate for adequate or more efficient representation. Our implementation does not suffer from the limitations of RDF
2. All statements in the database can be qualified by TimeSpan.
3. All string values (Name, Text) have a language indicator (such as @fr)
4. Many relationships apply to all kinds of entities, thus also to organizations.
5. LegalEntity includes Person and Organization, roughly equal to foaf: Agent.
6. All entity instances are identified by a URI, preferably a URI used across the Web.
7. ~ means inverse relationship

Entity	*<isa>* ~*<hasInstance>*	EntityType	For organizations, this would be the OrganizationType org:*classification*
Entity	*<hasID>*	(System, ID)	Organizations has identifier in org:identifier
Entity	*<hasName>*	(Name, NameStatus)	skos: *label*. NameStatus examples: PreferredName, AlternateName, OfficialLegalName, DoingBusinessAs
Entity	*<hasStartTime>*	PointInTime	
Entity	*<hasEndTime>*	PointInTime	
Entity	*<hasSuccessor>* ~*<hasPredecessor>*	Entity	See org:5.6
Entity .	*<isPartOf>* ~*<hasPart>*	Entity	org:*unitOf* ~org:*hasUnit*
Entity	*<isAbout>* ~*<coveredIn>*	Entity	NR *<hasPurpose>*
Entity	*<coveredIn>*	Document	E.g., the home page
Entity	*<hasPurpose>*	Entity	org:purpose BR *<isAbout>*
Entity	*<hasDescription>*	Text	NR *<hasShortDescription>* NR *<hasLongDescription>*
Entity	*<hasShortDesription.>*	Text	BR *<hasDescription>*
Entity	*<hasLongDescription>*	Text	BR *<hasDescription>*
Organization	*<hasHeadquarterLoc.>*	Location	Could be as specific as address org:5.4 has more detail
Organization	*<hasOffficialLanguage>*	Language	
Entity	*<hasNarrower>* ~*<hasBroader>*	Entity	skos:*narrower* ~skos:*broader* org:*hasSubOrganization* ~ org:*subOrganizationOf* NR *<hasPart>*, *<hasOrgFamMember>*, *<owns>*, *<hasSubsidiary>*
Organization	*<hasOrgFamMember>*	Organization	BR *<hasNarrower>*
Organization	*<owns>*	Organization	BR *<hasNarrower>*
Organization	*<hasSubsidiary>*	Organization	BR *<hasNarrower>*
Organization	*<org:linkedTo>*	Organization	
Organization	*<org:hasMember>* ~ *<org:memberOf>*	LegalEntity	
Organization	*<hasStaffMember>*	(Person, InOrgRole)	In org: the artificial class membership special case: org:*headOf*
Organization	<org:*hasPost*> ~ *<org :PostIn)*	Post	In US English: Position

Figure 2: *A partial organization ontology (an illustration)*

(1999-). This schema needs to be further extended to provide for all types of data required by one or more of the existing internal data systems for organization data that are to be integrated into or served by the OAD. As can be seen from the beginnings of the conceptual data schema, we envision an enriched OAD to include much more data than names and identifiers, such as location, type of organization, purpose and subject area of the organization, partnership agreements (similar in function to Related Term in a thesaurus), historical data, perhaps going even beyond the W3C recommendation in this respect.

Where needed, our data structure goes beyond the limitations of triples, which can be easily done in our implementation (see Section 3.3). We could export data in the form of triples, possibly losing some information. We also often use longer names for relationship types (properties) to increase clarity and understanding and to avoid ambiguity. For example, instead for skos:*narrower* we say *<hasNarrower>* to avoid confusion with *narrowerThan*, which is the inverse. For readability, the entity type concerned can be added, as in *<hasNarrowerOrganization>* (abbreviated *NO)* or *<hasNarrowerRelation ship>* (*NR*). Relationship types (properties) form a hierarchy; that hierarchy is stored in the same way as any other hierarchy in the system.

The conceptual data schema is designed to cover a much broader scope - dealing with subjects, places, time / historical periods, events, people, organizations and documents. Each of these entity types, for example, Organization is, for some searches, a search target in its own right and, for other searches, part of a query formulation. For instance, a search for documents that deal with an organization or a search for events in which an organization participates. This is why we formulate relationships with a domain and range broader than Organization so that the relationship, for example, *<isAbout>*, can be applied to many types of entities - documents, events, organizations, people, etc.

There is no clear distinction between authority data and other data by their nature; the distinction is rather based on how the data are used. From this line of thinking it follows that data to be used as authority data, such as a thesaurus, should not be kept in a separate "compartment" of a database to be consulted in formulating queries but should rather be fully integrated in a comprehensive database, any part of which may be used to find the information or entities wanted or to formulate queries to be applied to another part of the database.

In the long run the conceptual data schema presented in Figure 2 with the extension has the potential of growing into an ontology for all information systems in the WBG.

3.2. User interface and search

The interface design for using OAD should be largely the same as the interface for using a classification. Organizations form a hierarchy using the relationship type *<hasNarrowerOrganization>*, which is the union of the relationship types *<hasPart>*, *<hasOrgFamMember>*, *<owns>*, *<hasSubsidiary>*. In our design this would work as follows: when a user needs to search for an organization (either as a first step in finding information about it or to find the correct name and ID to use in cataloguing a document), the following happens:

- A window opens with a search bar on top. The user can search for organizations by name or, for example, by a combination of location and organization purpose or organization type. Or the user can just browse the classification tree in Explorer style as shown in Figures 3a - 3b;

- The results are displayed in the context of an organization tree (i.e. an organization or organizational unit that is part of another organization) would be shown under its parent organization. Nodes in the tree can be expanded in Explorer style;
- The user can then check one or more organizations for which to get more data or to use in a query (connected with OR) or to be entered in a cataloguing record. In the query, the organization would be represented by its URI (when searching a database using organization URIs), its system-specific identifier, or, for a free-text search, by an OR-combination of all the names associated with the organization. The user would have the options to do an inclusive search, where the query would include all the subordinate organizations/organizational units (parts or subsidiaries).

This design is efficient for users: they need to learn only one interface for finding organizations in an organization hierarchy and subjects in a subject hierarchy. It is also efficient for implementation because the same code is used for both purposes.

The hierarchy of organizations can be used for hierarchic query expansion. For example, one might want to search for all documents from any WBG member organization dealing with Uganda or on publications from any WBG member organization on irrigation projects in Africa (using hierarchic query expansion for Location as well).

☐ ▼**United Nations Family**
☐ ► UN General Assembly
☐ ► Security Council
☐ ► Secretariat
☐ ► Economic and Social Council
☐ ► International Court of Justice
☐ ► Trusteeship Council

☐ ▼**US Government Agencies**
☐ ► Departments
☐ ▼ Independent agencies
☐ ► Administrative agencies
☐ ► Civil Service agencies
☐ ► Commerce regulatory agencies
☐ ► Education agencies
☐ ► Energy and science agencies
☐ ► Foreign investment agencies
☐ ► Interior agencies
☐ ► Labor agencies
☐ ► Monetary and financial agencies
☐ ► Postal agencies
☐ ► Retirement agencies
☐ ► Federal Property and Seat of Government agencies
☐ ► Transportation agencies
☐ ► Volunteerism agencies
☐ ► Defense and Security agencies
☐ ► Civil Rights

Figure 3a: *A tree browse window with limited drill-down*

We also plan a display of full entries for individual organizations, giving alternate names and other information. The alternate names can be used for synonym query expansion, so that a search for World Bank would also find

International Bank for Reconstruction and Development
IBRD,
I.B.R.D.,
Banque internationale pour la reconstruction et le développement,
BIRD
Weltbank
Internationale Bank für Wiederaufbau und Entwicklung

- ▼ **United Nations Family**
  - ► UN General Assembly
  - ► Security Council
  - ► Secretariat
  - ▼ Economic and Social Council
    - ► Funds and Programmes
    - ► Research and Training Institutes
    - ► Other Entities
    - ▼ Specialized Agencies
      - ► FAO, Food and Agriculture Organization of the UN
      - ► ICAO, International Civil Aviation Organization
      - ► IFAD, International Fund for Agricultural Development
      - ► ILO, International Labour Organization
      - ► IMF, International Monetary Fund
      - ► IMO, International Maritime Organization
      - ► ITU, International Telecommunication Union
      - ► UNESCO, UN Educational, Scientific and Cultural Organization
      - ► UNIDO, United Nations Industrial Development Organization
      - ► UNWTO, World Tourism Organization
      - ► UPU, Universal Postal Union
      - ► WHO, World Health Organization
      - ► WIPO, World Intellectual Property Organization
      - ► WMO, World Meteorological Organization
      - ▼ World Bank Group
        - ► IBRD, International Bank for Reconstruction and Development
        - ► ICSID, International Center for Settlement of Investment Disputes
        - ► IDA, International Development Association
        - ► IFC, International Finance Corporation
        - ► MIGA, Multicultural Investment Guarantee Agency
  - ► International Court of Justice
  - ► Trusteeship Council
- ▼ **US Government Agencies**

Figure 3b: *A tree browse window with drill-down to WBG and below*

World Bank

LCCN permalink: http://lccn.loc.gov/n79043403

Variant(s)
International Bank for Reconstruction and Development
IBRD
World Bank Group. World Bank
Banque internationale pour la reconstruction et le développement
B.I.R.D.
BIRD
Banque mondiale
Mezhdunarodnyĭ bank dli͡a rekonstrukt͡sii i razvitii͡a
MBRR
Welt Bank
Weltbank
Internationale Bank für Wiederaufbau und Entwicklung
Banco Internacional de Reconstrucción y Fomento
Banco Mundial
hanākhān Lōk
Viśva Baiṅka
Lōka Băṅkuva
Ngân hàng Thế giới

Figure 4a: *World Bank and variants (from longer list at LC Authorities)*

World Bank. Agriculture and Natural Resources Department
permalink: http://lccn.loc.gov/nr95045186
Variant(s): AGR
World Bank. Agriculture & Natural Resources Department
World Bank. Agriculture and Natural Resources Dept.
See also: World Bank. Rural Development Department
Hierarchical superior: World Bank
Found in: World Bank Group dir., May 1996: (Agriculture & Natural Resources Department (AGR))
The World Bank website, Archives, viewed May 4, 2012: International standard archival authority record –
Agriculture and Rural Development sector (Agriculture and rural development department, 2002-;
Rural development department, 1997-2002;
Agriculture and natural resources department 1993-1997)

Figure 4b: *Authority record from LC*

Sometimes, historical information is important for dealing with documents. The WBG Archives needs to know which unit in the organization is responsible for an official document in order to determine access rights or proper disposal. But the unit that produced the document may have been changed, perhaps several times, in one of the many reorganizations in the WBG. Using *<hasSuccessor>*, perhaps several times in a chain, the system can find the present unit that "inherited" responsibility for the document.

As was mentioned above, a user may want to find organizations as the endpoint of a search. For example a user may want to find organization such that

> Organization *<hasPurpose>* Economic development AND
> Organization *<hasPurpose>* Africa

This search would find the WBG unit(s) dealing with Africa, other units in the UN family, the US Agency for International Development unit(s) dealing with Africa, government units in other countries and non-governmental organizations.

3.3. System implementation

The pilot system is being implemented using MarkLogic (http://www.marklogic.com/), a powerful NoSQL database management system that stores data in XML and has many features that support information ingestion and information retrieval.

Our integrated system design that treats authority and classification data for all kinds of entities - including subjects, places, times / historical periods, events, people, organizations and documents - following the same abstract scheme greatly facilitates development. There is one system module that displays a hierarchical structure, no matter whether it is a subject, place, or organization hierarchy and handles all user interaction (including type-ahead search, not shown in Figure 3). The module takes as input (1) a reference to the set of XML objects that represent all the entity instances to be included and their relationships and (2) a list of relationship types that are considered hierarchical.

Likewise, there is one system function that handles hierarchic query expansion and synonym query expansion for any entity type.

This unified approach not only simplifies system development but also provides a consistent user experience. We are now testing the usability of the pilot with favourable initial results.

4. Populating an organization authority database

We will first focus on three comprehensive external sources with complementary data, including many names under which an organization is known:

- Organization data extracted from DBpedia[1];
- Library of Congress Name Authority File, select headings of type "corporate name", searchable on the LC website[2];

1 DBpedia. Available at: http://wiki.dbpedia.org/.

- Library of Congress Authorities, Name Authority Headings (see Figure 4)[3];
- The Library of Congress > Linked Data Service > LC Name Authority File[4];
- Dun & Bradstreet (company names and identifiers, used in one WBG system, but presents copyright problems)[5].

Next we will work on ingesting organization names from WBG-internal data systems. This will be easier once we have the many names from external sources in the database.

Ingesting data about organizations from one source requires mapping the relationship types (properties) used in the source to the relationship types used in our OAD. This can be done manually.

Integrating data from multiple sources can be done by name matching. The Library of Congress and Dun & Bradstreet data have many variant names, so the chance for matching organizations from different sources is quite high. To guard against conflating data for two different organizations that have the same name, we will compare other data about an organization given in two sources (if such data are available) and flag for manual intervention cases where the data from two sources differ greatly. A certain error rate is unavoidable; the effort for checking all information manually would be far too great. Some errors will surface as the database is used and will then be corrected.

4.1. Import of organizations from DBpedia

For the extraction from DBpedia, we first selected entity instances that belong to one of the types listed in Table 1, checking the first three DBpedia properties listed in Figure 5. We supplemented this by selecting first Wikipedia articles under relevant categories, such as Economics organizations, Banks, government ministries from many countries, Islamist groups, and then the organization that is the subject of such an article. We extracted all triples for these entity instances; Table 1 gives some numbers.

Next, we produced a report of all the DBpedia properties that occurred in the triples and mapped these to the relationship types in the OAD conceptual data schema; some examples are shown in Figure 5.

With this mapping, we imported the DBpedia triples into the MarkLogic database. The TimeSpan in the MarkLogic objects is blank since DBpedia does not give that information.

The next step is to import Library of Congress authority data and determine the degree of match.

---

2 The Library of Congress Name Authority File (NAF). Library of Congress. Available at: http://id.loc.gov/authorities/names.html.

3 ibid.

4 ibid.

5 Dun & Bradstreet (D&B). Available at: http://www.dnb.com/company.html.

Table 1: *Data on the DBpedia extraction*

http://dbpedia.org/ontology/	
Organization	329,500
Company	88,049
EducationalInstitution	52,241
Broadcaster	29,628
Newspaper	5,248
GovernmentAgency	3,283
Legislature	1,081
MilitaryUnit	17,812
PoliticalParty	7,340
Non-ProfitOrganisation	3,494
TradeUnion	1,489
All	~540,000
44M triples, ~80 triples per organization	

DBpedia property (relationship type)	OAD schema relationship type
<http://www.w3.org/1999/02/22-rdf-syntax-ns#type>	*<isa>*
<http://dbpedia.org/ontology/type>	*<isa>*
<http://dbpedia.org/property/type>	*<isa>*
<http://dbpedia.org/property/companyName>	*<hasName>* | NameSratus: OfficialLegalName
<http://www.w3.org/2000/01/rdf-schema#label>	*<hasName>* | NameSratus: OfficialLegalName
<http://xmlns.com/foaf/0.1/name>.	*<hasName>* | NameSratus: OfficialLegalName
<http://dbpedia.org/ontology/parentOrganisation>	*<hasBroader>*
<http://purl.org/dc/terms/subject>	*<isAbout>*
<http://dbpedia.org/property/purpose>	*<hasPurpose>*
<http://www.w3.org/2000/01/rdf-schema#comment>	*<hasShortDescription>*
<http://dbpedia.org/ontology/abstract>	*<hasLongDescription>*
<http://xmlns.com/foaf/0.1/homepage>	*<hasWebAddress>*
<http://dbpedia.org/ontology/owner>	*<owns>* REVERSE

Figure 5: *Correspondence between the DBpedia and the OAD schema (examples)*

5. Conclusions

Authority control is at the heart of master data management. Using consistent identifiers for core entity types - for example, subjects/topics, diseases, procedures, organisms, chemical substances, products, types of costs/expenses, places, times/historical periods, events, people, organizations and documents -

is a prerequisite for linking data across the many applications in the entire enterprise and many external sources to prevent operational mistakes and performing powerful data analytics considering the complex interactions among many variables. We have outlined a unified approach to handling all kinds of authority data, focusing on the common problems of multiple names for the same thing and of interacting with hierarchical structures. We emphasized general definitions of entity types (classes) and relationship types (properties) that capture, with useful abstraction, structural elements that are common to multiple domains. This logical analysis lays the foundation for general software modules, saving development effort, and for a unified user experience. We are applying these principles in a pilot system to demonstrate their usefulness in a large organization with highly varied information requirements such as the World Bank Group.

Acknowledgements

We thank Rob Rudin, who is working on the software design and implementation of the unified authority database in MarkLogic and on data import; Helmut Nagy, Semantic Web Company, Vienna, Austria, who extracted the organization date from Wikipedia and Olivia Helfer who compiled the figures.

References

DBpedia. Available at: http://wiki.dbpedia.org/.

Dun & Bradstreet (D&B). Available at: http://www.dnb.com/company.html.

Dun & Bradstreet D-U-N-S Number. Available at: http://www.dnb.co.uk/dandb-duns-number.

GND Ontology. (2015). Gemeinsame Normdatei (Integrated authority file): namespace document 2015-05-19. [Edited by] Alexander Haffner. German National Library. Available at: http://d-nb.info/standards/elementset/gnd.

GoodRelations: the Web vocabulary for e-commerce. Available at: http://purl.org/goodrelations/.

GS1 company prefix. Available at: http://www.gs1.org/company-prefix.

Hoover's Company Information Database. Hoover's Inc., Dun & Bradstreet Company Available at: http://www.hoovers.com/.

The Library of Congress Linked Data Service: authorities and vocabularies. Library of Congress. Available at: http://id.loc.gov.

The Library of Congress Name Authority File (NAF). Library of Congress. Available at: http://id.loc.gov/authorities/names.html.

MARC 21 format for authority data. (1999-). Washington, DC: Library of Congress, Network Development and MARC Standards Office. Available at: http://www.loc.gov/marc/authority/ecadhome.html.

MARC 21 Concise Format for Classification Data. (2003). Concise edition. Library of Congress. Available at: http://www.loc.gov/marc/classification/eccdhome.html.

Okkam Entity Name System. Available at: http://api.okkam.org/.

Oracle Business Name Standardization Files. (2010). Master Index Standardization Engine Reference. Available at: http://docs.oracle.com/cd/E19182-01/821-0860/ref_sme-bn-config_c/index.html.

The Organization Ontology. (2014). W3C Recommendation 16 January 2014. Edited by D. Reynolds. Available at: http://www.w3.org/TR/vocab-org/.

SKOS. (2009). Simple Knowledge Organization System: reference. W3C Recommendation 18 August 2009. Edited by A. Miles; S. Bechhofer. Available at: http://www.w3.org/2009/08/skos-reference/skos.html.

SWB Online-Katalog (Südwestdeutschen Bibliotheksverbundes). Available at: http://swb.bsz-bw.de/.

Thing: organization. Schema.org. Available at: http://schema.org/Organization.

Thing: organization: corporation. Schema.org. Available at: http://schema.org/Corporation.

DAGOBERT SOERGEL is Professor, Department of Library and Information Studies, Graduate School of Education, University at Buffalo since 2009 and Professor, College of Information Studies, University of Maryland, 1970-2010 and Professore Onorario, Dipartimento di Ingegneria e Scienza dell'Informazione, University of Trento since 2007. He has been working in the area of classification (taxonomy, ontologies) and thesauri for over 50 years. He authored the still-standard text- and handbook *Indexing Languages and Thesauri. Construction and Maintenance* (Wiley 1974) and *Organizing Information* (Academic Press 1985), which received the American Society of Information Science Best Book Award, and more than 100 papers and presentations in information retrieval, classification / ontologies, digital libraries, sense-making and relevance. He was the chief architect for the *Alcohol and Other Drug Thesaurus* (http://etoh.niaaa.nih.gov/ AODVol1/Aodthome.htm) and the *Harvard Business Thesaurus*. He received the American Society for Information Science Award of Merit in 1997.

DENISA POPESCU is an IT Officer with the Information and Technology Solutions of the World Bank Group. Popescu led and worked on initiatives in the area of enterprise information integration of both structured and unstructured information, Master Data Management, reference data and taxonomies management and automatic metadata capture using semantic technologies. She holds a PhD in Business Administration from George Washington University. Popescu's research activities focus on the areas of knowledge transfer and learning, technology innovation, international regulatory standards and global governance.

Machine-learning methods for classification and content authority control in mathematics

Ulf Schöneberg
FIZ Karlsruhe - Leibniz-Insitut für Informationinfrastruktur, zbMATH, Berlin, Germany

Wolfram Sperber
FIZ Karlsruhe - Leibniz-Insitut für Informationinfrastruktur, zbMATH, Berlin, Germany

Abstract: The abstracting and reviewing service zbMATH (zbMATH, 1931-) is the most comprehensive bibliographic database of mathematical literature. The database uses reviews, keywords and classification for content analysis of mathematical publications. Controlled vocabularies and classification schemes are important for a uniform and standardised analysis of the content and precise information retrieval. Over the last few years, the zbMATH team has started developing machine-based concepts and tools to create controlled vocabularies and to improve the Mathematics Subject Classification (MSC) scheme. Concepts of natural language processing and other machine learning methods, especially neural networks, were adapted to the specific requirements of mathematical information, e.g., named mathematical entities and mathematical formulas. The tools are used for key phrase extraction and classification of mathematical publications. Basing on the extracted key phrases, a prototype for a controlled vocabulary for mathematics was created. The tools and the state of the art are described briefly. These activities will help - in cooperation with authority control for authors, series and institutions - to automate the zbMATH workflow and improve the usefulness and information retrieval capabilities of the database.

Keywords: zbMATH; mathematics; text classification; controlled vocabulary; authority control; key phrase extraction; machine learning methods; natural language processing; neural networks

1. Introduction

Mathematical science is increasing in content, importance, size and form. New forms of mathematical knowledge have evolved: mathematical software, models and simulations. But until now publications are the most important resource of mathematical knowledge and they are also the basis for knowledge management in mathematics.

Managing information is becoming more and more important for research and access to knowledge. Classification schemes, controlled vocabularies and ontologies are widely accepted tools for content analysis and authority control of content metadata. Tools and the process of content analysis are symbiotically connected: tools are necessary for uniform and standardised content analysis. On the other hand, the actual process of content analysis is necessary for the development of tools. The development of tools, as well as the content analysis and authority control by humans itself, is a labour- and cost-intensive effort. Moreover, the validity of content analysis depends on the subject and differs from subject to subject. Over the last few years, new machine learning methods for text analysis have been developed. In the following sections of this paper, content analyses of mathematical publications are discussed. Several machine-learning tools, adapted to the needs of mathematics are presented.

2. A historical remark

The origins of mathematics can be traced back thousands of years when it emerged from geometry, astronomy and trade as a solution to practical problems and the need to understand the phenomena of the real world. The first specific catalogues of mathematical knowledge - up to the present more or less presented in books - were published by the end of the 18th century (Scheibel, 1769-98; Murhard, 1787-1805). We can also observe that these catalogues were organized by subject, a form of classification scheme. The first journals specializing in mathematics were founded at the same time. They became the most important platform for scholarly communication in mathematics. Subsequently, the number of mathematical publications increased dramatically requiring new ways for the handling of knowledge. Therefore, a new kind of journal, the reviewing journal, was born providing the mathematical community with a fast survey about the progress, trends and results of mathematical research. The first volume of *Jahrbuch über die Fortschritte der Mathematik* was published in 1868. It marked the beginning of mathematical knowledge management (JFM, 1868-1943).

Mathematics has been an international science from its beginnings. Hence, JFM was conceived as an activity of the international mathematical community focused on worldwide mathematics literature. Today, the two leading reviewing databases in mathematics, *MathSciNet* (MathSciNet, 1940-) and *zbMATH* (zbMATH, 1931-), provide a more or less comprehensive reviewing service and search engine on mathematical literature. The reviewing journal *Zentralblatt MATH* was founded in 1931. With more than 3,000,000 entries (including the data of JFM), the database zbMATH is the most comprehensive bibliographic database in mathematics covering more than 200 years of information on mathematical literature (the oldest entry dates back to the year 1755).

The number of mathematical publications is permanently increasing. The first volume of JFM contained references to 867 publications. Currently, more than 100,000 mathematical articles and books are published annually. The constant increase in the number of publications has lead to the development of new methods for the access and management of mathematical literature in reviewing services and libraries. Methods and tools for organizing, cataloguing and content analysis have improved and refined over time. In the initial years, the JFM entries contained only the names of authors in a very reduced form (e.g., only surnames). Moreover, subject headings in JFM were changed annually which made a subject-oriented search for the user difficult.

Currently, the reviewing services are developing machine-based concepts for quality and authority control which are described below in more detail.

3. Bibliographic data and authority control in zbMATH

Methods and tools for standardisation and authority control, especially of authors' names and journal titles, have become more and more important. Authority control is essential for the quality and usability of bibliographic data. The mathematical reviewing services have developed their own databases for handling information about mathematical journals and for author identification. Moreover, bibliographic data in zbMATH are also being extended through new features. One current important extension of zbMATH data is to add the references to bibliographic data. This also necessitates an extraction, analysis and standardisation of the names of the authors and sources.

4. Content analysis and classification in zbMATH

4. 1. Challenges for content analysis in mathematics

Mathematical language is a natural language but often co-notated by terms and mathematical symbols. This means that we are confronted with the usual difficulties of natural languages, e.g., ambiguous terms. Moreover, we also have to analyse mathematical symbols and formulas. Symbols can be aggregated to arbitrary complex structures (formulas) which are more precise and informative than textual notations. Handling of symbols and formulas is a special requirement of mathematics.

As noted earlier, mathematical knowledge has been growing continuously over the last fifty years:

- The number of publications has been increased more than eightfold, zbMATH lists 13,440 entries for 1960, and 106,344 entries for 2010;
- Mathematical subjects are diversifying more and more. As a consequence, the mathematical vocabulary (terms and symbols) is constantly increasing;
- Mathematical theories and methods have been used in more and more application areas. Real processes must be translated into a mathematical language by mathematical modelling;
- New types of mathematical knowledge are emerging, e.g., mathematical software and simulations. Today, mathematical software and simulations are independent mathematical research areas as well as important bridges between mathematics and applications.

As a consequence, mathematical knowledge and mathematical terminology is continuously increasing and developing. New concepts and methods for mathematical knowledge management must be developed so as to support digital research environments in an adequate way. Realistically, this can no longer be achieved manually. Hence, automatic methods must substitute/ supplement the manual work.

4. 2. The MSC

In the sixties, a delivery service for Math Reviews was developed. The structure of the delivery scheme was widely accepted by the community and so it was also used for classifying mathematical publications by Zentralblatt MATH. Today, the Mathematics Subject Classification (MSC) is jointly maintained and updated by the editorial offices of *MathSciNet* and *zbMATH*. The MSC is a special form of authority control for the content of publications.

The MSC is a fine-grained classification scheme for mathematics and its applications: it has 63 top level classes, 528 second level classes and 5606 third level classes. Classes are characterized (only) by their label and position in the MSC graph. The granularity of classes is uneven, as the MSC scheme is often not detailed especially in application areas.

The MSC has a (partially) faceted structure. Main facets are document type and mathematical subjects; more specific facets could be objects, methods, theories, applications, etc.

The structure of MSC has been stable since its beginning but a permanent maintaining of the classification scheme reflecting the development of mathematics is necessary. Therefore, the MSC has been updated every ten years, the last update dating from 2010.

MSC classes are partially semantically overlapping. A few kinds of equivalency relationships were introduced in the MSC, namely the relationships "See also", "See", mainly as general similarity relationships; and "For ... see ...", "For ... see and also" for similarity regarding special aspects. The structure of the MSC influences significantly the classification process. Often, more than one MSC class is relevant for a publication. The most important code is marked as the primary MSC classification, all other codes are so-called secondary classifiers. The number of MSC codes and also the weighting are not really unique. The classification is the result of a decision process where authors, reviewers, and editors are involved. Especially if a few MSC codes are similar (have a significant overlap) the classification codes can vary significantly.

Over the last few years, the MSC scheme has been more formalized using Semantic Web technologies: a version of the MSC (MSC, 2010) based on the Simple Knowledge Organization System (SKOS, 2009) standard has been developed. The SKOS standard allows a clear distinction of the formal notation of a MSC class, e.g., 34A08 and the corresponding label, e.g., "Fractional differential equations". The SKOS formalization has some further important advantages. Multilingual labels can be added and a machine-based conversion to general classification schemes such as Universal Decimal Classification (UDC), Dewey Decimal Classification (DDC) or Library of Congress Classification (LCC), or to other science specific schemes such as ACM Computing Classification System are possible. Moreover, "other than" hierarchical relations can be expressed in a machine-understandable way (for more information see Ion & Sperber, 2012). Below we discuss further uses and authority control of MSC.

4.3. Content analysis and keywords

In the 70s, keywords were introduced as a new facility for content analysis in zbMATH. High-quality keywords have great potential for the searching and relevance ranking of search results.

zbMATH data cover more than the manually created (not distinct) 10,000,000 keywords. Typically, the keywords are not single words but phrases. Therefore we use the term 'key phrase' instead of 'keyword' in the following. The majority of these phrases are noun phrases (more than 90%). Key phrases in zbMATH data contain only a sequence of tokens but no relations to other phrases.

Up to now, key phrases in zbMATH have been created manually. The large number of key phrases and the huge effort involved in manual filtering is one of the main reasons for a controlled vocabulary for mathematics that has been missing up to now. In the following, we present a method to create key phrases and a controlled vocabulary for mathematics in a semi-automatic way.

Key phrases, controlled vocabularies and classification have a close correlation. This is used to develop classification methods based on key phrases.

Key phrases and classification codes are also used to improve and refine the bibliographic information in zbMATH, especially for the control of author information, e.g., to remove misspellings of author names, and to create profiles of mathematicians (structuring author's publications by subject).

Last but not least, key phrases, controlled vocabularies and MSC could play an important role in sophisticated tools for managing knowledge in mathematics, especially glossaries (ontologies) of mathematical knowledge containing definitions, semantic relations between mathematical objects or concepts and the corresponding mathematical symbols and formulas as well as further information. FIZ Karlsruhe is one of the initiators of the SMGloM project (SMGloM, 2014), an enhanced glossary for mathematics which, amongst other things, provides automatically generated support for the semantic identification of mathematical symbols and formulas.

4.4. Natural Language Processing (NLP)

Open source software for NLP, especially a dictionary for the English language and POS (part-of-speech) tagging software, which were developed at Stanford University (Stanford NLPG, 2004-) were used as a starting point of our work.

In the DeLiVerMATH project (Schöneberg & Sperber, 2013), led by FIZ Karlsruhe, Technische Informationsbibliothek und Universitätsbibliothek Hannover (TIB, 2015) and L3S Research Center (L3S, 2015), NLP tools were adapted for the needs of mathematics, covering the following:

- Identification and special treatment of mathematical symbols and formulas: mathematical publications are typically written in *TeX* code; mathematical symbols and formulas are enclosed in *$* signs which allows easy identification and mark-up of symbols and formulas;
- Building of special dictionaries for terms and named mathematical entities, acronyms in mathematics, and names of mathematicians: Today, English is the *lingua franca* of mathematics. In addition, mathematics has special words, e.g., *holomorphic*, named entities, e.g., *partial differential equations*, and acronyms, e.g., *LMIs*, the abbreviation for "linear matrix inequalities". The names of mathematicians are often used in notations of mathematical objects or concepts.

NLP tools were used for key phrase extraction and classification of zbMATH data. This means that methods and tools for key phrase extraction and classification were developed using the bibliographic information and not the full texts of publications. But a well-written review or an abstract should describe the subject, the mathematical objects or concepts which were investigated, the methods, the results and a comparison with existing results in a condensed and understandable way. Therefore, reviews and abstracts are an excellent starting point for key phrase extraction and classification.

The first step is the so-called tokenization of the text, the splitting of a text into small units, e.g., words. Instead of words, we use in the following the more general term "token" because symbols, especially mathematical symbol or formulas, are not words but they are essential for the content. Classifying tokens in NLP is called POS tagging. It assigns each token its type, e.g., adjective or noun. Different tagging schemes exist. The tagging schemes used in NLP differ in the number of tags which often also contain, besides the main categories (noun, verb, article, preposition, pronoun, adverb) of the English language, subcategories. We have used the widely accepted Penn Treebank POS scheme (Santorini, 1990) which has 45 tags for words and punctuation symbols, e.g., 'nouns' are more precisely classified as singular common nouns (NN), plural common nouns (NNS), singular proper nouns (NNP) or plural proper nouns (NNPS).

Remarks: Mathematical symbols and formulas do not have their own tags in the Penn Treebank POS scheme but we encode and decode each mathematical symbol or formula as a special token allowing unique identification of these terms. This is described in detail in Schöneberg & Sperber (2014). Today, the majority of mathematical publications use the English language. Therefore we have restricted text analysis to the English language.

The complete tagging of all tokens of a text encounters two difficulties:

- The type of a token can be ambiguous. Determining the real tag of such a token necessitates analysis of the context;
- The token is unknown. This means that the token is not currently in the dictionary.

Tagging of a document means assigning to each token a unique tag, by using dictionaries and statistical means. A Dynamic Programming method - in NLP the name Viterbi algorithm is used - is an important heuristic method for tagging based on the observed transition probabilities of sequences of *n* tokens which are called *n*-grams. These methods are based on the evaluation of manually tagged large training *corpora* and achieve high accuracy.

There exist a lot of different taggers: for tagging, we have worked with the Stanford POS tagger (Stanford, NLPG, 2004-) which is open source software. We have used the original Stanford POS tagger as core and have added further modules, e.g., a pre- and post-processor for the handling of formulas.

The module structure of our POS tagger is presented in Figure 1.

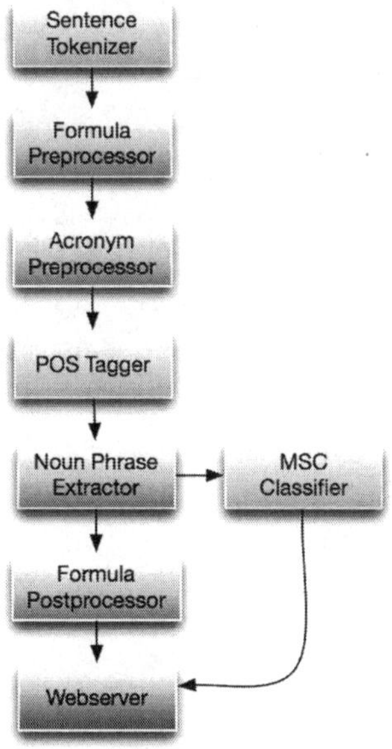

Figure 1: *The zbMATH scheme for POS tagging and classification*

As already indicated, we are especially interested in noun phrases. Noun phrases are the most important candidates of key phrases. In the next step of key phrase extraction, characteristic tag patterns for noun phrases, e.g., "adjective - singular proper noun - plural proper noun - mathematical expression", in a given document (review or abstract) were defined. A noun phrase chunker allows the identification of all sets of tokens with such kind of patterns.

The approach works well and is described in detail by Schöneberg & Sperber (2014). In the result, we get a set of noun phrases, but not only the key phrases characterizing the essential features of a document, e.g., we find also irrelevant phrases such as 'main theorem', 'important property', etc.

Therefore, the next step is to select semantically meaningful noun phrases. One method consists of comparing the extracted noun phrases with existing encyclopaedias. Existing digital encyclopaedias and glossaries (such as EoM, 2015; PlanetMath, 2015; WolframAlpha, 2015), Wikipedia and other Web services are good sources to identify named mathematical entities within the set of noun phrases. Moreover, this method cannot be used to remove meaningless noun phrases.

4.5. Neural Networks

Another approach is the use of Neural Networks (NNs). The classical approach in text analysis is the bag-of-words model. Therefore, the text is split into isolated tokens, e.g., words, symbols or formulas. A document vector is created which assigns each word the frequency of its occurrence. In other words, each document is reduced to a set of tokens and its frequencies, the structure and the order of tokens are removed. But frequencies alone don't provide any semantic information and do not provide any statements about the semantic similarity of tokens.

The analysis of the context of a token is a promising alternative to the bag-of-words model. Context analysis was also used successfully in the Viterbi algorithm to determine the correct tags of tokens. NN models analyse windows of tokens instead of frequencies of single tokens.

Quite simply, NNs are concepts which adapt the workflow of human brain to machines. Input information, e.g., the tokens of a text, are processed by a model of hidden neurons layers which are controlled by a machine learning process.

More specifically, NNs consist of an input layer with a number of (ordered) input nodes and a number of hidden layers. Each node of a certain layer is connected to each node in the next layer. The nodes of the hidden layers, the neurons, process the input information in a unique way. This relationship is - in mathematical language - a function. Therefore, a linear approach is assumed which can be formulated as a matrix-vector multiplication between the nodes of two sequent layers. The matrix elements are weights and characterize the influence of the node of a certain layer to a node of the following layer. At the start, these weights will be chosen randomly. The linear approach is an artificial restriction. To compensate it, a nonlinear transformation of the nodes is added to each node. Therefore the *softmax* function is often used which is a continuous and differentiable approximation of a step function. The top layer of the NN is the output. It classifies the value of output corresponding to the task, e.g., named entity recognition. The values of the output level will be compared with the corresponding values of the manually evaluated training set and used as the cost function which should be minimized. This leads to a hierarchical discrete optimization problem. Backpropagation is therefore employed in NNs, which means the iterative process to improve the weighting of the nodes in the hidden layers of the neural network. Therefore the cost function must be minimized which can be done by standard optimization methods, e.g., a gradient algorithm.

NNs work on the principle of "learning by comparing" (the output of a NN with a given training corpus). They are a unsupervised machine learning method. This means that NNs structure a set of objects without human intervention. An advantage of the use of NNs (and more generally machine learning methods) is their ability to process large datasets. New data can be added without problems. The 'only' tasks for humans are to define the model (what is the goal of the output classification) and to determine a 'good' training set as a base for the learning process.

Not every document collection is suitable for using NNs. It is necessary that the wording is nearly homogeneous in the collection (the use of the words in similar context should be the same with no enhancement or embellishment); that the collection is not too small and that the training corpus is representative for the set. All these conditions are fulfilled for zbMATH data.

There is an emerging number of publications which use NNs for NLP tasks (see, e.g., Collobert et al., 2011; and Mikolov et al., 2013). Especially, recurrent NNs which model structured time-dependent processes (which are derived from spoken language) are used. One impressive example for the use of NNs in text analysis is the word2vec application (word2vec, 2015). The task consists of determining similar words to a given token. Therefore, a sequence of *n* tokens of the document is investigated. The idea is to look in the collection for other tokens which could substitute the given token in the sequence. We have input zbMATH data into the open source software word2vec which leads to many semantically similar tokens, as can be seen the following table:

Table 1: *Similar tokens in the zbMATH corpus by word2vec*

blue	positive	linear	prime number	algebra	color
red	nonnegative	nonlinear	primes	ring	pixel
green	nonzero	quadratic	integers	module	texture
colored	$k>0$	bilinear	square-free	k-algebra	image
monochromatic	bounded	parametric	cardinality	C^*-algebra	luminance
2-coloring	$\alpha > 0$	differential	number theory	subalgebra	RGB

The word2vec software determines different kinds of semantically similar tokens, synonyms, also broader and narrower tokens (hypernyms, hyponyms), or meronyms.

This concept can also be used for phrases and analogies. A possible way would be to use Wikipedia's texts as training set for the zbMATH data.

4.6. Key phrases and controlled vocabulary

Key phrases are candidates for a controlled vocabulary. A controlled vocabulary could be used as a tool for the standardised creation of key phrases (e.g., by using the commonly used terms of a mathematical object or concept as key phrase) and also for eliminating phrases which are not meaningful.

4.7. Classification

A second important feature of standardised content analysis, besides key phrases and controlled vocabulary, is classification. In the DeLiVerMATH project (Schöneberg & Sperber, 2013) several methods for a machine-based text classification were investigated.

We have used extracted key phrases for classification, L3S and the full texts of the reviews and abstracts. Several techniques for classification, Support Vector Machines, Naive Bayes and Decision Trees were checked. The publications were classified by using an analysis of words and their frequencies in the reviews/abstracts or key phrases. Until now, symbols and formulas were not used for classification.

The quality of results was evaluated by the usual statistical parameters: precision, recall, and as a standard measure, the F1 score, a mean value of precision and recall. The main results of the evaluation are:

- The use of key phrases instead of the full text of reviews or abstracts is not significant. The results of the classification are similar;
- The quality is strongly influenced by the MSC scheme. Classification codes for classes which have minor overlapping with other classes yield good results, strong overlapping yields big differences between machine and human classification;

- For the best 10% of the top classes of the MSC, the F1 score is > 0.83, for all 0.66. So we could at least partially use the existing tool for automatic pre-classification;
- Not surprisingly, we could observe that overlapping of classes is mirrored by similar vocabularies.

We see further chances to enhance the tools and the methods for content analysis and authority control by combining text analysis and classification, e.g., by building controlled vocabularies for a more precise description of the MSC classes. Such vocabularies could contribute to a more objective and precise classification.

5. Summary

The approved traditional tools for content analysis and authority control, such as controlled vocabularies and classification schemes, are also important in the digital age for structuring collections, content analysis and retrieval of publications. However, the ever-growing large corpora of scientific publications require the use of computers and computing technologies.

Machine learning methods, especially NLP and NNs are new concepts and approaches providing efficient methods for text analysis and classification. They were briefly introduced.

Still, such methods must be adapted to the special needs of the subject. In mathematics, formulas are a specific challenge. Some prototypical use cases for the use of machine-learning techniques were discussed. We are optimistic that such kinds of method could be used for a more efficient workflow and improvement of the quality of the zbMATH database.

References

Collobert, R. et al. (2011). Natural language processing (almost) from scratch. *The Journal of Machine Learning Research*, 12 (2/1), pp. 2493-2537. Available at: http://arxiv.org/pdf/1103.0398v1.pdf.

EoM (2015). *Encyclopedia of mathematics*. Available at: http://www.encyclopediaofmath.org.

Ion, P.; Sperber, W. (2012). MSC 2010 in SKOS - the transition of the MSC to the Semantic Web. *Newsletter of the European Mathematical Society*, 84, pp. 55-57. Available at: http://www.ems-ph.org/journals/newsletter/pdf/2012-06-84.pdf.

JFM (1868-1943). *Jahrbuch über die Fortschritte der Mathematik*. Available at: http://www.emis.de/MATH/JFM/.

L3S (2015). *L3S Research Center*. Available at: http://www.l3s.de.

MathSciNet (1940-). *MathSciNet: mathematical reviews*. American Mathematical Society. Available at: http://www.ams.org/mathscinet.

Mikolov, T. et al. (2013). Distributed representations of words and phrases and their compositionality. *Advances in Neural Information Processing Systems,* 26 (NIPS 2013).

Available at: http://papers.nips.cc/paper/5021-distributed-representations-of-words-and-phrases-and-their-compositionality.pdf.

MSC (2010). *Mathematics Subject Classification*. American Mathematical Society. Available at: http://www.msc2010.org.

Murhard, F. W. A. (1787-1805). *Literatur der mathematischen Wissenschaften*. Leipzig. Available at: http://www.planetmath.org.

Santorini, B. (1990). *Part-of-speech tagging guidelines for the Penn Treebank Project* (3rd rev.). Available at: http://repository.upenn.edu/cgi/viewcontent.cgi?article=1603&context=cis_reports.

Scheibel, J. E. (1769-98). *Einleitung zur mathematischen Buecherkenntnis*. Breslau: J.E. Meyer.

Schöneberg, U.; Sperber W. (2014). POS tagging and its applications for mathematics text analysis in Mathematics. In: *Intelligent Computer Mathematics. International Conference, CICM 2014, Coimbra, Portugal, July 7-11, 2014: proceedings*. Edited by S.M. Watt et al., Heidelberg: Springer. (LNAI, 8543), pp. 213-223. Available at: http://arxiv.org/pdf/1406.2880.pdf.

Schöneberg, U.; Sperber, W. (2013). The DeLiVerMATH project: text analysis in mathematics. In: *Intelligent Computer Mathematics. MKM, Calculemus, DML, and Systems and Projects 2013, Held as part of CICM 2013, Bath, UK, July 8-12, 2013. Proceedings*. Edited by J. Carette et al. Heidelberg: Springer. (LNAI, 7961), pp. 379-382. Available at: http://arxiv.org/pdf/1306.6944.pdf.

SKOS (2009) Simple Knowledge Organization System: reference. W3C Recommendation 18 August 2009. Edited by A. Miles; S. Bechhofer. Available at: http://www.w3.org/2009/08/skos-reference/skos.html.

SMGloM (2014).*Semantic multilingual glossary on mathematics*. Available at: https://mathhub.info/smglom/smglom.

Stanford NLPG (2004 -) *Stanford log-linear Part-Of-Speech tagger*. The Stanford Natural Language Processing Group. Available at: http://nlp.stanford.edu/software/tagger.shtml.

TIB Hannover (2015). *Die Technische Informationsbibliothek und Universitätsbibliothek Hannover*. Available at: http://www.tib.uni-hannover.de.

WolframAlpha (2015). *WolframAlpha computational knowledge engine*. Available at: http://www.wolframalpha.com.

word2vec (2015). DL4J Deep Learning for Java. Available at: http://deeplearning4j.org/word2vec.html.

zbMATH (1931-). *Zentralblatt MATH*. Available at: http://www.zbmath.org.

ULF SCHÖNEBERG works as software developer in the editorial office of zbMATH. His research interests include natural language processing methods for text analysis and neural networks methods and their use for test analysis.

WOLFRAM SPERBER is working as an editor at zbMATH. Previously he has worked in mathematical research, especially optimal control of partial differential equations and numerical methods for the solutions of these equations. His research interest is the content analysis of mathematical information, with an emphasis on machine-learning methods. Currently he is working on machine-learning methods for content analysis, tools for formula search, and concepts for semantic glossaries in mathematics.

4. Classifications in subject access authority control

Subject authority control supported by classification: the case of National Library of the Czech Republic

Marie Balíková
Czech National Library, Prague, Czech Republic

Abstract: From the very beginnings of library automation, subject authority control has been considered an important bibliographic tool in the Czech National Library (CNL). Effective subject access cannot exist without standardised access points. Subject authorities are considered an indispensable reference tool in supporting the selection of subject access points and normalizing content indexing. Most importantly, they are heavily relied upon when it comes to customisation of links between bibliographic records and subject access points in order to create a user-friendly subject browsing and searching environment. Because of the fact that the Universal Decimal Classification (UDC) is widely used in Czech Libraries it has become a readily available language independent subject framework which can be complemented by a more user-friendly subject heading system. In this context, the subject authority control offers a means of enhancing subject headings' access points with terminology and the semantic links available in UDC. Furthermore classification is used to enrich relationships between authority records themselves. The author will discuss in more detail the different aspects and advantages of subject authorities in which a classification and a subject heading system complement one another and the way this is implemented in the CNL.

Keywords: library systems; subject authority control; Czech National Library; Universal Decimal Classification; UDC; bibliographic records; semantic relationships

Invited talk, paper not submitted.
Presentation materials are available on the conference website: http://seminar.udcc.org/2015.

MARIE BALÍKOVÁ is Head of National Subject Authorities, Indexing and Classification Department of the National Library of the Czech Republic; she is responsible for the national subject authority files and the implementation of the subject analysis international standards, as well as the Conspectus Categorisation Scheme in Czechia. She chairs the Working Group on Subject Access and is a member of the National Cataloguing Policy Committee in Czechia. She is a member of the Standing Committee of the IFLA Classification and Indexing Section, a member of the Executive Committee of UDC Consortium and a member of UDC Editorial Team. She also participated in several projects covering the subject analysis area: M-CAST (Multilingual Content Aggregation System based on TRUST Search Engine), UIG (Uniform Information Gateway), MUS (Musica Subject Gateway), KIV Subject Gateway (Subject Gateway for Library and Information Science). Currently she works on the national project INTERMI (Interoperability in memory institutions in Czechia).

Multilingual subject access and classification-based browsing through authority control: the experience of the ETH-Bibliothek

Jiri Pika
UDC Editorial Team, Zurich, Switzerland

Milena Pika-Biolzi
ETH-Zurich, Zurich, Switzerland

Abstract: The paper provides an illustration of the benefits of subject authority control improving multilingual subject access in NEBIS - Netzwerk von Bibliotheken und Informationsstellen in der Schweiz. This example of good practice focuses on some important aspects of classification and indexing. NEBIS subject authorities comprise a classification scheme and multilingual subject descriptor system. A bibliographic system supported by subject authority control empowers libraries as it enables them to expand and adjust vocabulary and link subjects to suit their specific audience. Most importantly it allows the management of different subject vocabularies in numerous languages. In addition, such an enriched subject index creates re-usable and shareable source of subject statements that has value in the wider context of information exchange. The illustrations and supporting arguments are based on indexing practice, subject authority control and use of classification in ETH-Bibliothek, which is the largest library within the NEBIS network.

Keywords: subject authority control; subject index; OPAC; NEBIS; Universal Decimal Classification; UDC; ETH-Bibliothek; multilingual subject index

1. Introduction

There is very little that we can say in praise of subject indexing that has not already been said. We know that the objective of subject indexing is to help users retrieve and browse information resources about unpredictable ranges of topics and their combinations. These may appear in textual documents irrespective of their language or format, or may be expressed by images, music, objects or events. Much of this information will not appear anywhere in the formal description of documents and cannot be captured by computing upon collections or their metadata. Whenever feasible and affordable, content analysis and subject indexing are the best ways of capturing knowledge. Yet subject cataloguers seem to be under continuous pressure to justify the value of their work and their tools. Sadly, we often see that the effort put into subject analysis and classification to help search or browse subjects is rarely made available to users. In spite of advances in database technology and graphical user interfaces, library systems have been failing to exploit the value of subject information hidden in bibliographic databases. Research over the past ten years indicates that little improvement has been made in OPAC interfaces with regards to subject searching, in particular classification browsing (Casson, Fabbrizzi & Slavic, 2011; Slavic, 2006). There are, of course, some positive developments, especially in the domain of academic libraries (Schallier, 2007; Papy & Leblond, 2007; La Barre, 2013). What is notable in these rare success stories is that an improvement in subject retrieval can usually be linked to both the use of classification and the availability of the subject authority control tools supporting its use.

As subject specialists at ETH (Eidgenössische Technische Hochschule) Bibliothek we have been privileged to work with a system which provides our users with a very good subject browsing and searching interface. This is to a great extent thanks to our comprehensive subject index and good management of subject authorities.

The ETH library has been associated with excellence in subject indexing and multilingual information retrieval with regards to ETHICS (ETH Information Control System). This was an advanced in-house library system developed and used in the ETH library from 1983 to 1999. ETHICS was often commended for its sophisticated support for classification-based searching and browsing and multilingual subject access.[1] So much so that its UDC-based, multilingual subject authority file was also used in GERHARD - German Harvest Automated Retrieval and Directory as a terminology and classification base for the indexing of Web resources[2].

In 1999, ETHICS migrated to Aleph to support Netzwerk von Bibliotheken und Informationsstellen in der Schweiz (NEBIS). The subject index from ETHICS, was successfully implemented in the new environment and it evolved into a shared subject NSI (NEBIS Subject Index) used and maintained by member libraries within the network known as NEBIS (Pika, 2007).

In this paper we argue that the use of classification and subject indexing are only as good as the authority tools supporting them and enabling their usability in catalogue searching and browsing. We will illustrate this point by showing how authority control in NSI can help manage a synthetic classification such as UDC and its local extension as well as subject headings in three languages attached to each class.

2. Subject searching in NEBIS

The ETH-Bibliothek collection contains more than 2.8 million (print) documents classified by UDC in over 50 languages with the greatest proportion of

---

1 Reports on ETHICS can be found in Buxton (1990), Hug & Nöthiger (1988), Loth & Funk (1990); Grünewald (1994), Frâncu (2003, 2015); Slavic-Overfield (2005).

2 GERHARD was fully automatic indexing and classification system of academic resources on the German Web (developed as a research project at the University of Oldenburg 1997-2002). It allowed for browsing the web using UDC with an interface that instead of UDC notation displayed captions from the ETHICS subject index (Möller et al, 1999).

documents in English, followed by documents in four official languages of the Swiss Confederation which are German, French, Italian and Rhaeto-Romance. ETH-Bibliothek is the largest and most important library for the field of science and technology in Switzerland. The library's tradition of detailed content indexing derives, to a large extent, from the significance of its collection for the Swiss academic and research community. Nowadays, the ETH collection represents the most significant part of the NEBIS catalogue[3] which provides access to 7.9 million books and journals in 140 libraries of the NEBIS network.

The OPAC interface in NEBIS allows users to search in English, German and French. What is, however, special for this catalogue is that once users have made their search with a simple natural language term, they are presented with a result list that offers access to a subject authority record. At this point the user can opt for semantic search expansion through hyperlink for broader, narrower and related terms.[4] Figure 1 shows options displayed to users if they choose to explore the subject 'diamond'. This particular entry shows options for expanding the search to broader (Carbon group in Mineralogy) and related subjects (Synthetic diamonds) which are derived from the UDC hierarchy and class relationships (see also).

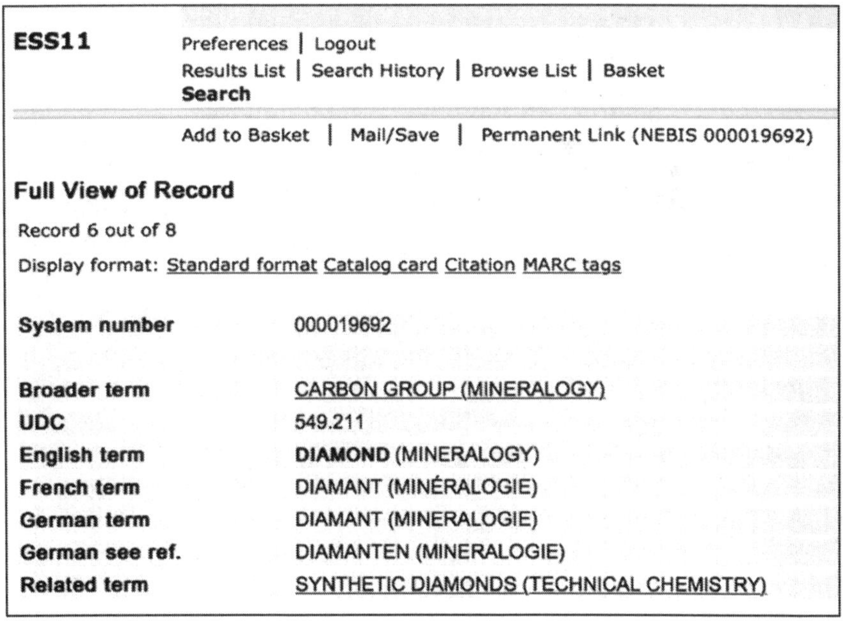

Figure 1: *Catalogue view of the subject authority record for 'diamond'*

3 NEBIS is available at: http://www.nebis.ch/eng/.

4 Casson, Fabrizzi & Slavic (2011) argue that such "two-step searching" should be norm in subject searching in library catalogues.

The interface of the subject authority records illustrates a particular approach not only of applying UDC and its combination with subject descriptors, but also the choice of NEBIS' browsing method by which users can navigate through a classification without being aware of the classification scheme they use. At this point we ought to point out that the strength of our catalogue is not in the graphical user interface such as it is, which is made available, in the current interface version, by the OPAC vendor. Rather it is to do with the underlying subject authority data which at any point in the future can be displayed with a better and more user-friendly interface.

Clearly, in order to enable any level of sophistication in browsing and searching, the indexing of documents has to be supported by a data management system that allows for the storing and managing of classification notations, relationships between classes and multilingual subject descriptions. Once established, such a vocabulary management tool allows for the development of subject index to suit local or regional needs as well as being adaptable for information exchange on the global network. In further sections we will explain in more detail the role of classification, in this case UDC, its local ETH extensions and adaptation (in terms of vocabulary and syntax) and the assignment of natural language terms to UDC classes.

3. Approach to subject indexing in the ETH-Bibliothek

3.1 Making best use of UDC

Similar to many large academic libraries in Europe, the majority of the ETH collection is not available in open access and the only way to view its content is through a subject metadata search. Therefore, it comes as no surprise that ETH-Bibliothek not only applies very detailed subject indexing but also makes sure that its catalogue provides advanced browsing and searching functionality. Given the content and the size of the collection the UDC scheme, with its detailed science and technology schedules, seems to suit the library's needs very well. ETH is particularly interested in the UDC's synthetic feature and provision for extensions with alphabetical terms and local classification. The possibility to manage smaller semantic units of complex classification notation in indexing and searching is very important for the objectives of the library's catalogue as it allows easier linking of multilingual subject terms to classification notations.

Figure 2 illustrates the many levels of synthesis applied in ETH in indexing using UDC. The general principle in indexing is to express complex subjects by connecting UDC notations in such a way that they can be easily decomposed into smaller semantic components. Numbers denoting different fields and

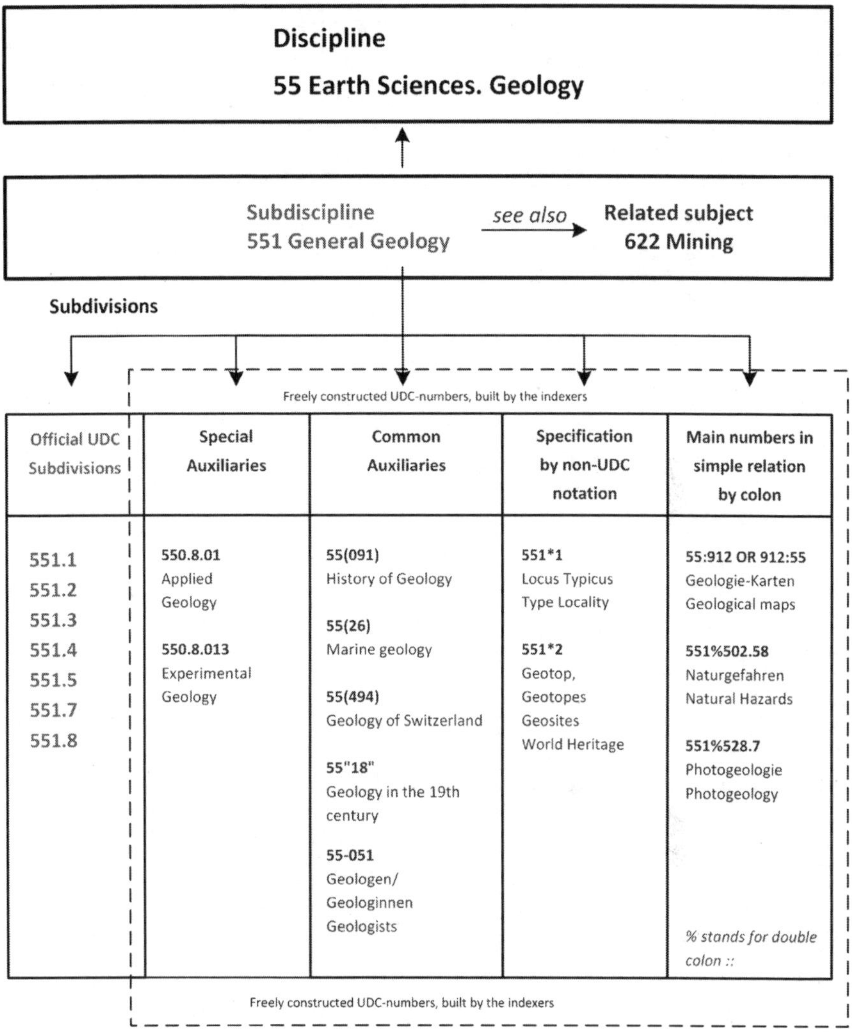

Figure 2: *The application of UDC in ETH-Bibliothek*

disciplines are connected by using colon or double colon combination[5]. Furthermore, each UDC number within its own hierarchy can be combined with common auxiliaries (place, time, form, person, etc.) and special auxiliary subdivisions developed for that particular field. Last but not the least, ETH-Bibliothek develops and includes its own local extensions which are allowed in

5 Double colon :: in UDC denotes fixed order of main UDC numbers in a complex classmark. This is used to indicate pre-coordination that would lose its intended meaning, if the order would be permuted. For technical reasons in the ETH's NEBIS Subject Index we replace :: sign (official UDC symbol for fixed order) system with % (percentage) e.g., 622.21%622.323 *Petroleum concessions.*

UDC following the asterisk symbol. In addition to this, ETH uses the comma (not an official UDC symbol) for direct extensions of UDC hierarchy e.g. UDC class 622.228 *Abandoned mines. Reopening, re-equipping of mines*, which does not have a further subdivision, is extended as 622.228,1 *Abandoned mines*. The asterisk and comma symbols denote the point at which standard UDC notation finishes and local extensions start (cf. Pika, 2007). The policy of local extensions is very typical of ETH-Bibliothek and is driven by the need to include more specific or emerging terminology not yet developed in the UDC scheme.

It is notable that the ETH-Bibliothek indexing policy favours synthesis to its full extent as this assumes co-ordination of subjects, i.e. post-coordinate searching in the catalogue. When dealing with complex subjects it is recommended, whenever possible, to link two classes (existing in the authority file as separate entries), rather than opt for a simple notation representing a complex subject, even if this exists in the schedule or can be created via parallel division. For instance, 622 *Mining* and 552.523 *Clay* to express 622:552.523 *Mining : Clay,* rather than 622.361 *Clay mining.*[6] This is one of the main sources of the index expansion and growth, which is helped, to a large extent, by the library's practice of assigning multiple classmarks (simple or complex) to a single document.

3.2 Managing natural language terms

Libraries often combine classification with an alphabetical indexing language. A typical scenario would include a classification complemented with a subject-heading system which is developed and maintained as a separate indexing language. In this case libraries tend to use less detailed classmarks primarily for systematic shelf arrangement, browsing and in supporting collection planning and management. Subject authority files are then utilised to intellectually map two systems and align their complementary functions in information retrieval. During this process, subject indexers would have to reconcile the synthetic nature of UDC and its propensity to post-coordination with the pre-coordinated nature of subject-heading systems (cf. Balikova, 2007: 203).

In the case of ETH and its subject index, the situation is very different. The NSI started its life in ETH as a very detailed and complex subject index to classification whereby UDC classmarks are used as placeholders for numerous search terms in German, French and English. The NSI authority file uses UDC to establish semantic and associative relationships and UDC class descriptions to expand the subject index with synonyms and related subjects.

NSI has been populated by natural language terms, i.e. subject descriptors in a particular way. If a complex class or concept such as "chemical composition of the

6 More examples are provided in Pika (2007).

upper atmosphere" or "chemical reactions in the atmosphere" or "convection cells in earth mantle" is to be easily found in the alphabetical index, some additional entries, including synonyms, are added to assist the user and their search strategies. Such a class description may need several descriptive terms per language, often reaching over 20 terms per class. In the first instance terminology is taken from the UDC schedules, and the original captions then get extended by synonyms, term inversions, abbreviations, etc., that are ranked according to their importance. 'Descriptors' have the status of the authoritative, main term (usually taken from UDC schedules), quasi-synonyms serve as extensions if narrower classes are not available. At the end, one lists technical terms, specialist jargon, popular science terminology, abbreviations and related/associated terms. Chosen descriptors are listed according to their importance. The ultimate goal is to help users find subjects with ease, irrespective of whether they use jargon or a colloquialism or search in English, German or French.

NSI has evolved for over thirty years and although today it could be easily described as a descriptor or subject heading system, its nature remains strongly classification-oriented. NSI subject terms, over 64,000 of them, are all conceptually closely linked to the UDC hierarchy and to the syntactically expressive nature of its notation.

4. Managing vocabulary through subject authority control in NEBIS

In Figure 3 we can see how UDC class 549.211 is connected with its verbal components in three languages. MARC field 150 holds the descriptors in three languages, whereas MARC field 450 keeps synonyms, plural/singular forms, acronyms, etc.; its main function is to help browsing in the NEBIS-OPAC index. All these fields are linked to UDC class 549.211, entered in MARC field 072. Its hierarchical position is described within field 550 which holds the notation of the broader class, in this case 549.21. Its description *Carbon Group / Mineralogy* can be seen in the OPAC view of the descriptor 'diamond' (see Figure 1).

In Figure 4, below, we can see an authority record showing the management of the relationships between classes. It shows an example of Rhone Glacier and we can see its classmark in MARC field 072: (282.244.311*RHONEGL). MARC fields 150 holds the descriptors in three languages for Rhône Glacier, whereas MARC field 450 keeps inverted terms, or linguistic variations. All these fields are linked to two UDC class numbers: (282.244.311) *Rhone (West European rivers)* and (234.311.4) *Valais Alps (Western Alps),* both appearing in MARC field 550.

The Rhone Glacier is hydrologically a part of the Rhone river system, and as a geographical entity it lies in Western Alps. Therefore it is appropriate to have it placed in two hierarchies. OPAC displays both classes as Broader Terms (Figure 5).

Leader	LDR		00452nz---2200169n--4500
Control No.	001		000022564
Control No. ID	003		ETHICS-SSR
Date and Time	005		19840411000000.0
Fixed Data	008		990813---a-z---a-----------------------
Former RecID	090	a	00022564
		b	SSR
Former CAT	099	a	PIKA
		c	19980908
		l	E01
		h	13:55:19
Topical Term	150	a	DIAMANT (MINERALOGIE)
		9	ger
Topical Term	150	a	DIAMOND (MINERALOGY)
		9	eng
Topical Term	150	a	DIAMANT (MINÉRALOGIE)
		9	fre
Seef.Trac.Topic	450	a	DIAMANTEN (MINERALOGIE)
		9	ger
SAF.Trac.Topic	550	a	549.21
		w	g
UDC	072	a	549.211

Figure 3: *Subject editing screen in NSI*

Fixed Data	008		990813---a-z---a-----------------------
Former RecID	090	a	00000586
		b	SSR
Topical Term	150	a	RHONE-GLETSCHER (VIERWALDSTÄTTER ALPEN)
		9	ger
Topical Term	150	a	RHONE GLACIER (VIERWALDSTÄTTER ALPS)
		9	eng
Topical Term	150	a	GLACIER DU RHÔNE (ALPES DES QUATRE-CANTONS)
		9	fre
Seef.Trac.Topic	450	a	RHÔNE, GLACIER DU RHÔNE (ALPES DES QUATRE-CANTONS)
		9	fre
Seef.Trac.Topic	450	a	ROTTEN-GLETSCHER (VIERWALDSTÄTTER ALPEN)
		9	ger
SAF.Trac.Topic	550	a	(282.244.311)
		w	g
SAF.Trac.Topic	550	a	(234.311.4)
		w	g
UDC	072	a	(282.244.311*RHONEGL)

Figure 4: *Relating the descriptor Rhone Glacier to two classes*

System number	000000461
Broader term	SWISS RHONE (WEST EUROPEAN RIVERS)
Broader term	VALAIS ALPS (WESTERN ALPS)
UDC	**(282.244.**311*RHONEGL)
English term	**RHONE GLACIER (VIERWALDSTÄTTER ALPS)**
French term	**GLACIER** DU RHÔNE (ALPES DES QUATRE-CANTONS)
German term	RHONE-GLETSCHER (**VIERWALDSTÄTTER** ALPEN)
French see ref.	RHÔNE, **GLACIER** DU RHÔNE (ALPES DES QUATRE-CANTONS)
German see ref.	ROTTEN-GLETSCHER (**VIERWALDSTÄTTER** ALPEN)

Figure 5: *Recording relationships between classes*

5. Indexing interface in NEBIS

The interface in the NEBIS cataloguing module combines browsing of several indexes with editing functions. New subject descriptors can be created and linked to the new UDC class record and then linked to the relevant documents. Upon saving, new subject terms become instantly visible in the OPAC. Following content analysis, one can assign a classification number to documents through the alphabetical index by browsing and selecting as many relevant descriptors as necessary.

The indexing process itself starts by inspecting the bibliographic description of the new document which is displayed on an internal cataloguing interface and which also enables searching for related documents (through title, author or ISBN search) and cross-matching these items. After opening the classification interface and introducing the set of MARC fields 691, for ETH Subject Topics, the search for the best suitable subjects can be started. While looking for suitable subjects there are several ways to proceed, but basically there are two prominent methods: an alphabetical search in the subject index and a systematic search in the UDC structure. The best way is a combination of both. Figure 6 illustrates the ease with which one may assign a descriptor by choosing an appropriate topic from the alphabetical search.

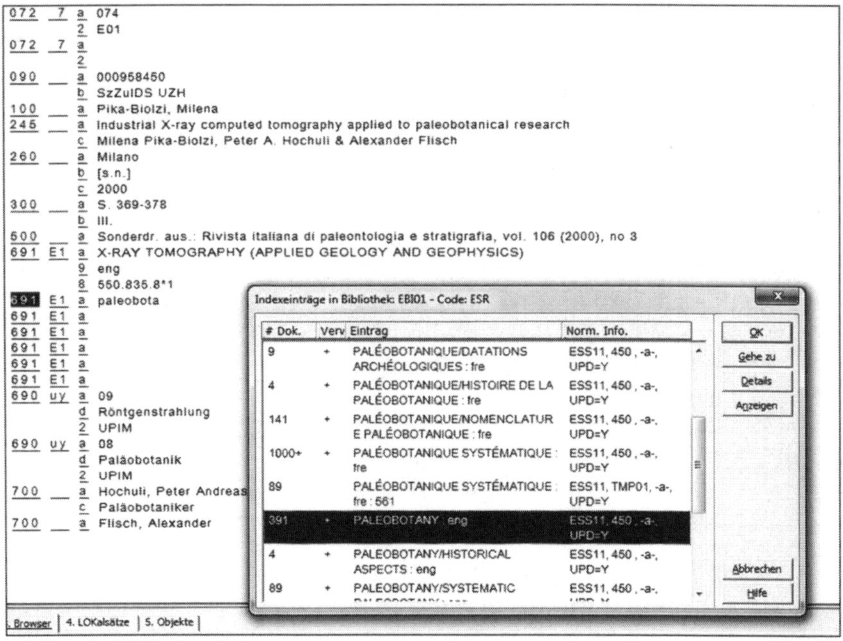

Figure 6: *Selection of an index term from the NSI in the process of subject cataloguing*

It is outside of the scope of this paper to show all the functionalities and features of the NSI system (cf. Pika, 2007). Our objective with this paper was simply to draw attention to an example of good practice in subject indexing and the importance of supporting tools. We hope that the value for both users and librarians in such a well developed system is self-evident.

4. Conclusion

Almost three decades ago the indexing specialists in ETH-Bibliothek recognized the importance of subject authority control in managing the relationship between classification and alphabetical subject access in order to improve information retrieval in its OPAC. The ETH-Bibliothek approach, now part of the wider NEBIS network, still stands as an example of good practice in exploiting subject data in information retrieval.

Authority control helped in accomplishing independent control over verbal access to classification. This made it possible to implement multilingual verbal access and enhance search term development. Most importantly, the NSI authority control tool helped with the implementation and management of two complementary indexing systems: subject descriptors and UDC with its local extensions and enhancements.

In this paper we tried to draw attention to the importance that an authority control tool can play in not only empowering subject searching in OPAC but also in supporting the daily practice of subject cataloguing. As the NSI grows it is becoming semantically and structurally stronger and ever more capable in supporting resource discovery in the large collection it serves.

Acknowledgements

We would like to thank our colleagues from ETH-Bibliothek Zürich, students from the MAS LIS courses at the University of Zürich, colleagues from Classification Societies, the UDC editorial team and in particular Aida Slavic for many stimulating and challenging discussions, and for sharing ideas about classification systems.

References

Balikova, M. (2007). UDC in Czechia. *Extensions and Corrections to the UDC*, 29 (2007), pp. 191-227. Available at: http://hdl.handle.net/10150/105205.

Buxton, A. B. (1990). Computer searching of UDC numbers. *Journal of Documentation*, 46 (3), pp. 193-217.

Casson, E.; Fabbrizzi, A.; Slavic, A. (2011). Subject search in Italian OPACs: an opportunity in waiting? In: *Subject access: preparing for the future.* Edited by P. Landry et al. Berlin: De Gruyter, pp. 37-50.

Frâncu, V. (2003). *Multilingual Access to Information using an Intermediate Language : proefschrift voorgelegd tot het behalen van de graad van doctor in de Taal- en Letterkunde aan de Universiteit Antwerpen*. Available at: http://arizona.openrepository.com/arizona/handle/10150/106319.

Frâncu, V.; Dediu, L.-I. (2015). TinREAD – an integrative solution for subject authority control. In: *Classification & authority control: expanding resource discovery: proceedings of the International UDC Seminar, 29-30 October 2015, Lisbon, Portugal. Edited by A. Slavic, M. I. Cordeiro. Würzburg: Ergon Verlag*, pp. 123-133.

Grünewald, F. (1994). Anwendung UDK in ETHICS. In: *Bang voor onderwerpsluiting*. Edited by G. Riesthuis et al. Antwerpen, VVBAD, pp. 46-52.

Hug, H.; Nötiger, R. (1988). ETHICS: an online public access catalogue at ETH Bibliothek, Zurich. *Program*, 22 (2) 1988, pp. 133-142.

Hug H.; Walser, M. (1990). Retrieval in the ETH database using the UDC. In: *Tools for knowledge organization and the human interface: proc. of the 1st International ISKO Conference, Darmstadt, 14-17 August 1990*. Edited by R. Fugmann. Frankfurt/Main: Indeks Verlag, 1990. (Advances in knowledge organization 1), pp. 216-219.

La Barre, K. (2013). Sempre avanti? Some reflections on facted interfaces. In: *Classification & visualization: interfaces to knowledge: proceedings of the International UDC Seminar, 24-25 October 2013, The Hague, The Netherlands*. Edited by A. Slavic, A. Akdag Salah, S. Davies, 177-190. Würzburg: Ergon Verlag. pp. 91-103.

Loth, K. (1996). Überlegungen zu einer computergerechten Reorganisation der UDK. *Extensions and Corrections to the UDC*, 18, pp. 9-13.

Loth, K.; Funk, H. (1990). Subject search on ETHICS on the basis of UDC. In: *The UDC : essays for a new decade*. Edited by A. Gilchrist; D. Strachan. London: Aslib, pp. 35-47.

Möller, G. et al. (1999). Automatic classification of the World Wide Web using Universal Decimal Classification. In: *23rd International Online Information Meeting*, London, 7-9 December 1999: proceedings. Edited by B. McKenna. Oxford: Learned Information Europe, pp. 231-237.

Papy, F.; Leblond, C. (2007). L'interface de recherche d'information du Visual...Catalog: un outil innovant à "double détente". *Documentaliste-Sciences de l'Information*, 44 (4), pp. 288-298. Available at: http://www.cairn.info/revue-documentaliste-sciences-de-l-information-2007-4-page-288.htm#no1.

Pika, J. (2002). Anwendung der UDK in NEBIS in der Schweiz : ein Ausblick. [talk given at the seminar] Jahrestagung der Gesellschaft für Klassifikation (GfKl), Universität Mannheim, 23. Juli 2002. Available at: http://www.ethbib.ethz.ch/pub/nebisUDK.pdf.

Pika, J. (2007). Universal Decimal Classification at the ETH-Bibliothek Zürich - a Swiss perspective. *Extensions and Corrections to the UDC*, 29, pp. 229-251.

Schallier, W. (2004). What a subject search interface can do? *Extensions and Corrections to the UDC*, 26, pp. 18-28. Available at: http://hdl.handle.net/10150/105315.

Slavic, A. (2006). The level of exploitation of Universal Decimal Classification in library OPACs: a pilot study. *Vjesnik bibliotekara Hrvatske*, 49 (3-4): pp. 155-182. [English translation available at: http://hdl.handle.net/10150/105346].

Slavic-Overfield, A. (2005). *Classification management and use in a networked environment: the case of the Universal Decimal Classification*. Doctoral thesis, London: University College London, University of London. Available at: http://discovery.ucl.ac.uk/1334914/.

JIRI PIKA is a member of the UDC Editorial Team and works on the revision of Earth Sciences and on the German UDC editions (UDC Summary, UDC Abridged Edition and Deutsche UDK Online). Up until 2014 he was a librarian - subject specialist in Earth Sciences at the ETH-Bibliothek (Swiss Federal Institute of Technology in Zurich). During this period he worked on document indexing using UDC and developed a number of local extensions to classification including a mnemonic Earth Sciences Classification for a major open-stacks Earth Science Department Library (ETH). Jiri was also teaching indexing and classification at the master degree programme in Library and Information Science offered in collaboration between Zurich University and University Library in Zurich from 1998-2014. Jiri holds PhD degree in Natural Sciences from the ETH Zurich (1982).

MILENA PIKA-BIOLZI is a curator of the Geological-Palaeontological Collections of the ETH-Zürich (Earth Science Department). As a palaeontologist she initiated and designed several exhibitions dealing with phenomena in geology and palaeontology, based on material from ETH Geological-Palaeontological Collections. She was also in charge of the conceptual design of the *focus*Terra exposition at the Earth Science Department, which is now one of major attractions in museum landscape of city of Zurich. During her time as a curator she started to set-up Data Base for all the specimen of the Geological-Palaeontological Collections of the ETH-Zurich, now accessible online. Milena was also teaching Palaeoclimatology and Stable isotope Geology at the master degree programme in University of Parma (Italy) between 1986-2012. Milena holds a Doctoral degree from University of Parma and the PhD degree in Natural Sciences from the University of Zurich (1984).

Development of a classification-oriented authority control: the experience of the National and University Library in Zagreb

Ana Vukadin
National and University Library in Zagreb, Croatia

Abstract: The paper presents experiences and challenges encountered during the planning and creation of the Universal Decimal Classification (UDC) authority database in the National and University Library in Zagreb, Croatia. The project started in 2014 with the objective of facilitating classification data management, improving the indexing consistency at the institutional level and the machine readability of data for eventual sharing and re-use in the Web environment. The paper discusses the advantages and disadvantages of UDC, which is an analytico-synthetic classification scheme tending towards a more faceted structure, in regard to various aspects of authority control. This discussion represents the referential framework for the project. It determines the choice of elements to be included in the authority file, e.g. distinguishing between syntagmatic and paradigmatic combinations of subjects. It also determines the future lines of development, e.g. interlinking with the subject headings authority file in order to provide searching by verbal expressions.

Keywords: Universal Decimal Classification; UDC; analytico-synthetic classification; authority control; National and University Library in Zagreb

1. Introduction

Universal Decimal Classification (UDC) has been used in the National and University Library in Zagreb since the early 1980s for systematic shelf arrangement, indexing and retrieving of information resources, and subject access to the national bibliography. However, the consistency in the application of the standard among and within different library departments and collections was maintained manually, without the help of an authority file, which often lead to unsatisfactory results, especially due to the fact that in the Library UDC notations are assigned to various kinds of material, from printed monographs and journal articles to electronic resources and recorded music, each of which has its own specific demands. Another challenge was data updating, which is regularly required in cases when indexing policies change or a new edition of the standard is published, and is difficult to perform without adequate machine support.

In order to meet the issues of indexing consistency at the institutional level, in 2014 a database was created that contains all locally used UDC notations, as well as instructions for their building and use. At the same time the importance of data consistency was recognized not only in regard to the improvement of subject access to the Library's material, but also for eventual sharing and re-use in a wider environment. Therefore the creation of the UDC database is seen as the first step towards a real classification authority file. It is hoped that in the next stages of the project it can be connected to the other Library's databases, e.g. exported to the library management system or linked via a web application.

Taking into account the complexity and costs of authority work, the necessity of such a tool was widely discussed. During the past decade the Department for subject cataloguing has been putting much effort into the development of a subject heading authority file, based on the adaptation of Library of Congress Subject Headings (LCSH), and into its alignment with current indexing principles and standards. Starting from 2011 all authorized subject headings have been assigned UDC notations, which serve both as a classification tool, providing disciplinary context for subject terminology, and as a search tool for professionals that helps them choose or compose the notation during the process of subject analysis.[1] The inclusion of UDC notations in subject heading authority records significantly improved the consistency of classification data in the bibliographic database. Nevertheless, this system could not replace a real classification authority file, not only due to the fact that subject headings were introduced in the library only in 1997, which means a great amount of older library material is still retrievable by subject only through UDC, but also because the additional benefits of having independent UDC authorities were considered, such as the increased possibility of classification data updating or their improved visibility in a wider context. It should also be noted that almost all libraries in Croatia use UDC, while the use of subject headings and thesauri greatly varies, therefore in any future cooperative library network or web service subject access will probably be best provided through UDC as an intermediary between different controlled vocabularies. For all these reasons, a UDC authority file is recognized as an important tool both at the institutional level and in a networked environment.

While the further development of the authority file will clearly depend on technical and, above all, financial issues, the importance of some kind of a referential framework that establishes the main lines of development and continually serves as a guideline was recognized right from the initial stage. For this reason great attention has been paid to a clear and consistent indexing policy that would support the maximum use of classification authorities. Some observations concerning the indexing policy and its application in the UDC database are presented below.

---

1 Depending on the specificity of the topic, both simple and composed notations are used in authorized subject heading records. If a subject heading corresponds to more than one UDC class, multiple notations are added in order to ensure cross-disciplinary access and exhaustivity of the subject.

2. UDC and authority control

Notwithstanding recently published standards and guidelines such as ISO 25964 or IFLA's *Guidelines for Subject Access in National Bibliographies*, the field of subject authority control has been much disregarded, particularly if compared to the standardisation activities in descriptive cataloguing and name authority control (Cordeiro, 2001). As much as the availability of classification schemes in machine-readable formats was exploited in scheme management very early by publishers (Slavic, Cordeiro & Riesthuis, 2008; Slavic, 2008), the functionalities required by analytico-synthetic systems such as UDC developed only gradually in MARC formats. For all these reasons the challenges of classification data management in libraries resulted in a heterogeneous practice regarding both information organization issues and technical solutions.

In the case of the National and University Library the principal questions concerning the development of an indexing policy that would support the use and re-use of UDC authorities were: what are the advantages of UDC as an analytico-synthetic scheme and how can these advantages be used to their full potential in terms of authority control? What are the possible drawbacks of using this system? The answers had a decisive role in determining which elements should be included in UDC-oriented authority control.

2.1 Authority vs. flexibility

One well known advantage of analytico-synthetic classifications is that they allow for great specificity in indexing even for subjects that were not anticipated at the time of the creation of a scheme. Such classifications can be implemented in indexing scenarios and for specialized topics that were neither planned nor considered of significance for the majority of users, cultures or languages. This means that irrespective of bias or delay in updates of its knowledge base, the scheme can be used to generate new and specific subjects. This is one of the main reasons why, for instance, UDC serves libraries well in multicultural and multilingual contexts as well as collections in a specialized library environment. In order to express complex or specialized subjects, main numbers in UDC are combined or extended by facets of concepts that are shared between different areas of knowledge (common auxiliaries), or by domain-specific facets (special auxiliaries).

What has just been put forward as an advantage needs to be leveraged against well known issues brought about by this flexibility. There are three well known practical problems for which authority control tools seem indispensable:

First, classification allows different ways of expressing the same subject with a small shift in semantics that requires local indexing policies and guidelines. For example, in 51-051(092) 'biographies of mathematicians' the focus is on mathematics, i.e. the content of these biographies will be of interest primarily to mathematicians, while in 929:51 'biographies of mathematicians' the emphasis is on biography, i.e. factual information about a person's life.

Second, UDC allows for flexibility in citation order. Some general classification theory rules are applied in practice: the treated subject is always listed first, followed by the subject of treatment (Ranganathan's picture-wall rule). Nevertheless it seems that it has always been more important for UDC to be able to retrieve all subjects in complex UDC notations than to be concerned with the order of subjects.

Third, there is the problem with the co-existence of the new and old structure due to the continuous revision of UDC which converts the remaining enumeration of pre-combined subjects in the schedules into a faceted structure. Facets of new general concepts are being introduced with the intention of replacing repetition of this concept throughout the schedules (Williamson & McIlwaine, 2009; Vukadin & Slavic, 2013). The objective in the revision is to achieve a single notational representation for general, frequently used concepts. However, during this long process of revision there may be alternative ways of expressing the same concept or category. For instance, professions are generally expressed by main numbers extended by the common auxiliary -051 *Persons as agents, doers, practitioners*, e.g. 616-051 'medical staff'. However, in class 7 the notations for professions are still composed by main numbers combined with special auxiliaries .07, e.g. 78.071 'musicians'. In a few cases the profession can also be expressed in an enumerative way, e.g. 023.5 'library staff'.

It is obvious that a balance must be found between the adaptability of a classification system to various indexing needs and the consistency required by the authority control. Namely, how much uniformity is needed to ensure the necessary level of predictability, without compromising the flexibility which is one of the system's greatest strengths? How much control is too much?

The issue can partly be addressed by the distinction between syntagmatic and paradigmatic combinations of concepts. Syntagmatic combinations usually describe occasional, *ad hoc* relationships. In natural language they are represented by a phrase or a syntagm, such as 'feminism and sport', 'public views on healthcare reform', or 'the impact of marketing on charities' fundraising efficiency'. Paradigmatic combinations express relationships that are constantly valid and are usually represented (as well as searched) by a well-established terminology, e.g. 'cultural policy' (*nota bene*, not the same as 'culture and politics'!), 'sociology of religion', or 'urban climate'.

In general, syntagmatic aspects pertain to the syntax of an individual subject indexing language and are not the concern of authority control (Tartaglia, 2004). Although in practice it is not always easy to distinguish between the two (Svenonius, 2000), the general distinction does matter, not only at the conceptual level, but also in the pragmatic context of verbal searching, as will be shown later. In UDC notations both types of combinations are governed by the same syntactic rules. However, in syntagmatic combinations the sequence is by nature more flexible and should not be part of authority control. In many cases it is the indexer who gets to decide which concept should be placed in the first position, because this may vary depending on the predominant subject or disciplinary point of view, as shown above. On the other hand, paradigmatic combinations should be included into the authority file in strict citation order. Needless to say, the inclusion of synthesized notations into a database presupposes the possibility of facet searching, i.e. each compositional element ought to be identifiable and retrievable.

Another question concerns predictability of the established citation order. For instance, if 'sociology of religion' is to be represented by the compound notation 316.74:2, i.e. with the number for 'sociology' at the first position, do all sub-disciplines of sociology have to be represented in the same way? What about, for instance, the sociology of literature, which belongs more to literature studies than to sociology? In general, as much as the predictability plays a key role in ensuring the internal logic of a system and thereby in facilitating searches, such a high level of uniformity is not necessary if there are equivalence relationships (*see* references) between terms, possibly in the form of direct links. Equivalence relationships also redeem the internal inconsistency of the standard which is due to the ongoing process of revision.

2.2 Notation vs. natural language terms

A classification authority file ought to contain captions in order to enable users to search and browse using natural language. However, as stated above, in the process of revision many enumerated UDC classes were removed and some of these, though not all, were replaced by examples of combination consisting of a main number and an auxiliary. While this evidently facilitated the management of the scheme, it also reduced the possibility of a detailed vocabulary (Broughton, 2010). On the other hand, many complex concepts with simple and precise corresponding terms in natural language were never part of the schedules either in enumerative form or as examples of combination, since it is impossible for a faceted scheme to list all possible subjects and their combinations. This is particularly true of named entities (e.g. diseases, biological species, historical events, holidays, etc.), that are usually reduced to the level of concepts in classification systems (Buizza, 2011). However, in the case of faceted classifications the inclusion of a precise terminology (which includes, but is not limited to named entities) represents an additional issue due to their structural principle (Broughton, 2010). For instance, in UDC the terms 'acute-phase proteins' or 'Turner syndrome' would correspond to the long and complex notational combinations, respectively 577.112.82:616-002 and 616-007.1-055.2. Therefore in the schedules such topics often remain irretrievable either by notation or by caption.

Bearing this in mind, the need to include the pre-coordinated paradigmatic combinations into the UDC authority file becomes even more obvious. Authority control not only ensures citation order in paradigmatic sequences, but also enables their retrieval by verbal expressions. If verbal labels by which these concepts are generally known cannot be imported from the schedules, another controlled vocabulary (a thesaurus, a subject headings system, a terminological database etc.) can be used as the source. Mapping and interlinking of the classification and subject headings authority files is an even more efficient way of enhancing subject access. Subject headings can serve as a search term index for the classification authority file, especially in the case of terminology that is not found in the scheme, while in return being enriched by the improved semantic structure. The bibliographic record is provided with more access points and the two fundamental aspects of subject cataloguing are integrated. However, the number and variety of mapping methodologies between subject heading systems and classification systems (Chan & Zeng, 2002) calls for a well-considered approach.

2.3 General vs. specific

The relations between notation and natural language terms raise another dilemma, that of the level of specificity required in authorized compound notations. For example, in the National and University Library in Zagreb the subject of the 'Hvar rebellion', a sixteenth-century popular revolt against the nobility on the Croatian island of Hvar, is expressed by the compound UDC notation 323.269.6(497.583)(210.7Hvar)"1510/1514" ('rebellions' + 'central Dalmatia' + 'island of Hvar' + 'from 1510 to 1514'). This is a very detailed notation, however there are various ways to reduce it, some of which would perhaps better serve the collocation task, e.g. 'rebellions' + 'island of Hvar' + 'history', or 'rebellions' + 'central Dalmatia' + 'sixteenth century'. It is a challenge to find a balance between the indexing needs of the individual library (including time and costs) and the level of specificity ideal for data sharing on the Web. For example, should local and national topics be indexed with a higher level of specificity? In different institutions that use the same indexing system not only can different citation order and level of specificity be practiced, but also different facets can be chosen for grouping together the concepts. This leads to the conclusion that automatic mapping in a networked environment will achieve results only on a very broad level.

The purpose of assigning classification notations to subject heading authorities should also be reconsidered in this context. Namely, does it aim to describe the subject heading (i.e. to translate it as precisely as possible into the notational system) or to map it to the notations used in the bibliographic records? What goals are achieved by either of the two tasks? It seems that in the latter case, although the specificity of the notation may not always equal those of the subject heading, the basis is built for a more efficient interlinking of bibliographic data, subject heading authority data and classification authority data, leading to an improvement in the quality of indexing and thus to better retrieval results.

3. UDC database in the National and University Library in Zagreb

The observations discussed above form a referential framework for the development of a UDC authority file in the National and University Library. As stated above, the current stage of development is represented by a MySQL database that serves primarily as a searching tool for indexing specialists, but it is expected to be made interoperable with the other Library's databases.

The notations and captions in the database are based on the Croatian Abridged Edition of UDC Master Reference File (MRF) 2011, which is the version of the standard currently used in the Library. The translation was undertaken in 2013 for the purpose of publishing the Abridged Edition in the Croatian language and was done by subject specialists both in and outside the Library. The database contains single main numbers, common and special auxiliary numbers, captions, and selected examples of combination. The content has been imported from the UDC Pocket (i.e. Abridged) Edition Translator and adapted to local indexing needs. For example, some subdivisions of common auxiliaries of place have been removed, while more specific subdivisions concerning national and regional history, culture, administrative division, etc. have been imported from the complete UDC MRF 2011. Furthermore, composite notations used in local indexing practice have been added. As argued above, these mostly refer to paradigmatic combinations of subjects. Besides authorized sequences in compound notations, consistent use is ensured by application notes containing revised and updated instructions and guidelines that have been documenting local practice since 1990s. New entries are proposed by indexing specialists, discussed by the editorial team and, if approved, entered into the database by the editor-in-chief.

The hierarchical notational structure can be browsed. The database also contains cross-references, *see* references, and application notes. At the time of writing, the database contained 10,358 records divided into three types: single main and auxiliary numbers with captions, 'including' captions, and composite notations. The data can be searched by any or all of the three categories. The inclusion of the 'including' captions was considered particularly important in the context of verbal searching. It is proposed that verbal expressions for compound notations that could not be found in UDC MRF be taken from the Library's subject heading authority data.

3.1 Searching by compositional elements

When a composite notation is entered into the database, compositional elements or the type of combination can be specified by choosing an option from a drop-down list: a) the combination of main numbers and auxiliaries, b) the combination of two or more main numbers, c) the auxiliary introduced by a facet indicator. In this way compound notations can be searched either as a whole or by individual compositional elements. For example, the query -051 *Persons as agents, doers, practitioners* will return all complex notations in which this auxiliary is contained, e.g. 141.72-051 'feminist theorists' or 639.09-051 'veterinarians'. Similarly, all combinations of main numbers that contain, e.g., the number 82 'literature' in any citation order, such as 316.74:82 'sociology of literature' or 82:111.852 'aesthetics of literature', will be retrieved.

3.2 Verbal searching

The UDC database can be searched by notations and captions using Boolean operators OR and AND. The captions can be linked to the OPAC view of the bibliographic records via the MARC 21 field 080, thus enabling online searches by UDC in the bibliographic database to be performed using verbal expressions. Enhanced access could be ensured by connecting the UDC database with the subject heading authorities, especially when the appropriate verbal expression is not available in the schedules. As argued above, the initial step toward this was taken by assigning UDC notations to authorized subject headings. This kind of intellectual mapping was done by editors of the subject heading authorities as a part of the authorizing process, with semantic equivalence or proximity as the principal criterion. However, until 2015 subject heading authorities were assigned UDC marks based on the complete UDC MRF 1998, so revision of authority records is needed.

4. Conclusion

Indexing consistency in libraries has a key role in ensuring not only better search results at the local level, but also improved machine-readability and interoperability of data in a wider environment. Since indexing needs can differ considerably across different library departments and collections, experience has shown that the manual maintenance of consistency does not provide satisfactory results. Therefore in the National and University Library in Zagreb, a UDC database was created with the principal goal of providing the control of notations used in bibliographic records. In its current stage, the database is primarily a searching tool, not a real authority file; however, bearing in mind the possibilities for its future development, great attention has been paid to the indexing policy behind it. The advantages of the analytico-synthetic principles of UDC have been analysed in order to be exploited to their full potential in terms of authority control. The question of maintaining the flexibility of the system while fulfilling the principal goals of authority control was partly addressed by proposing a distinction between syntagmatic and paradigmatic combinations for the purpose of authorization.

The possibilities of verbal searching, already improved by linking UDC captions to the bibliographic records in the OPAC, can be significantly enhanced by connecting authorized classification data to subject heading authorities. The potential of using subject heading authorities provided with UDC notations as the basis for this mapping is currently being explored. Two tasks important for data updating remain to be realized: establishing *see* references between old and revised notations (revised either at the level of the standard or the indexing policy) and the connection of the UDC database to other data in the Library's catalogue. The latter is undoubtedly the most important step in fulfilling the goals of authority control. A fully functional authority file has the potential to become an intermediary in the development of Web portals or services aiming at providing unique access to the cultural heritage held in various memory institutions, both in Croatia and abroad.

Acknowledgements

Many kind thanks to Lidija Jurić, Marko Orešković and Davor Polonijo for providing me with all the necessary details for this paper.

References

Broughton, V. (2010). Concepts and terms in the faceted classification: the case of UDC. *Knowledge organization*, 37 (4), pp. 270-279.

Buizza, P. (2011). Indexing concepts and/or named entities. *JLIS.it. Italian Journal of Library, Archives, and Information Science*, 2 (2). Available at: http://leo.cineca.it/index.php/jlis/article/view/4707.

Chan, L. M.; Zeng, M. L. (2002). Ensuring interoperability among subject vocabularies and knowledge organization schemes: a methodological analysis. *IFLA Journal*, 28 (5/6), pp. 323-327.

Cordeiro, M. I. (2001). From library authority control to network authoritative metadata sources. In: *Subject retrieval in a networked environment: proceedings of the IFLA Satellite meeting held in Dublin, OH, 14-16 August 2001 and sponsored by the IFLA Classification and indexing section, the IFLA Information technology section and OCLC*. Edited by I. C. McIlwaine. München: K. G. Saur. (UBCIM publications – new series 25), pp. 131-139.

Slavic, A.; Cordeiro, M. I.; Riesthuis, G. (2008). Maintenance of the Universal Decimal Classification: overview of the past and preparations for the future. *International Cataloguing and Bibliographic Control*, 37 (2), pp. 23-29.

Slavic, A. (2008). Faceted classification: management and use. *Axiomathes*, 18 (2), pp. 257-271.

Svenonius, E. (2000). *The intellectual foundation of information organization*. Cambridge, Mass.; London: The MIT Press.

Tartaglia, S. (2004). Authority control and subject indexing languages. *Cataloging and Classification Quarterly*, 39 (1/2), pp. 365-377.

Vukadin, A.; Slavic, A. (2013). Challenges of facet analysis and concept placement in universal classifications: the example of architecture in UDC. In: *Knowledge organization in the 21st century: between historical patterns and future prospects:*

proceedings of the Thirteenth International ISKO Conference, 19-22 May 2014, Krakow, Poland. Edited by W. Babik. Würzburg: Ergon Verlag. (Advances in knowledge organization 14), pp. 236-243.

Williamson, N.; McIlwaine, I. C. (2009). UDC medical sciences project: progress and problems. *Extensions and Corrections to the UDC*, 31, pp. 33-36.

ANA VUKADIN works in the National and University Library in Zagreb as a subject cataloguer and an editor of the subject headings authority file. She is the editor-in-chief of the Croatian cataloguing code. Ana is a PhD candidate at the Department for Information Science at the University of Zadar and is currently working on her thesis on bibliographic modelling of transmedia resources. She also collaborates with the UDC Editorial Team on the revision of class 7 The Arts.

5. Strategies and innovation with classification in libraries

TinREAD – an integrative solution for subject authority control

Victoria Frâncu
"Carol I" Central University Library, Bucharest, Romania

Liviu-Iulian Dediu
IME Romania Ltd, Bucharest, Romania

Abstract: The paper introduces TinREAD (The Information Navigator for Readers), an integrated library system produced by IME Romania. The main feature of interest is the way TinREAD can handle a classification-based thesaurus in which verbal index terms are mapped to classification notations. It supports subject authority control interlinking the authority files (subject headings and UDC system). Authority files are used for indexing consistency. Although it is said that intellectual indexing is, unlike automated indexing, both subjective and inconsistent, TinREAD is using intellectual indexing as input (the UDC notations assigned to documents) for the automated indexing resulting from the implementation of a thesaurus structure based on UDC. Each UDC notation is represented by a UNIMARC subject heading record as authority data. One classification notation can be used to search simultaneously into more than one corresponding thesaurus. This way natural language terms are used in indexing and, at the same time, the link with the corresponding classification notation is kept. Additionally, the system can also manage multilingual data for the authority files. This, together with other characteristics of TinREAD are largely discussed and illustrated in the paper. Problems encountered and possible solutions to tackle them are shown.

Keywords: authority control; authority files; subject headings; Universal Decimal Classification; UDC; TinREAD

1. Introduction

Access to information on the Internet can be free, open to any user, anywhere, and it only takes patience and time to get a required piece of information using the vast resources available through search services such as Google. This, frequently, raises the questions: Is the information we get from Google accurate and reliable enough? Can we find it there at any time? Can we get better structured information from Google?

We know that we can get good quality information from libraries and that systematic catalogues are source of valuable subject information. This is so even if we speak of traditional manual classification and subject indexing before library catalogues became available online. Many library theoreticians, practitioners and computer specialists have been discussing the issue of how to make better use of the intellectual work already put into indexing by generations of librarians through deploying better technological solutions (see, e.g., Riesthuis & Bliedung, 1990; Frâncu, 2003; Frâncu & Sabo, 2010; Doorn & Polman, 2010; Dediu, 2012). This has become even more challenging with the change of the information seeking behaviour and the new information infrastructure.

This paper discusses the approach to improving subject access implemented in TinREAD (The Information Navigator for Readers), an integrated library system. The main feature of TinREAD is that it is designed to handle the assignment of verbal index terms mapped to classification numbers in bibliographic records by means of authority files. The system supports subject authority control that links two types of authority files: subject headings and Universal Decimal Classification (UDC).

2. Historical background

The UDC proved to be a useful tool as its notation can be used to impose consistency in indexing as well as to control natural language terms linked to it to facilitate searching. Much of what we aim to achieve in improving subject authority control in modern OPACS is likely to have already been implemented and tested in early automation examples of UDC (Rigby, 1981).

Projects dating back to 1965 deployed UDC as a way of improving subject information retrieval in bibliographic databases. Some of the most widely cited examples include AUDACIOUS (Freeman & Atherton, 1968), ETHICS (Grünewald, 1994) and the Basic Semantic Reference Structure (Schmitz-Esser, 1999). These projects are of interest to our research for the following reasons: a) they use classification to provide indexing consistency b) they allow searching of individual semantically discrete elements of complex UDC notation b) they use classification as a basis for a word search system, i.e. they enable multilingual information access by adding terms in different languages to UDC notation.

AUDACIOUS (Automatic Direct Access to Information with the Online UDC System) was a project on creating a remote access to files containing 2,330 issues of Nuclear Science Abstracts indexed by UDC (Freeman & Atherton, 1968). This was the first online retrieval system offering advanced searching options via UDC notation and index terms in English associated to the UDC class marks. It enabled documents to be indexed and searched by means of natural language terms while UDC hierarchically expressive notation made provision for truncation i.e. semantic broadening of searching and advanced searching using Boolean operators. Boolean operators combined English terms and UDC notation and also different elements of complex UDC notation. The UDC being a hidden form of indexing, the users of the system could address their queries in natural language words without regard to the original indexing language used.

Clearly, UDC was considered well suited to support a sophisticated online searching and the outcome of the experiments in 1960-1970s influenced, to a great extent, the future applications of the scheme in automated systems (Francu, 2003).

ETHICS (Eidgenössischen Technischen Hochschule Information Control System) was an in-house library system which explored and made use of UDC to support online searching of the ETH-Library in three languages. Grünewald (1994) claims that the structure of the UDC operating in the ETH library system is slightly different from the UDC basic structure, which may cause impediments in information transfer. Besides, he suggests that, for such a purpose, a table of concordance should exist in order to prevent whatever consequences this shortcoming might have. In spite of this, ETHICS stood, at its time, as the best example of an online catalogue and a sophisticated multilingual information storage and retrieval system working in English, French and German and which was based on the UDC scheme. In terms of subject access ETHICS was probably the most advanced online library catalogue of its time (cf. Buxton, 1990). It comes as no surprise that Clavel-Merrin & Lehtinen (1998) used ETHICS to illustrate their approach to subject access. Their argument was that an ideal indexing system should allow indexers to analyse subjects and assign subject headings to documents using their own language and allow users to search information by entering subject headings in their own language, irrespective of the document's language. The example they have chosen is from a version of ETHICS catalogue used in the Swiss National Library between 1983 and 1989 (Figure 1). In the example, indexing terms are interfiled in English (E), French (F) and German (D) in alphabetical display:

REGISTRE-MATIERES ALPHABETIQUE:	LANGUE REG-MAT.: A
1 ADAPTATION/BEWEGUNGSADAPTATION (ANATOMIE U.PHYSIOLOGIE)	D O,Q
2 ADAPTATION/BOTANY	E O,Q
3 ADAPTATION/BRIGHT TO DARK ADAPTATION (VISION)	E O,Q
4 ADAPTATION/CELLULAIRE A L'ENVIRONNEMENT (CYTOLOGIE)	F O,Q
5 ADAPTATION/CELLULAR ADAPTATION	E O,Q
6 ADAPTATION/CLIMAT (ANATOMIE ET PHYSIOL.)	F O,Q
7 ADAPTATION/CLIMATIQUE ET EDAPHIQUE (PHYTOGENETIQUE)	F O
8 ADAPTATION/COLORATION (ANIMAL ETHOLOGY)	E O,Q
9 ADAPTATION/CULTIVATED PLANTS	E O
10 ADAPTATION/CULTURAL	E O
11 ADAPTATION/DARK ADAPTATION (VISION)	E O,Q
12 ADAPTATION/DE L AGRICULTURE	F O
13 ADAPTATION/DUNKELADAPTATION (PHYSICLOGISCHE OPTIK)	D O,Q
14 ADAPTATION/ECOLOGIE VEGETALE	F O,Q,E,U
15 ADAPTATION/EVOLUTIONARY FACTORS (BIOLOGICAL EVOLUTION)	E O,Q,U

Figure 1: *Example of index terms in three languages in ETHICS (from Clavel-Merrin & Lehtinen, 1998:73)*

A different, although comparable system was designed by Schmitz-Esser (1998) for multilingual access to information provided by an international exhibition. The Basic Semantic Reference Structure (BSRS) was created to assist information retrieval and was based on the outline for a lexicographic, multilingual, computerized, universal thesaurus for linguistic engineering and information retrieval which was proposed in 1993 by the German Committee on Thesaurus and Classification Research in Jena, Germany. The BSRS included terms and expressions in four languages and, moreover, its structure was semantically controlled. It is sufficient to remind the impressive number of semantic relations between the terms of the system to realize how complex the system was. In addition to that, BSRS had a provision for adding equivalent entries from the authority files to bibliographic classifications such as UDC or Dewey Decimal Classification (DDC). This could serve, Schmitz-Esser argues, as a conceptual bridge between the proposed format and other ordering systems. We recognize here an instance of integration of indexing languages dating quite long before any discussion of standardisation on this topic was started.

From the practical solutions applied by the developers of older systems like AUDACIOUS, ETHICS and BSRS some new UDC-based information retrieval systems emerged, of which we can mention here DOBIS/LIBIS as implemented at the KU Leuven University Library (Schallier, 2007) and NEBIS, a system currently used in a network of around 140 libraries in Switzerland (Pika, 2007)[1].

Schallier (2007: 186) talks about the need of intelligent ways of integrating and combining formal and subject metadata and recommends that the library user should be shown only what he wants to know. He concludes that the user should be central in further developments of the UDC and that metadata such as UDC should enrich visibility of information (idem: 188). Pika (2007: 229), in the same spirit, explains how users of the ETH Library, after 25 years of using the UDC, hardly noticed the presence of classification. He goes on arguing that descriptors attached to a single UDC number connect them to related document titles regardless of the language. Both LIBIS and NEBIS provide multilingual access to information, a characteristic which significantly enhances retrieval.

TinREAD, which will be introduced in Sections 4 and 5, is very much inspired by the example of good practice of subject access and authority control from the systems described above. We will explain methods of implementing classification authority control and support to multilingual access via the use of search terms from different subject heading systems within TinREAD.

3. Why do information retrieval systems need authority control?

Authority control is a method by which a library normalizes the form of headings used in the bibliographic records. Subject authorities provide enhanced access to information by bringing together, i.e., linking different forms of index terms under a single authorized form. When developed as a vocabulary

1 ETHICS was replaced by an integrated library system and NEBIS catalogue (http://www.nebis.ch/eng/).The multilingual UDC-based multilingual subject authority file with over 60,000 entries was integrated and continues to be developed as NEBIS Subject Index (cf. Pika 2007, Pika & Pika-Biolzi, 2015).

management tool proper, subject authorities hold semantic relationships between subject terms within the vocabulary structure (hierarchy, equivalency and association) and allow integration and mapping of index terms from different controlled vocabularies and in different languages. Thus they can make best use of combination of indexing languages which support different function in information retrieval (e.g., classification and alphabetical indexing languages). Ideally, when implemented in information retrieval, subject authorities will provide multiple access points to subjects and enable semantic searching expansion.

Standard data formats for subject vocabularies are central in implementing subject authority control in bibliographic systems. Although their development started relatively late MARC formats for classification data have an important role in improving management of classification data in library systems (Guenther, 1994; MARC 21 Format for classification data (2000).

The conceptual aspect of subject data in bibliographic systems is dealt within the Functional Requirements for Subject Authority Data (FRSAD) (2011). It is notable that the proposed model stresses the importance of integrating controlled vocabularies which is facilitated through the authority control:

> "Subject access to information has been a significant approach of users to satisfy their information needs. Research results have demonstrated that the integration of controlled vocabulary information with an information retrieval system helps users perform more effective subject searches. This integration becomes possible when subject authority data (information about subjects from authority files) are linked to bibliographic files and are made available to users." (Functional requirements for subject authority data (FRSAD), 2011: 8).

Integrating classification and thesaurus terms or subject headings is of a particular interest to information systems mainly because it brings added value to a library catalogue. It represents an added value to what was previously implemented in traditional systematic catalogues and leads to an improved recall and precision in information retrieval. With both types of subject access available, i.e. classification and word systems, the users of the library system can search with words and also have the overview of hierarchies of the classification scheme.

4. TinREAD (The Information Navigator for Readers)

TinREAD is an integrated library system that is, like most library systems, designed to support bibliographic standards and functionalities proposed in relevant international standards (MARC Formats for Authority Data, for Bibliographic Data, for Classification Data, for Community Information, and MARC Format for Holdings Data). TinREAD can support simultaneously more than one national MARC format including ROMARC, the Romanian MARC format, CNMARC and CHMARC, two Chinese MARC formats, plus LIDO[2],

2 LIDO – Lightweight Information Describing Objects. Available at: http://www.lido-schema.org

SPECTRUM[3] and CIDOC-CRM[4]. Each of these can have their own authority, bibliographic and holdings records. Additionally, the system can convert imported bibliographic records from their original format into the format the cataloguer works with. For example, one can import a record for a monograph from a Chinese catalogue and convert it in real time into UNIMARC or MARC21.

When it comes to implementing thesaurus data in TinREAD there is a number of integration and interoperability issues to take into consideration. In order to enable an appropriate treatment of thesauri in UNIMARC-A and MARC21-A, TinREAD has a supplementary set of fields defined for the purpose of accommodating specific semantic relations (for example, a repeatable field 975 for related terms from a different classification scheme and a repeatable field 690 for LCSH equivalents). The system provides support for mapping for those who use different thesauri (including multilingual) and, more important for our purposes, enables mapping terms with classification notations.

Classification data is held either in field 675, derived from UNIMARC-A, or in field 83, from MARC21-A, and captions are cross referenced to a UNIMARC subject heading field. Classifiers introduce the metadata for each access point by the corresponding subject heading. One classification notation can be used to search simultaneously into more than one corresponding subject heading systems. This feature is meant to keep the consistency of the search terms and helps in maintaining accurate subject authority records. A major advantage of the above mentioned development of classified catalogues is that re-indexing the classified documents can be avoided therefore an important amount of time and intellectual work is preserved. Hence, the indexing process becomes less difficult and the one-to-one relationship between the natural language terms and classification notations improves indexing consistency.

It has been proved that a higher degree of specificity results in increased relevance of the documents retrieved. This can become a real advantage to classification-based thesauri as long as they are derived from the correct use of the classification notations with which their terms are associated. The rules for building complex UDC notations have to be rigorously observed in order to ensure good quality of automatically assigned indexing terms.

It has often been said that intellectual indexing is, unlike automated indexing, both subjective and inconsistent (Fidel, 1994). The system we describe here makes these two ends meet: it uses both the intellectual indexing (as input UDC notations assigned to documents in the past) and the automated indexing resulting from the integration of the UDC-based thesaurus. Each UDC notation is represented by a UNIMARC subject heading record as authority

---

3 SPECTRUM – a standard designed to manage and develop museum collections. Available at: http://www.collectionstrust.org.uk/spectrum-resources

4 CIDOC – Conceptual Reference Model (CRM) provides an extensible ontology for concepts and information in cultural heritage and museum documentation. Available at: http://cidoc-crm.org/

data. Another advantage of the system is that it can also manage multilingual and multi-script subject data in its authority files.

5. Description of the methodology used in creating authority records

This paper is trying to answer three questions: 1) How to link UDC data and thesaurus terms? 2) How to link subject authority records to bibliographic records and control the result? 3) How to make this result available to users? We have to start with what, in the system creators view, was the most appropriate choice from: a fixed concordance between a UDC class and a set of descriptors from a thesaurus, or an authority file including corresponding verbal terms according to the semantic factoring of each meaningful part of a complex UDC number. The system developers' choice was for the second variant and the reasons are described below.

Based on previous research work conducted in the field of mapping UDC numbers with terms from a controlled vocabulary (Riesthuis, 1997, Frâncu, 2003), TinREAD can provide separate authority files in MARC classification format and link them with bibliographic records in order to improve the quality of indexing. Subject-oriented data is held in fields 6xx for classification and in 9xx for subject headings or thesaurus terms. The authority records include two types of data: classification data from the UDC tables and verbal terms from more than one subject heading system, be they created as the system's local controlled vocabulary or as equivalents of the aforementioned vocabularies. In Figure 2 below, an authority record is shown. Along with the UDC number and the appropriate local heading it includes links to similar subject headings from LCSH and RAMEAU.

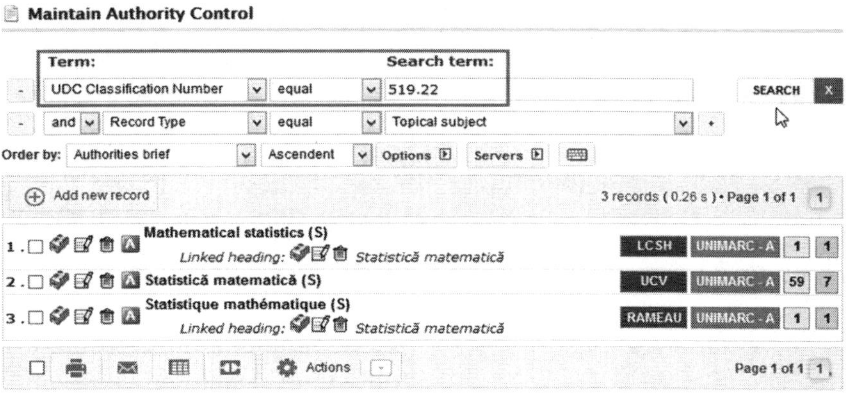

Figure 2: *A multiple language subject authority record in TinREAD*

As stated earlier, the MARC format for subject authority control has specialized fields for these two categories of data and these authority records are further linked to the corresponding bibliographic records in the system. As long as a UDC number is assigned to a 675 field, the system automatically provides its corresponding subject heading in a 606 field.

Figure 3: *UNIMARC thesaurus structure with authorized access points in other languages*

The system works the other way around, also. Whenever an indexer enters a descriptor in a 606 field, a corresponding UDC number is entered in a 675 field. Figure 3 shows a different version of the same authority record with the specific 9xx fields for a thesaurus syndetic structure plus the linking fields 750 for other language terms, or other script variants, according to the UNIMARC-A format.

Concluding, we deal with three connected entities: the bibliographic record, the subject authority record and the UDC notation (which is either simple or compound). The example in Figure 4 below, illustrates the way TinREAD manages complex UDC numbers and their relationship to subject headings.

TinREAD can handle compound UDC numbers by semantic factoring of each meaningful sequence of digits. These component parts are treated in separate files and subject headings are mapped to them according to their significance in the UDC tables. Each term in the subfields of field 250 has its own authority record and this is demonstrated by the existence of a different ID number stored in a $3 subfield for each significant component part as shown in Figure 3. The example chosen to illustrate the management of compound UDC numbers is illustrated, as already said, in Figure 4. The use of subfields in the MARC classification format is adapted in such a way that our purpose is accomplished. One should mention the correspondence between the concepts expressed by the UDC component parts and the associated descriptors from which the indexer has to make a choice.

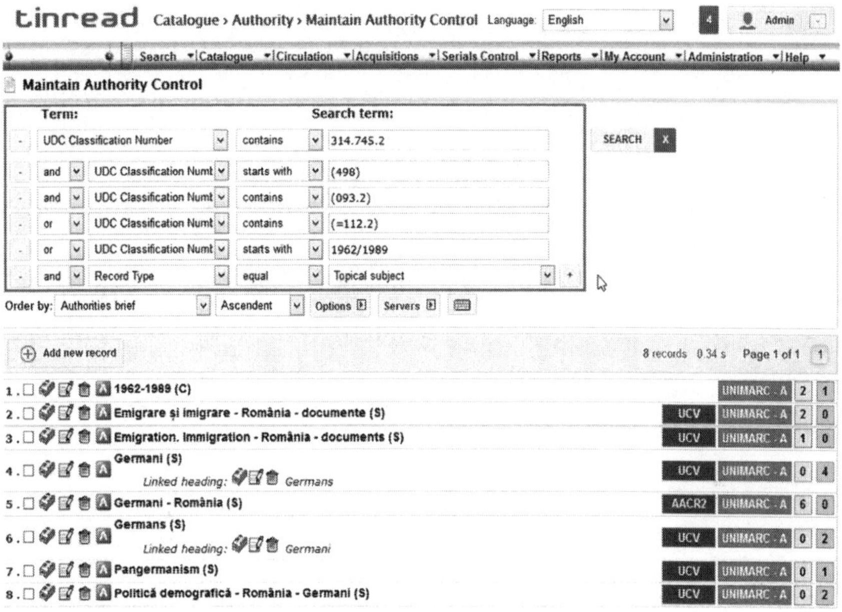

Figure 4: *Authority record showing the management of compound UDC numbers*

6. Concluding remarks

In this paper we have demonstrated the capacity of TinREAD to support each subject element which has a meaning as a contextual entity. In so doing TinREAD is substantially assisting indexers in selecting the appropriate subject access points. Another useful feature of the system is its capacity to allow global changes for any of the data elements including the subject fields, which is a real advantage for the indexers.

From the end-user point of view TinREAD has a number of advantages such as: the possibility to see all the subject headings in the OPAC version of the bibliographic record and also to visualize the authority records including both subject headings and UDC notations. Furthermore, other documents that were indexed under the same terms and UDC numbers are simultaneously displayed, therefore allowing navigation. The system also generates and displays a subject cloud which can be visualized at the bottom of the search screen.

References

Buxton, A. B. (1990). Computer searching of UDC numbers. *Journal of Documentation*, 46 (3), pp. 193-217.

Clavel-Merrin, G.; Lehtinen, R. (1998). Multilingual and multi-character set data in library systems and networks: experiences and perspectives from Switzerland and Finland.

In: *Multi-script, multilingual, multi-character issues for the online environment* (1998). *Proceedings of a workshop sponsored by the IFLA Section on Cataloguing, Istanbul, Turkey, August 24, 1995*. Edited by J. D. Byrum; O. Madison. München: Saur. pp. 67-91.

Dediu, L. I. (2012). *Managementul serviciilor pentru utilizatori în bibliotecile contemporane*. Bucureşti: Editura ANBPR.

Doorn, M.; Polman, K. (2010). From classification to thesaurus ... and back?: subject indexing tools at the library of the Afrika-Studiecentrum Leiden. *Knowledge Organization*, 37 (3), pp. 203-208.

Fidel, R. (1994). User-centered indexing. *Journal of the American Society for Information Science*, 45 (8), pp. 572-576.

Francu, V. (2003). *Multilingual Access to Information using an Intermediate Language : proefschrift voorgelegd tot het behalen van de graad van doctor in de Taal- en Letterkunde aan de Universiteit Antwerpen*. Available at: http://arizona.openrepository.com/arizona/handle/10150/106319.

Francu, V.; Sabo, C. N. (2010). Implementation of a UDC-based multilingual thesaurus in a library catalogue: the case of BiblioPhil. *Knowledge Organization*, 37 (3), pp. 209-215.

Freeman, R. R.; Atherton, P. (1968) File organization and search strategy using UDC in mechanized reference retrieval systems. In: *Mechanized Information Storage, Retrieval and Dissemination : proceedings of the FID/IFIP Joint Conference, Rome, June 14-17, 1967*. Edited by K. Samuelson. Amsterdam: North-Holland Publishing, pp. 122-159.

Functional requirements for subject authority data, a conceptual model (FRSAD). (2011). IFLA Working Group on Functional Requirements for Subject Authority Records (FRSAR). Edited by M. L. Zeng, M. Žumer, A. Salaba. Berlin/München: De Gruyter Saur. Available at: http://www.ifla.org/files/assets/classification-and-indexing/functional-requirements-for-subject-authority-data/frsad-final-report.pdf.

Guenther, R. S. (1994). The Library of Congress Classification in the USMARC format. *Knowledge Organization*, 21 (4), pp. 199-202.

Grünewald, F. (1994). Anwendung UDK in ETHICS. In: *Bang voor onderwerpsluiting*. Edited by G. Riesthuis et al. Antwerpen, VVBAD, pp. 46-52.

MARC 21 Format for classification data. (2000). Library of Congress. Available at: http://www.loc.gov/marc/classification/eccdhome.html.

Pika, J. (2007). Universal Decimal Classification at the ETH-Bibliothek Zürich - a Swiss perspective. *Extensions and Corrections to the UDC*, 29, pp. 229-251.

Pika, J.; Pika-Biolzi, M. (2015). Multilingual subject access and classification-based browsing through authority control: the experience of ETH-Bibliothek, Zürich. In: *Classification & authority control: expanding resource discovery: proceedings of the International UDC Seminar, 29-30 October 2015, Lisbon, Portugal*. Edited by A. Slavic, M. I. Cordeiro. Würzburg: Ergon Verlag, pp. 99-110.

Riesthuis, G. J. A.; Bliedung, S. (1990). Thesaurification of the UDC: preliminary report. In: *The UDC: essays for a new decade*. Edited by A. Gilchrist, D. Strachan, D. London, Aslib, pp. 85-97.

Riesthuis, G. J. A. (1997). *Decomposition of complex UDC notations*. In: *Knowledge Organization for Information Retrieval* : the Sixth International Study Conference on Classification Research held at University College London, 16-18 June 1997. The Hague: FID, (FID 716), pp. 139-143.

Rigby, M. (1981). *Automation and the UDC: 1948 - 1980.* 2nd ed. The Hague: FID, 1981 (FID 565).

Schallier, W. (2007). Why organize information if you can find it? UDC and libraries in an Internet word. *Extensions and Corrections to the UDC*, 29, pp. 183-190.

Schmitz-Esser, W. (1998). Defining the Conceptual Space for a World Exhibition – First Experiences. In: *Structures and relations in knowledge organization: proceedings of the Fifth International ISKO Conference, Lille, 25-29 August 1998.* Edited by W. Mustafa Elhadi, J. Maniez, S. Pollitt. Würzburg: Ergon Verlag, 1998. (Advances in knowledge organization 6), pp. 146-152.

VICTORIA FRÂNCU holds a PhD in Library and Information Science from the University of Antwerp (Belgium) and a bachelor degree in Literature from the University of Bucharest. She works as a librarian at the "Carol I" Central University Library in Bucharest and, as visiting lecturer, teaches at the Library and Information Science Department of the Bucharest University. Her research interests are in subject indexing, indexing languages, classification and thesauri on which she extensively published and presented at international conferences. Victoria Frâncu is a member of the International Society for Knowledge Organization (ISKO) and became a member of the Universal Decimal Classification Consortium (UDCC) Editorial Team.

LIVIU-IULIAN DEDIU is Director of the IME Romania Ltd. (Information Management & Engineering Romania Ltd.). He holds a PhD in Library and Information Science Department from the University of Bucharest. His research interests are in library systems and automation of library procedures in general. He was previously an associate director at "V.A. Urechia" County Library of Galati (1997-2007) where he worked on reorganization of library services and upgrade of the library automation system. As a member and president of the National Association of Romanian Public Libraries, he has been actively involved in the development of national library programmes.

Alignment in medical sciences: towards improvement of UDC

Olívia Pestana
Faculty of Arts, University of Porto, Porto, Portugal

Abstract: A classification scheme represents a powerful indexing and retrieval tool. Obsolete terminology and misalignment between widely used systems is key impediment to better use of classification. This paper looks into the issues caused by delay in the revision of UDC class of medical sciences and possible solutions. Following a short description of the Universal Decimal Classification (UDC) and of the National Library of Medicine (NLM) Classification, the author analyses the notations and captions included in 61 class of the UDC Summary. All the classes, subclasses and special auxiliary subdivisions are covered in order to find compatible notations between both schemes, out-of-date vocabulary and out-of-date subdivisions of UDC. As a result of this study and in light of the most recent developments in medical sciences, one subdivision is questioned and several vocabulary expressions included in the caption fields are proposed to be changed or updated.

Keywords: medical sciences; revision; Universal Decimal Classification; UDC; UDC Summary; National Library of Medicine Classification; NLM

1. Introduction

According to Doris H. Clarck (1990), subject authority control is aimed at ensuring "the use of consistent vocabulary that exactly matches both that of the user and that of the document". In American library tradition one can find the expression "controlled vocabularies" often associated only with thesauri and subject headings lists (cf. Wyman, 1999). However, the notion of term control in subject indexing and retrieval is relevant for all indexing languages as they all operate with a pre-prepared *vocabulary* and *syntax rules*. Whether this "vocabulary' is expressed with natural language or notational symbols does not change the process of subject analysis or indexing. Hjørland (1997), points out that information retrieval languages represent the results of subject analysis and, therefore, there is no real difference between subject indexing and classification. Considering bibliographic classifications as a powerful search tool, we are aware that end-users may encounter some difficulties when using classifications in their searches. According to Slavic (2006), the conclusions of some studies revealed that the Web environment and library catalogues offer many cases that justify the use of classification for knowledge browsing and search expansion. However, there is a need for classification data to be exposed in such a way as to reduce the users' effort to a minimum and the notations to be clearly expressed.

In Portugal most libraries use the Universal Decimal Classification (UDC) following recommendations from the National Library of Portugal. Hospital libraries and some medical colleges use also NLM Classification. We could consider that this is because there is no charge for obtaining the data; equally this classification is used worldwide in the medical sector and is known by the majority of medical professionals. However, medical libraries also hold a significant amount of non-medical literature and the NLM Classification needs to be complemented with other general knowledge schemes. NLM Classification manual suggests the use of Library of Congress Classification for supplementary, i.e., non-medical subjects. The use of NLM classification as a single scheme for both medical and non-medical topic is not a recommended practice.

It seems that in countries where UDC is the most widely used scheme, its application in all medical libraries would be more clear to users and would give better results when searching across catalogues and information systems. In addition, the growing experiences with information retrieval in the web environment could be enhanced with a wider use of UDC.

2. Problem statement

UDC Class 61 Medical sciences contains scientifically obsolete terminology and was listed for an urgent revision 25 years ago. The revision project started back in 1994 by Ia C. McIlwaine and Nancy Williamson. The revision assumed the complete restructuring of class 61 into a faceted schedule. The practical consequences of this revision method is that the new class cannot be introduced gradually and cannot replace the old schedule until the entire revision process is complete (McIlwaine, 1995; Williamson, 1995; McIlwaine & Williamson, 2008).

There is a group of problematic issues to be explored and solved in such a revision:

- The use of special auxiliary tables should be discussed - in the current edition of UDC there are numerous special auxiliary tables in class 61. There are only two special auxiliary tables in the new proposal for diseases in 615 and for regions and parts of the body in 616; yet, the doubt remains about including or not more subtopics,
- It is necessary to determine precisely how much space would be needed to handle each of the subclasses, considering the possibility of expanding some subjects,
- There is the possibility of moving medicine to class 4 which is currently vacant (McIlwaine & Williamson, 2008; Benito, 2007).

Due to this complexity, the revision has not been yet completed and is taking significantly longer than originally planned. Clearly the application of UDC in classifying medical literature is compromised. At the same time, extensive and profound changes in class 61 can cause a considerable amount of work in adjusting catalogues to the new schedules. And this work would certainly need special effort from library technical services in order to complete the transition to new notations.

In order to understand the existing tables and eventually suggest other approaches for the revising of class 61, the author undertook a comparative analysis of UDC and NLM Classification, which is described bellow.

3. Comparative analysis of UDC class 61 and NLM Classification

3.1. The NLM Classification: short introduction

NLM Classification schedules are based on an alphanumeric scheme and are developed in accordance with Medical Subject Headings[1] (MeSH), the NLM's thesaurus. It is composed by two groups: Preclinical Sciences and Medicine and Related Subjects, using, respectively, schedules QS-QZ and W-WZ, excluded from LCC (See Appendix 1). In turn, various LCC schedules are needed to complement NLM Classification for subjects not included in its tables, requiring knowledge of and practice with them.

NLM Classification has only one auxiliary table - Table G - used for geographical subdivisions, which use is restricted to classes annotated with "Table G" in the schedules. In some cases, Table G is required only in certain approaches to the subject, and generic approaches, for example, are not covered. For example, QS Human Anatomy, Histology subdivision, includes "QS 511 History (Table G)" and "QS 511.1 General coverage (Not Table G)".

NLM Classification representations are intentionally broader than those found in UDC, showing captions that do not enumerate all the related subjects. It is clear that this classification has a direct connection with MeSH, considering that MeSH descriptors appear in the index.

There are schedules, and sections within some schedules, containing a group of numbers that are not considered true subject numbers, as they are defined for aspects different from the core subjects of a class. The range from 1 to 39 is used to classify the main subject of a class by, for example, publication type (e.g., 17 corresponds to Atlases. Pictorial works) or with a special emphasis as education (18) or research (20.5).

3.2. Description of the study and results

All classes, subclasses and special auxiliary subdivisions available in the UDC Summary (2011) were analysed in order to find compatible notations between both schemes, as well as possible out-of-date UDC vocabulary and subdivisions. The comparative table is available in Appendix 2. In some cases it was necessary to analyse numbers in lower levels of the hierarchy (not available in the UDC Summary) in order to better understand the context of a given class. Vocabulary doubts or inconsistencies were clarified with the help of the NLM online version of MeSH and also of the *Medical dictionary* available in the MedlinePlus website, a service of the NLM.[2]

---

1 Available at http://www.ncbi.nlm.nih.gov/mesh

2 Available at http://www.nlm.nih.gov/medlineplus/mplusdictionary.html.

The NLM Classification analysis followed the recommendations explained in the classification tables and in the introduction to this classification available in the NLM website dedicated to this product[3]. In some cases, due to the completely different structure of each classification table, it was difficult to provide a compatible number from NLM Classification. It is a broader classification, as far as its vocabulary is concerned. The representation of specific concepts may be complex. Nevertheless, some numbers in UDC correspond to a group of NLM Classification notations, even if they are dispersed across the schedules.

As a result of the analysis, it is possible to conclude that UDC numbers from classes 613 and 614 are well detailed and appropriated for the representation of subjects in a specialized library and in universal use. These classes consider a substantial and useful group of subjects not covered by the NLM Classification. Some UDC subclasses, however, include vocabulary that has no direct connection to the upper class. The number 614.39, representing the subject "National health services", for example, is subordinated to number 614.3, which represents "Sanitary inspection and control". In this case, the emphasis should be on the health care organization model or system and not on inspective or regulatory aspects.

Classes 611, 612 and 616 present some redundancy, despite the intentional focus on the anatomical, physiological and pathological approaches. As a result, the final presentation of a catalogue may feature the dispersion of closely related subjects. On the other hand, there are numbers that have no connection to upper classes or that present a deficient articulation of their vocabulary. For example, subclasses 612.41 and 612.42 (not in the UDC Summary) are used to classify subjects related to haematopoietic system and lymphatic system, respectively. These systems are not considered as glandular systems and the association to secretion or excretion may be too biased.

Subclass 612.7 includes "Motor functions. Organs of locomotion. Voice. Integument". It is difficult to associate integument to the preceding subjects. Class 615 is related to "Pharmacology. Therapeutics. Toxicology". The representativeness of subjects related to Physiotherapy, Physical therapy, or Radiotherapy (see 615.8), requires a deeper and distinctive use of these themes. Neurology, neuropathology, nervous systems and related diseases are mentioned in class 616.8. In this hierarchy, one can find 616.89 for Psychiatry and related subjects. Being a distinctive specialty, this number should be in a different hierarchy, at the same level of Neurology or Orthopaedics, for example.

Numerous special auxiliary tables were found, confirming previous studies that already identified this problem: the amount of special auxiliaries contributes to thematic redundancy, and may cause some dispersion when classifying documents with the same subject.

---

3 Retrieved from http://www.nlm.nih.gov/class/.

3.3. Some suggestions for the revision of UDC class 61

Based on the results of our study, it is possible to put forward a group of suggestions for the revision of UDC class 61:

- classes 613 and 614 should be maintained, considering that they explore and represent important subjects in a clear way.
- classes 611 and 612 should be reviewed in connection to class 616, in order to avoid possible redundancy or extremely close semantics in captions. This review could consider the use of the systems' approach presented in the NLM Classification in classes from WD to WL. On the other hand, the structure of NLM Classification provided by classes WC and from WM to WW could be followed in order to complete the coverage of medical specialties in their specificities and related pathologies. Vocabulary used in the 612 and 616 classes should be, consequently, reviewed so that specific aspects would pass to subsequent numbers.
- NLM Classification options provided by numbers from 1 to 39 (used in some tables) could be followed, considering that they express the same subjects in each upper class, and may facilitate user searching.
- class 615.8 shouldn't include Physiotherapy, Physical therapy and Radiotherapy. These subjects could be included in class 616, associated to each pathology.
- there is an urgent need to review the position of class 616.89 (Psychiatry). In the current UDC structure, it will be complex to relocate this number. A possible suggestion is its inclusion in 616.8 caption, resulting, for example, in the following sequence: Neurology. Neuropathology. Nervous system. Psychiatry. Pathological psychiatry. Psychopathology.

4. Conclusion and future development

This paper provided a comparison of two different classification schemes regarding their structure, vocabulary organization and also their types of notations. The main objective of the author was to explore and propose the updating of UDC in alignment with NLM Classification, and to clarify which notations could be promptly updated.

Revision of UDC Medical Sciences would contribute to widening the use of this classification, especially as a retrieval language. NLM Classification is aligned with Medical Subject Headings, enhancing its use and vocabulary proximity. But there is no doubt that the universal coverage of UDC is a strong advantage that can make the difference. The international use of UDC is made easy by its synthetic notational system that lend itself to an easy extension, while revision by improving captions and mapping into other documentary languages is also feasible.

The proposed UDC revision would allow for better interoperability among catalogues, not only because it would better represent recent advances in medical diagnosis and therapies, but also because inconsistencies would be reduced when merging records from a diverse group of libraries. On the other hand, redundancies in the same catalogue would be, for sure, minimized.

The revision proposal could be enhanced by means of libraries' collaboration in the process. It would be useful to involve a group of libraries using UDC in order to obtain consistent information about the level of usage of some class 61 numbers. This action would help in the identification of numbers that were never used or used less frequently, thus contributing to decide about the elimination or revision of certain numbers in order to free some subclasses for further relocation.

The proposal revealed in this work was developed on the basis of a comparison with another bibliographic classification. It would be interesting to undertake the same study using classifications directly related to health care. The International Classification of Diseases is used for coding diagnosis and procedures in the health care sector. It is used worldwide and is the basis for many decisions related to health services funding and reorganization. Exploring its detailed vocabulary could help update the UDC vocabulary. These and other developments could certainly contribute to clarify the effective revision needs of UDC Class 61.

References

Benito, M. (2007). Better consistency of the UDC system : moving Medicine from section 61 to section 4. *Extensions and Corrections to the UDC,* 29, pp. 311-316.

Clarck, D. H. (1990). *Authority control : principles, applications, and instruction.* Chicago: American Library Association.

Hjørland, B. (1997). *Information seeking and subject representation: an activity-theoretical approach to information science.* Westport, Connecticut: Greenwood Press.

McIlwaine, I. C. (1995). UDC centenary - present state and future prospects. *Knowledge Organization*, 22 (2), pp. 63-69.

McIlwaine, I. C.; Williamson, N. J. (2008). Medicine and the UDC: the process of restructuring. In: *Culture and identity in knowledge organization. Proceedings of the Tenth International ISKO Conference 5-8 August 2008 Montréal, Canada 2008.* Edited by C. Arsenault, J. T. Tennis. (Advances in Knowledge Organization, 11), pp. 50-55.

UDC Summary (2011) Multilingual Universal Decimal Classification Summary. The Hague: UDC Consortium. (UDCC Publication No. 088). Available at: http://udcdata.info/.

Slavic, A. (2006). UDC in subject gateways: experiment or opportunity? *Knowledge Organization*, 33 (2), pp. 67-85. Also available at: http://dlist.sir.arizona.edu/1556/.

Williamson, N. J. (1995). The development of a notational system for a restructured UDC. In: *Proceedings of the 6th ASIS SIG/CR Classification Research Workshop*, pp. 227-236. Edited by R. P. Schwartz et al. Available at: https://journals.lib.washington.edu/index.php/acro/article/view/12671.

Williamson, N.; McIlwaine, I. C. (2009). UDC Medical Sciences Project: progress and problems. *Extensions and Corrections to the UDC,* 31, pp. 33-36.

Wyman, L. P. (1999). *Indexing specialties : medicine.* Medford, NJ: Information today.

OLÍVIA PESTANA is Assistant Professor at the Faculty of Arts of the University of Porto, Portugal. Previously she worked for almost two decades as head librarian at a regional hospital. She holds a PhD in Information and Communication in Digital Platforms. Her teaching and research areas are in the management and organization of information, including subject cataloguing and authority control. She is the author of several papers in the fields of health information, health information services and information management.

Appendix 1

Outline of the NLM Classification[4]

PRECLINICAL SCIENCES

QS	Human Anatomy
QT	Physiology
QU	Biochemistry. Cell Biology and Genetics
QV	Pharmacology
QW	Microbiology and Immunology
QX	Parasitology
QY	Clinical Pathology
QZ	Pathology

MEDICINE AND RELATED SUBJECTS

W	General Medicine. Health Professions
WA	Public Health
WB	Practice of Medicine
WC	Communicable Diseases
WD	Disorders of Systemic, Metabolic or Environmental Origin, etc.
WE	Musculoskeletal System
WF	Respiratory System
WG	Cardiovascular System
WH	Hemic and Lymphatic Systems
WI	Digestive System
WJ	Urogenital System
WK	Endocrine System
WL	Nervous System
WM	Psychiatry
WN	Radiology. Diagnostic Imaging
WO	Surgery
WP	Gynecology
WQ	Obstetrics
WR	Dermatology
WS	Pediatrics
WT	Geriatrics. Chronic Disease
WU	Dentistry. Oral Surgery
WV	Otolaryngology
WW	Ophthalmology
WX	Hospitals and Other Health Facilities
WY	Nursing
WZ	History of Medicine. Medical Miscellany

4 Available at: http://www.nlm.nih.gov/class/OutlineofNLMClassificationSchedule.html

Appendix 2

Alignment of UDC top classes with NLM

UDC	*Compatible NLM classes*	*Comments*
61 Medical sciences		
611/612 Human biology		
611 Anatomy. Human and comparative anatomy	QS Human Anatomy	NLMC: Classify works on anatomy of a part of the body with the part.
612 Physiology. Human and comparative physiology	QT Physiology QT 104-172 ..Human Physiology	NLMC: Classify physiology of a part of the body with the part
612.1/.8 Systematic physiology		
612.1 Blood. Cardiovascular, circulatory system	WH Hemic and Lymphatic Systems WG Cardiovascular System	NLMC: Classify works on morphology, physiology, and clinical aspects of diseases of blood in WH (Hemic and Lymphatic Systems); WG for works on the cardiovascular system;
612.2 Respiration. Breathing. Respiratory system	WF Respiratory System WF 102 Physiology of respiration WF 110 Biochemistry of respiration and the respiratory system	
612.3 Alimentation. Eating. Digestion. Nutrition	WI 102 Physiology. Biochemistry. Digestion QU 145-220 Nutrition. Vitamins	
612.4 Glandular system. Secretion. Excretion	WK Endocrine System WI 802 Physiology. Secretions (Pancreas) WJ 303 Urinary secretion. Anuria (General)	
612.5 Animal heat. Thermal processes Including: Body temperature. Effects of heat and cold. Hyperthermia. Hypothermia	QT 165 Body temperature regulation WD 670 Hypothermia. Frostbite	

UDC	*Compatible NLM classes*	*Comments*
612.6 Reproduction. Growth. Development Including: Sexual intercourse, coitus. Parturition. Puberty. Ageing. Death	WQ 205 Fertilization. Development of ovum. General physiology of reproduction WS 103 Normal physical growth and development WS 450 Puberty WT 116 Longevity. Life expectancy. Death	
612.7 Motor functions. Organs of locomotion. Voice. Integument. Including: Muscular actions. Function of skin	WE Muscles. Fascia WV 501 Anatomy. Physiology. Physiology of speech WV 530 Vocal cords WR 102 Physiology. Chemistry and metabolism of the skin. Sensory functions. Skin temperature	
612.8 Nervous system. Sensory organs Including: Cerebral functions. Sight (vision). Hearing (audition). Smell (olfaction). Taste (gustation). Touch (tactile sense)	WL Nervous system WL 700-710 Sense Organs WW 105 Visual perception. Space perception WV 272 Physiology of hearing. Auditory perception. Tinnitus. Function tests WV 301 Anatomy. Physiology. Olfaction	
613 Hygiene generally. Personal health and hygiene	QT 180 Hygiene (General)	
613.2 Dietetics. Nutrition principles applied to feeding and foods	QT 235 Diet	
613.3 Drinks. Curative drinks. Medicinal waters. Liquid diet	WB 442 Water. Mineral waters	
613.4 Personal hygiene. Clothing	WU 113 Oral hygiene QT 245 Clothing	
613.5 Hygiene of dwellings	Not included	
613.6 Occupational health hazards. Occupational health and hygiene	WA 400-495 Occupational Medicine, Health and Hygiene	
613.7 Health and hygiene of leisure, recreation, sleep	QT 250-275 Leisure Activities. Sports. Sports Medicine	
613.8 Health and hygiene of the nervous system. Health and ethics	QV 89 Narcotics WM 101 Mental health WM 290 Tobacco use disorder	
613.9 Health and hygiene in relation to age, sex, ethnicity	WA 306 Men's health WA 309.1 Women's health (General, not Table G) WS 460 Adolescent hygiene WT 120 Geriatric hygiene	

UDC	*Compatible NLM classes*	*Comments*
614 Public health and hygiene. Accident prevention	WA 4 Works on general hygiene WA 250-295 Accident and Injury Prevention. Disasters	
614.1 Population. Depopulation	Not included	
614.2 Public and professional organization of health Including: Hospitals generally. Regulation of medical profession, of doctors	W General Medicine. Health Professions	
614.3 Sanitary inspection and control Including: Inspection of foods, medicines	WA 672 General Sanitation and Environmental Control WA 695 Food. Food supply. Food inspection	
614.39 National health services	WA 540 National and state health administration (Table G)	UDC number should be, eventually, in a different hierarchy
614.4 Prevention and control of communicable (infectious, contagious) diseases. Prevention of epidemics Including: Quarantine	WA 110 Prevention and control of communicable diseases. WA 230 Quarantine	
614.6 Cemetery hygiene. Disposal of the dead	WA 840-847 Mortuary Practice	
614.7 Hygiene of air, water, soil. Pollution and its control	WA 750 Air sanitation and hygiene WA 778-790 Waste	
614.8 Accidents. Risks. Hazards. Accident prevention. Personal protection. Safety	WA 250-295 Accident and Injury Prevention. Disasters	
614.9 Animal health. Veterinary hygiene	QW 70 Veterinary microbiology	
615 Pharmacology. Therapeutics. Toxicology	QV Pharmacology QV 600-667 Toxicology	
615.1 General and professional pharmacy	QV 701-737 General Pharmacy and Pharmaceutics	
615.2 Medicaments according to their principal action	QV 60-370 (Classify works on an individual drug according to its principal action)	
615.3 Medicaments according to their origin	QV 738-772 Drug Standardization. Pharmacognosy. Medicinal Plants	
615.4 Pharmaceutical preparations. Medical material. Equipment	QV 773-835 Pharmaceutical Processes. Packaging. Labeling	

UDC	*Compatible NLM classes*	*Comments*
615.8 Physiotherapy. Physical therapy. Radiotherapy. Other nonmedicinal therapeutic treatment Including: Massage. Mechanotherapy. Physical agents. Nature cures. Naturopathy. Electrotherapy. Radiotherapy. Electrotherapeutics. Psychotherapy. Work therapy. Curative voyages. Dietotherapy etc. Folk medicine. Popular, household remedies	WB 460-556 Physical and Occupational Therapy QZ 269 Radiotherapy WB 537 Massage WB 935 Naturopathy	
615.9 General toxicology. General studies of poisons and poisoning (intoxication)	QV 600-667 Toxicology	
616 Pathology. Clinical medicine Application Note: Details by special auxiliaries 616-001/-009 and 616-01/-099		
616-001/-009 Special auxiliary subdivision for morbid processes		
616-001 Traumata. Injuries. Wounds	Classified in each system	
616-002 Inflammation. Irritation. Engorgement (hyperaemia). Mucous congestion	Classified in each system	
616-003 Regressive and reparative processes	Classified in each system	
616-004 Sclerosis. Hardening (induration). Cirrhosis	Classified in each system WI 725 Cirrhosis	
616-005 Local circulatory disorders	QZ 170 Circulatory disorders	
616-006 Tumours. Neoplasms. Blastomata. Choristomata. Hamartomata. Oncology	QZ 200-380 Neoplasms. Cysts	
616-007 Defective structural development. Physiological deformities. Malformations. Hemiterata. Oversized, undersized organs. Teratology. Monsters. Abnormalities	WE 883 Deformities Classified in each system	

UDC	*Compatible NLM classes*	*Comments*
616-008 Functional and metabolic disorders	WD 200-226 Metabolic Diseases	
616-009 Neural (nervous) disorders	WL 200-405 Central Nervous System. Disorders. Therapeutics	
616-01/-099 Special auxiliary subdivision for general aspects of pathology	Classified in each system	
616-01 Various aspects of disease, patients and medical intervention	W General Medicine. Health Professions	
616-02 Aetiology. Science of the causes of disease	QZ 40-109 Pathogenesis. Etiology	
616-03 Various forms of disease, of treatment, of administration of medicaments	Classified in each system	
616-05 Persons and personal characteristics in pathology. Characteristics of the patient	Classified in each system	
616-06 Complications. Consequences. Repercussions. Concurrence, simultaneous state. Correlation. Previous illnesses. Previous state of health. Antagonism of two diseases	Classified in each system	
616-07 Semeiology. Symptomatology. Signs and symptoms. Examination. Diagnosis. Propaedeutics	Classified in each system	
616-08 Treatment Including: Care of the patient. Nursing. Operative treatment. Operative technique. Surgery. Surgical anaesthesia	WY 101-145 Nursing Specialties WY 150-170 Nursing in Special Fields of Medicine WO 178-198 Principles of Care. Procedures WO 200-460 Anesthesia	
616-091 Pathological anatomy. Morbid anatomy	QS 504-532 Histology QZ 33 Comparative pathology QZ 35 Postmortem examination	
616-092 Pathological physiology. Processes, mode of action of diseases. Pathogenesis. Study of origin of diseases	QZ 40-109 Pathogenesis. Etiology	
616-093 Microbial techniques	QW 1-300 Microbiology	
616-094 Microbial morphology	QW 1-300 Microbiology	

UDC	Compatible NLM classes	Comments
616-095 Microbial physiology	QW 1-300 Microbiology	
616-097 Immunogenicity	QW 501-949 Immunology	
616-098 Microbial physics, chemistry, metabolism, catabolism	QW 1-300 Microbiology	
616-099 Poisoning. Intoxication	WA 465 Industrial poisons and poisoning	
616-71/-78 Special auxiliary subdivision for medical and surgical instrumentation and equipment		
616-71 Medical instruments and equipment in general Including: Diagnostic, measuring, testing and recording instruments and devices	W 26 Equipment and supplies Also classified in each system	
616-72 Surgical and therapeutic instruments	WO 162 Surgical equipment, instruments and other supplies	
616-74 Reinforcement and reparative materials and equipment	WU 170-190 Dental Chemistry and Materials	
616-76 Corrective and protective appliances, aids etc.	WU 500-530 Prosthodontics WV 274 Hearing devices. Cochlear implants. Cochlear implantation WW 350-358 Corrective Devices	
616-77 Prosthetic materials and parts. Artificial organs etc.	WO 162-176 Surgical Equipment. Artificial Organs WU 500 General works. Dental prosthesis	
616-78 Machines and mechanical apparatus	Redundant Also classified in each system	
616.1/.9 Special pathology		
616.1 Pathology of the circulatory system, blood vessels. Cardiovascular complaints Including: Cardiology. Cardiovascular diseases. Thrombosis. Heart, cardiac diseases	WG 120-170 Cardiovascular Diseases, Diagnosis and Therapeutics WG 200-460 Heart. Heart Diseases WG 500-700 Blood Vessels. Vascular Diseases	

UDC	*Compatible NLM classes*	*Comments*
616.2 Pathology of the respiratory system. Complaints of the respiratory organs Including: Otorhinolaryngology (ear, nose and throat). Lungs, pulmonary diseases	WF 140-900 Diseases of the Respiratory System WV 140 Otorhinolaryngologic diseases	
616.3 Pathology of the digestive system. Complaints of the alimentary canal Including: Diseases of the mouth, stomach, intestines, liver	WI 140-150 Diseases. Diagnosis. Signs and Symptoms (WI Digestive system)	
616.31 Stomatology. Oral cavity. Mouth. Diseases of the mouth and teeth Including: Odontology. Diseases of the teeth. Dentistry. Orthodontics	WU Dentistry. Oral Surgery	
616.4 Pathology of the lymphatic system, haemopoietic (haematopoietic) organs, endocrines Including: Endocrinology	WH Hemic and Lymphatic Systems WK Endocrine System	
616.5 Skin. Common integument. Clinical dermatology. Cutaneous complaints	WR Dermatology	
616.6 Pathology of the urogenital system. Urinary and sexual (genital) complaints. Urology Including: Diseases of the kidneys, bladder, male reproductive organs	WJ Urogenital System	
616.7 Pathology of the organs of locomotion. Skeletal and locomotor systems Including: Clinical osteology and myology. Diseases of the bones, muscles	WE Musculoskeletal System	
616.8 Neurology. Neuropathology. Nervous system Including: Diseases of the nervous system	WL Nervous System	
616.89 Psychiatry. Pathological psychiatry. Psychopathology. Phrenopathies. Psychoses. Mental abnormality. Morbid mental states. Behavioural and emotional disturbances	WM Psychiatry	UDC number should be in a different hierarchy, at the same level of Neurology, or Orthopaedics, for example.

UDC	*Compatible NLM classes*	*Comments*
616.9 Communicable diseases. Infectious and contagious diseases, fevers Including: Sexually transmitted diseases (STDs), e.g. HIV infection, AIDS	WC Communicable Diseases	
617 Surgery. Orthopaedics. Ophthalmology	WO Surgery WE 168-190 Orthopedics. Reconstructive Orthopedics. Bone Transplantation WW Ophthalmology	
617.3 Orthopaedics in general	WE 168-190 Orthopedics. Reconstructive Orthopedics. Bone Transplantation	
617.7 Ophthalmology. Eye disorders and treatment	WW Ophthalmology	
618 Gynaecology. Obstetrics Including: Midwifery. Tocology. Pregnancy (gravidity). Childbirth. Delivery. Parturition. Physiology and pathology of labour, puerperium and post-partum period	WP Gynecology WQ Obstetrics	

Commerce, see also Rhetoric: cross-discipline relationships as authority data for enhanced retrieval

Claudio Gnoli
University of Pavia Science and Technology Library, Pavia, Italy

Rodrigo De Santis
Paraná Federal Institute of Education Science & Technol., Irati, Brazil

Laura Pusterla
University of Pavia Science and Technology Library, Pavia, Italy

Abstract: Subjects in a classification scheme are often related to other subjects in different hierarchies. This problem was identified long ago by Hugh of Saint Victor (1096?-1141). Still with present-day bibliographic classifications, a user browsing the class of architecture under the hierarchy of arts may miss relevant items classified in building or in civil engineering under the hierarchy of applied sciences. To overcome these limitations we have developed SciGator, a browsable interface to explore the collections of all scientific libraries at the University of Pavia. Besides showing subclasses of a given class, the interface points users to related classes in the Dewey Decimal Classification, or in other local schemes, and allows for expanded queries that include them. This is made possible by using a special field for related classes in the database structure which models classification authority data. Ontologically, many relationships between classes in different hierarchies are cases of existential dependence. Dependence can occur between disciplines in such disciplinary classifications as Dewey (e.g. architecture existentially depends on building), or between phenomena in such phenomenon-based classifications as the Integrative Levels Classification (e.g. fishing as a human activity existentially depends on fish as a class of organisms). We provide an example of its representation in OWL and discuss some of the details.

Keywords: relationships; existential dependence; query expansion; disciplines; phenomenon-based classification; Dewey Decimal Classification; DDC; Integrative Levels Classification; ILC

1. Introduction

The most typical structure of all classifications (be they synthetic or not, discipline-based or not, aimed at classifying books or other objects) is a hierarchical tree of classes. Every concept is subsumed under a more general one, and so on, thus forming one big pyramidal graph. This structure offers many benefits for both navigation between concepts and search of classified items: for example, by a single search for a truncated notation a user can retrieve all items classified in the selected class or in any more specific class.

On the other hand, the real world is obviously more complex than a single big pyramid. Concepts are related in many ways, not just by vertical dominance.

While the hierarchical structure is an effective facility for displaying some relationships, it also hides other relationships that may be relevant too.

This problem was identified long ago by Hugh of Saint Victor (1096?-1141), the Saxon theologian and philosopher whose classification of knowledge had a profound impact on Western knowledge organization in the subsequent centuries. As recently reported by Olson (2010: 134), while discussing his system Hugh observed that e.g. a class such as commerce could be classified not only among the practical arts, but in principle also under rhetoric, as "a peculiar sort of rhetoric [...] for eloquence is in the highest degree necessary to it". In other words, despite any classification of knowledge into separate disciplines, or more generally into separate main classes, a subject listed in any given class is often related to different classes as well.

Beyond Hugh's particular examples, which are obviously related to the culture of his time, this logical problem still affects any classification of the present day, and the retrieval of information resources through it. Indeed, due to the hierarchical structure of classifications, each subject has to be listed under one branch or another, no matter how many others have some semantic relationship with it. As users will browse bibliographic items classified under a certain branch, they will be missing potentially relevant ones classified under related branches.

This paper explores strategies to cope with this problem in both conceptual classification structures and their implementation as authority data in online catalogues or digital libraries. We will start by discussing the classical application of a disciplinary classification in library catalogues (Section 2), and present a web-based library tool for exploring classes and relationships between them in science and technology domains (Section 3). Then we will transcend the special case of discipline-based library classifications, by considering non-hierarchical relationships in the more general perspective of ontology (Section 4) and their representation in the Web Ontology Language (OWL) (Section 5).

2. Cross-discipline relationships in libraries

In traditional library classifications, relationships other than hierarchical are usually expressed in the schedules as "see also" links, pointing users from a given place in the scheme to a different one belonging to another hierarchy (Green, 2011). As most library classifications are based on disciplines, such relationships can be described as cross-discipline ones: an example in the Dewey Decimal Classification (DDC) is the relationship between class 378 for university, belonging to the discipline of education, and class 727.3 for university buildings, belonging to the discipline of architecture. "See also" references are also common in verbal subject headings lists, such as the Library of Congress Subject Headings, and are basically equivalent to "related terms" (RT) recorded in thesauri.

In terms of authority control, cross-discipline relationships can be recorded in special fields of the classification reference database accounting for relationships of a class with others in a different hierarchy. The UDC Master Reference File includes field 125 for references to the notation of other classes, which "represent[s] 'see also' reference, i.e. it points to related classes".

In reviewing the requirements of interfaces to classifications, Slavic (2006) lists "hyperlinks on class numbers, see also reference" among the possible functions of browsing and classified display; she emphasizes that "a systematic (classification) display can be adapted for search expansion, enhancing both recall and precision, through exploiting hierarchical and associative relationships, provided that semantic linking in the vocabulary is fully supported by vocabulary data".

Despite the opportunity to leverage this kind of authority data for retrieval, most library catalogues hardly provide any kind of link in their browsable lists of classes, as a wide survey of Italian online catalogues has shown (Casson, Fabbrizzi & Slavic, 2011). Display of related concepts to be used for query expansion has been demonstrated with a faceted thesaurus (Binding & Tudhope, 2004; Tudhope et al., 2006).

Similar cross-disciplinary references would also be very useful on library shelves arranged by some classification scheme. Unfortunately, applications of this kind are not common. A recent suggestion was to provide shelves containing a given DDC class with QR codes pointing to related classes in the online catalogue (Green, 2013), so that users can leverage their smartphones to navigate across the classification tree, and integrate the material space of the library with the digital space of its catalogue. An Italian institution making use of QR codes to connect signage at open shelves with the catalogue, and paying attention to illustration of the structure of DDC to users, is the Library of Social Sciences at the University of Florence (Fabbrizzi, 2014). In this implementation, display of cross-discipline relationships is delegated only to the catalogue:

> "each classified subject has relationships with other subjects, especially those which share one or more concepts within different disciplines [...]. If these relationships are recorded in the catalogue, it is possible to give the users the opportunity of a network of search paths that otherwise would not be evident due to the organization by disciplines" (Fabbrizzi, 2014: 115).

3. SciGator: an interface for exploring cross-discipline relationships

The Science and Technology Library of the University of Pavia was founded in 2009 by merging pre-existing smaller libraries, as part of a reorganization process. It gathers information resources mainly concerning engineering, architecture, natural science and mathematics. More resources in the related disciplines of physics, chemistry, pharmacology, and medicine are gathered in the separate Science Library and Medical Library. As all these libraries are increasingly adopting DDC for shelving, providing classification data in the catalogue is an important way to overcome the scattering of information resources across several institutions and buildings.

Besides searching the university catalogue by authors and titles, users can access information on the collections through the university libraries website: http://biblioteche.unipv.it/BST. Since 2015, this includes a browsable interface called SciGator, which allows navigation across DDC classes used in all three scientific libraries mentioned above. Only classes assigned to a significant number of owned documents (i.e., some 5 or more shelfmarks) are displayed. Data from local classifications previously used for shelving older resources in the same libraries are also included, and mapped to approximately equivalent DDC classes.

The relevant classification data are stored in a MySQL database that can be queried by a dynamic web page written in PHP. These include:

- DDC class notation;
- caption in Italian;
- caption in English;
- scope notes;
- related DDC classes from different hierarchies;
- equivalent classes from local schemes.

A book to be shelved often deals at one time with subjects listed in several places in DDC schedules, e.g. with 624 civil engineering, 690 building and 720 architecture. Although a single class has to be chosen for the shelfmark, based on the disciplinary perspective prevailing in the book, links to others will be suggested in the SciGator interface. Table 1 lists cross-discipline relationships that have been found to be relevant to the particular collections of these libraries (irrespective of whether they are recorded as "see also" relationships in the published editions of DDC or not).

Once a user has identified a relevant class, he/she can start three different kinds of search, each marked by a different icon, for corresponding items in the online catalogue:

- search all records having this class, or a subclass of it, in the Shelfmark field of location data, that is, all documents shelved in this class in any of the library sections that are already organized by DDC;
- search the records above, plus records having this class, or a subclass of it, in the Classification field of bibliographic description data (often assigned by other libraries) irrespective of their shelfmarks;
- search the records above, plus records having one of the related classes, or a subclass of them, in either the Shelfmark or the Classification field.

In all three cases, results are sorted in reverse order of publication data, assuming that most recent documents on the given subject can be more relevant for a majority of users. Also, results can be further refined by the standard search options available in the catalogue (only documents in one selected library, only documents of a selected type, only documents published

Table 1: *Cross-discipline relationships in the scientific libraries in Pavia*

004 computer science	←	519.4 numerical analysis
004 computer science	←	621.39 computer engineering
005.1 programming	←	511.3 mathematical logic
152.1 sensoryperception	←	612.8 physiology of nervous system
304.5 genetic factors in social processes	←	591.5 ethology
338 microeconomy	←	650 management
344 social and environmental laws	←	333.7 natural resources
344 social and environmental laws	←	363 security and social problems
344 social and environmental laws	←	618 public health
346 private and civil law	←	710 land planning
363.7 pollution and environmental problems	←	577 ecology
519.4 numerical analysis	←	515 calculus
569.9 palaeontology of hominids	←	599.9 physical anthropology
581.3 plant genetics	←	576.5 general genetics
599.935 human genetics	←	576.5 general genetics
610.72 medical statistics	←	519 statistics
611 human anatomy	←	571.3 comparative anatomy
612.015 medical biochemistry	←	572 biochemistry
612.64 human embriology	←	571.8 embriology
616.052 medical genetics	←	599.935 human genetics
616.89 psychiatry	←	153 mental processes
620.2 applied acoustics	←	534 physics of sound and vibrations
621.3 electrical engineering	←	537 electromagnetism
621.31 electric energy	←	333.7 natural resources
621.36 optical engineering	←	535 optics
621.4 engines	←	536 thermology
622 mining engineering	←	551 geology
624.176 earthquake engineering	←	551.22 seismology
627 hydraulic engineering	←	532 fluid dynamics
627 hydraulic engineering	←	551.48 hydrogeology
628.5 pollution control technologies	←	363.7 pollution and environmental problems
630 agriculture	←	580 botany
631.53 plant reproduction	←	581.3 plant genetics
632 agrarian pathology	←	581.2 plant pathology
660.6 biotechnology	←	572 biochemistry
660.6 biotechnology	←	610.28 biomedical instrumentation
663.2 oenology	←	634.8 viticulture
664 food technology	←	641 food science
681 precision tools and circuits	←	621.3815 components
690 building	←	624 civil engineering
696 interior plants	←	628 sanitary engineering
711.4 city planning	←	307 communities
720 architecture	←	690 building
725.5 health buildings	←	610.28 biomedical instrumentation
727.3 university buildings	←	378 university education
728 houses	←	307 communities
912 cartography	←	551 geology

within a selected range of years, only documents within the resulting set having a specific author or word in the title, etc.). However, experience suggests that few users pay attention to such refinement options.

Clearly, the second and third search options will yield an increasing number of results as compared to the first one. Indeed, more inclusive options produce a higher recall, especially in the case of the expanded query that includes several related classes. This will avoid missing relevant documents that have been assigned related classes, but at the same time will reduce precision and increase information overload: for example, some documents on building techniques may be irrelevant to a user only looking for information on the artistic aspects of architecture.

To face this situation, we have identified two strategies, that have been embodied in the search interface:

- making expanded query only an option, with clear instructions concerning its specific purpose, rather than making it the default search mode;
- limiting expansion to a single step in the graph of relationships; e.g., selecting civil engineering will also include building (as it depends on civil engineering), but not architecture (as it depends on building).

The latter strategies build on reported experience with testing query expansions by thesauri (Tudhope, Alani & Jones, 2001). While all concepts in a knowledge organization system can be virtually connected in a single graph, as one moves from one node to the next, the relationship becomes less and less strict. As a result, concepts connected through more than one or two steps, although having some semantic relationship with the concept searched, may be scarcely relevant to most users.

For this purpose, it is useful to have a closer look on the nature of the relationships between classes in a classification system. This is discussed in the next section.

4. Existential dependence between classes

Relationships other than hierarchical, such as "see also" relationships in classifications or RTs in thesauri, are usually described as "associative". Association may be based on several categories of meaning, for example a shared place or a shared time (like with the relationship between night and stars). However, these kinds of loose relationships seem to be of limited use in information retrieval. On the other hand, many relationships across a classification scheme that appear to be more significant for retrieval, such as the relationship between building and architecture, can be described as cases of existential dependence.

Existential dependence is a kind of ontological dependence (Lowe, 2015) in which the extension of a class depends on another for its own existence. Architecture cannot exist if there are no buildings where it can be applied. Buildings in turn cannot exist if there are no engineering principles to create them. Classes related by existential dependence often belong to different hierarchies in a classification scheme. To take another example, while knowledge on crops may belong to the hierarchy of agriculture, it also depends on botanical knowledge on cereals listed under biology, and on meteorological knowledge on climates listed under Earth sciences. This often makes it useful to provide users with links to such related classes, in order to search information resources, or to navigate between them, in more efficient ways.

As most bibliographic classifications, such as the UDC or the DDC, are organized according to disciplines, existential dependence in them takes the form of a link between disciplines: agriculture depends on botany and on meteorology.

Ultimately, dependence between disciplines can be reduced to dependence between phenomena: the existence of crops depends on the existence of some plants and of some climates. In phenomenon-based classifications, such as the Integrative Levels Classification (ILC)[1], this relationship can thus take the form of a link between classes of phenomena. Such links can also be represented as semantic factors concurring to the meaning of the class of phenomena (Gnoli, 2013); indeed, in a vocabulary or a formalized ontology one could define crops as the result of cultivating some kinds of plants, hence the concept of plants will be a semantic factor needed in the definition of crops. The ILC database structure includes a field for semantic factors. Another project of a phenomenon-based classification, the Basic Concepts Classification, plans to make wide use of synthetic notations derived from notations of the "basic concepts" forming the more complex concepts required (Szostak, 2014). As this may eventually result in long and complex classmarks, clearly a balance has to be found between what is expressed by post-coordinate synthetic notation and what is recorded as pre-coordinate semantic factors in the database.

5. OWL representation of relationships

This kind of authority data, together with the other structural elements of the classification, can also be represented as linked data for the purposes of interoperability. SKOS may be a natural option here, although this format has only a limited capability of representing the sophisticated structure of faceted classifications (Gnoli et al., 2011). Other RDF formats may then be considered, such as the more powerful Web Ontology Language (OWL) (Zeng, Panzer & Salaba, 2010). In the following, we provide an OWL example of representation of existential dependence between classes of such a phenomenon-based classification as ILC.

In ILC, the class `v` "technologies" have subclasses including `vc` "fishing", `vd` "mining" and `vf` "forestry". Other main classes of ILC are `m` "organisms" with subclasses including `mq` "animals" and `g` "bodies" with subclasses including `gx`

1 Integrative Levels Classification (ILC) is available at http://www.iskoi.org/ilc/ilc.php.

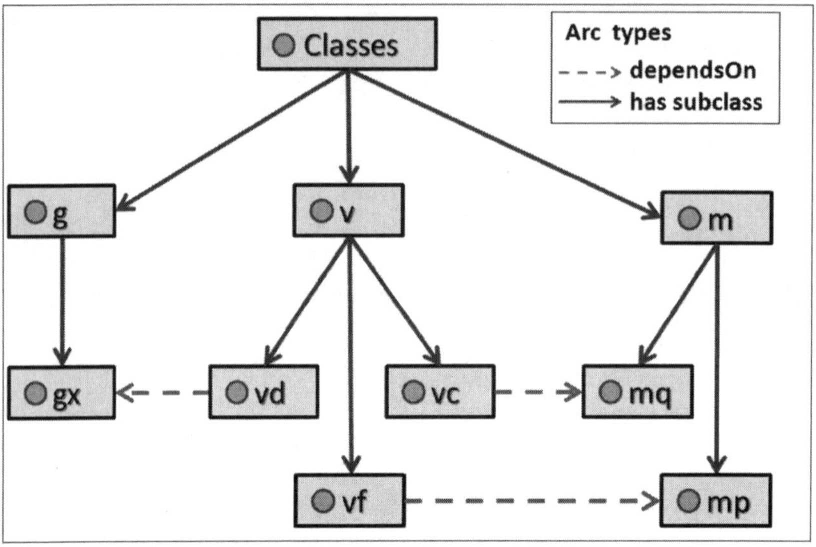

Figure 1: *Graphical representation of some ILC classes and their dependence relationships*

"crystals". Dependence relationship allows us to express that vc "fishing" depends on mq "animals"; vd "mining" depends on gx "crystals"; and vf "forestry" depends on mp "plants", as graphically represented in Figure 1.

The OWL code for classes v "technologies", vc "fishing" and the dependence property dependsOn are presented below.

Class v "technologies":

```
<owl:Class rdf:about="http://www.iskoi.org/ilc/ilc_ontology#v">
     <rdfs:label>v</rdfs:label>
     <rdfs:comment xml:lang="en">technologies</rdfs:comment>
     <rdfs:subClassOf rdf:resource="http://www.iskoi.org/ilc/
             ilc_ontology#Classes"/>
</owl:Class>
```

Class vc "fishing":

```
<owl:Class
rdf:about="http://www.iskoi.org/ilc/ilc_ontology#vc">
     <rdfs:label>vc</rdfs:label>
     <rdfs:comment xml:lang="en">fishing</rdfs:comment>
     <rdfs:subClassOf rdf:resource="http://www.iskoi.org/ilc/
             ilc_ontology#v"/>
     <owl:Restriction>
             <owl:onProperty rdf:resource="http://www.iskoi.org/
                     ilc/ilc_ontology#dependsOn" />
             <owl:allValuesFrom rdf:resource="http://www.iskoi.
                     org/ilc/ilc_ontology#mq" />
     </owl:Restriction>
</owl:Class>
```

Property `dependsOn`:

```
<owl:TransitiveProperty rdf:about="http://www.iskoi.org/ilc/
     ilc_ontology#dependsOn">
     <rdfs:label xml:lang="en">dependsOn</rdfs:label>
     <rdfs:range rdf:resource="http://www.iskoi.org/ilc/
            ilc_ontology#Classes"/>
     <rdfs:domain rdf:resource="http://www.iskoi.org/ilc/
            ilc_ontology#Classes"/>
</owl:TransitiveProperty>
```

The type `TransitiveProperty` asserts that the property `dependsOn` is able to be inherited for the whole hierarchy. It means that a class at a greater degree of specificity, e.g. `mqvhj` "salmoniformes", will automatically keep the dependence relationship with `vc` "fishing", throughout degrees `mq` "animals", `mqv` "chordates" and `mqvh` "ray-finned fish".

However, the transitivity of `dependsOn` has a side effect: it also expresses that `v` "fishing" could also depend on `mqvtoc` "canidae", or, in other words, that we would be able to fish a dog. A solution can be to create another property in class `mq`, called `fishable`, to set its value for each subclass, defining whether an animal can be "fishable" or not, and to set a new restriction for property `dependsOn` in class `vc` "fishing":

```
<owl:Restriction>
     <owl:onProperty rdf:resource="#isFishable" />
     <owl:hasValue rdf:resource="true" />
</owl:Restriction>
```

It is indeed possible in OWL to define properties unlimitedly and to represent different types of relationships between classes, properties and individuals (beyond the usual "is-a" and "is-part-of" relationships). On the one hand, this makes the initial work of creating a new scheme more complicated. On the other hand, it allows the model to be more flexible and powerful, allowing the representation of sophisticated schemes, which seems to be promising in the case of ILC.

6. Conclusion

Knowledge organization systems, including classifications, can imply complex and rich graphs of relationships between concepts. The classical hierarchical structure and display of classification schemes only show some of them, that is, the relationships between more general and more specific classes of the same branch. This is already a powerful tool, for both navigation and search, as it allows, e.g., using truncated notation in queries to retrieve all subclasses in the branch in one search.

On the other hand, non-hierarchical relationships between classes, such as existential dependence, are lost in most interfaces. We have shown how these can be represented to enhance both exploration of the whole classification scheme and recall in search. To achieve this, we had to operate on both a conceptual plane, by evaluating which and how many relationships should be used without obtaining retrieval of scarcely relevant information, and a technical plane, by recording the relevant relationships in a suitable database structure as part of classification authority data. We have also shown how such representation can be translated into RDF structures for uses in the Semantic Web.

A more precise and rich representation of relationships as authority data, than what is usually implemented, has the potential of providing users with more powerful tools for knowledge discovery, and making them more aware of the complex network of connections that form the corpus of human knowledge.

Acknowledgements

The paper benefits from discussions during first author's Erasmus Staff Training in May 2013 at the University of South Wales Hypermedia Research Unit, led by Douglas Tudhope, and from practical work at the University of Pavia Science and Technology Library, directed by Anna Bendiscioli.

References

Binding, C.; Tudhope, D. (2004). KOS at your service: programmatic access to knowledge organization systems. *Journal of Digital Information*, 4 (4). Available at: https://journals.tdl.org/jodi/index.php/jodi/article/view/110/109.

Casson, E.; Fabbrizzi, A.; Slavic, A. (2011). Subject search in Italian OPACs: an opportunity in waiting? In: *Subject access: preparing for the future*. Edited by P. Landry et al. Berlin: De Gruyter, pp. 37-50.

Fabbrizzi, A. (2014). An atlas of classification: signage between open shelves, the Web and the catalogue. *JLIS.it: Italian Journal of Library, Archives and Information Science*, 5 (2), pp. 101-122. Available at: http://leo.cineca.it/index.php/ jlis/article/view/10068.

Gnoli, C. (2013). Facets, levels, and semantic factoring. *SRELS Journal of Information Management*, 50 (6), pp. 751-762.

Gnoli, C. et al. (2011). Representing the structural elements of a freely faceted classification. In: *Classification & ontology: formal approaches and access to knowledge: proceedings of the International UDC Seminar 2011, 19-20 September, The Hague, Netherlands*. Edited by A. Slavic, E. Civallero. Würzburg: Ergon, pp. 193-206.

Green, R. (2011). See-also relationships in the Dewey Decimal Classification. *Knowledge Organization*, 38 (4), pp. 335-341.

Green, R. (2013). Is this all they have? In: *025.431: the Dewey blog*. Available at: http://ddc.typepad.com/025431/2013/09/.

Lowe, E. J. (2015). Ontological dependence. Revised version. In: *Stanford encyclopedia of philosophy*. Available at: http://plato.stanford.edu/entries/dependence-ontological/.

Olson, H. (2010). Earthly order and the oneness of mysticism: Hugh of Saint Victor and Medieval classification of wisdom. *Knowledge Organization*, 37 (2), pp. 121-138.

Slavic, A. (2006). Interface to classification: some objectives and options. *Extensions and Corrections to the UDC*, 28, pp. 24-45.

Szostak, R. (2014). The Basic Concepts Classification as a bottom-up strategy for the semantic Web. *International Journal of Knowledge Content Development & Technology*, 4 (1), pp. 39-51.

Tudhope, D.; Alani, H.; Jones, C. (2001). Augmenting thesaurus relationships: possibilities for retrieval. *Journal of Digital Information*, 1 (8). Available at: https://journals.tdl.org/jodi/index.php/jodi/article/view/181/160.

Tudhope, D. et al. (2006). Query expansion via conceptual distance in thesaurus indexed collections. *Journal of Documentation*, 62 (4), pp. 509-533.

UDC. (2012). *Data elements in UDC MRF exports*. The Hague: UDC Consortium. available at: http://www.udcc.org/files/udc_data_elements_mrf11.pdf.

Zeng, M.; Panzer, M.; Salaba, A. (2010). Expressing classification schemes with OWL 2: exploring issues and opportunities based on experiments using OWL 2 for three classification schemes. In: *Paradigms and conceptual systems in knowledge organization: proceedings Eleventh International ISKO Conference, 23-26 February 2010, Rome, Italy*. Edited by C. Gnoli and F. Mazzocchi. Würzburg: Ergon, pp. 356-362.

CLAUDIO GNOLI is a librarian at the Science and Technology Library, University of Pavia. His research interest is in classification theory and he participates actively in the work of the UDC Editorial team (UDC Consortium) and the International Society for Knowledge Organization. He has published papers on this subject in several international journals and conference proceedings. He is a member of the editorial boards of the Universal Decimal Classification Consortium (UDCC) and of the journal *Knowledge Organization* and was a vice-president of the International Society for Knowledge Organization (ISKO).

LAURA PUSTERLA is a librarian at the Science and Technology Library, University of Pavia, where she works on cataloguing and systematic shelf-arrangement. She has recently graduated in Archive, Documentation and Library Science at the University of Pavia with a final paper on indexing historical documents, supervised by Paul G. Weston.

RODRIGO DE SANTIS VIEIRA DA SILVA holds a master degree from the Brazilian Institute of Information in Science and Technology (IBICT). He is Professor at the Paraná Federal Institute of Education Science and Technology. His research interests are in information science and technology, knowledge organization and their application to the domain of music. Rodrigo participates in the Integrative Levels Classification project and was a founder of the Aquela Música! project for a semantic database of Brazilian popular music.

Managing classification in libraries: a methodological outline for evaluating automatic subject indexing and classification in Swedish library catalogues

Koraljka Golub
Department of Library and Information Science, School of Cultural Sciences, Faculty of Arts and Humanities, Linnaeus University, Växjö, Sweden

Joacim Hansson
Department of Library and Information Science, School of Cultural Sciences, Faculty of Arts and Humanities, Linnaeus University, Växjö, Sweden

Dagobert Soergel
Department of Library and Information Studies, Graduate School of Education, University at Buffalo, United States

Douglas Tudhope
Hypermedia Research Group, University of South Wales, United Kingdom

Abstract: Subject terms play a crucial role in resource discovery but require substantial effort to produce. Automatic subject classification and indexing address problems of scale and sustainability and can be used to enrich existing bibliographic records, establish more connections across and between resources and enhance consistency of bibliographic data. The paper aims to put forward a complex methodological framework to evaluate automatic classification tools of Swedish textual documents based on the Dewey Decimal Classification (DDC) recently introduced to Swedish libraries. Three major complementary approaches are suggested: a quality-built gold standard, retrieval effects, domain analysis. The gold standard is built based on input from at least two catalogue librarians, end-users expert in the subject, end users inexperienced in the subject and automated tools. Retrieval effects are studied through a combination of assigned and free tasks, including factual and comprehensive types. The study also takes into consideration the different role and character of subject terms in various knowledge domains, such as scientific disciplines. As a theoretical framework, domain analysis is used and applied in relation to the implementation of DDC in Swedish libraries and chosen domains of knowledge within the DDC itself.

Keywords: Dewey Decimal Classification; DDC; automatic indexing; evaluation methodology; domain analysis

1. Introduction

Searching based on a topic or subject using free keywords or controlled terms is one of the most common types of end-user searching and, at the same time, one of the most challenging. Controlled subject index terms from thesauri, subject heading lists and classification systems support established objectives of library catalogues and provide many benefits compared to free-text indexing (see, e.g., Taylor, 1995). (Semi)-automated subject indexing and classification represent one potential solution to retain the established objectives of bibliographic systems in the light of the ever-increasing number of digital documents (Svenonious, 2000: 30) in hybrid and digital libraries, repositories and other digital collections. An example of a recent project is exploring procedures and solutions for automatic assignment of German subject headings for online publications (Junger, 2014).

In order to improve searching for information in Swedish, especially in libraries and research output collections like SwePub (http://swepub.kb.se), we proposed a three-year project to find out to what degree it is possible to apply automated subject indexing and classification based on controlled indexing languages like the Dewey Decimal Classification (DDC) and Swedish Subject Headings (Svenska ÄmnesOrd – SAO), as well as indexing using keywords extracted from the resource itself. Furthermore, the aim is to determine the value of those automatically assigned index terms, in combination and comparison with end-users' and cataloguers' index terms, in the process of information retrieval by end-users.

We proposed using DDC as the main standard because is has just been introduced to Swedish libraries as the new national standard, replacing the Swedish classification scheme SAB (Svanberg, 2013); the uptake of DDC may also be facilitated by good methods for (semi-) automated indexing and other findings of the project. The major reason why DDC has been introduced to Sweden is that it is used in over 135 countries and could support multilingual search and access. The latter has been recently discussed by Mitchell, Zeng & Žumer (2014) where they explored the Swedish translation of DDC 22 (among others) in the context of the Functional Requirements for Subject Authority Data (FRSAD) conceptual model and its potential to address real-world discovery problems in multilingual and multicultural environments.

This paper discusses the methodology for evaluating automatic indexing and classification in the given context. Most experiments and studies on automated subject classification apply methods that do not take into account the subjective nature of aboutness in their evaluation, often also excluding end-users and cataloguers (Golub et al., (accepted for publication); Gunnarsson, 2011). The methodology draws on the evaluation framework suggested in Golub et al. (accepted for publication). In addition, as a theoretical framework, domain analysis, based on Hjørland & Albrechtsen (1995) and Hjørland (2002), is used and applied in relation to: (1) the implementation of DDC in Swedish libraries and (2) chosen domains of knowledge within the DDC itself.

The remainder of the paper is structured as follows:

- Section 2, Background, gives a brief overview of automated subject indexing and evaluation challenges;
- Section 3, Aims and objectives, discusses the aims and objectives of the proposed project;
- Section 4, Methodology, describes the suggested evaluation approach in the Swedish context;
- Section 5, Concluding remarks, sums up the significance of the project for the Swedish library world.

2. Background

2.1. Terminology

Subject indexing often refers to assignment of index terms from controlled vocabularies like subject headings and thesauri and *subject classification* typically refers to the assignment of pre-combined classes from classification schemes. However, for the sake of brevity here we use *subject indexing* to refer to the assignment of index terms from subject headings and thesauri, the assignment of classes from classification schemes and the assignment of uncontrolled keywords.

The terms *automatic* and *automated* have both been used in related literatures, but we choose to use the former as it tends to be more commonly used. A variety of terms are found to refer to automatic indexing, including *text categorisation, document categorisation, document indexing, document clustering, document classification* and others. While there may be differences between some of these approaches as discussed below, in this paper we use the general term *automatic subject indexing.*

2.2. Automatic subject indexing

Automatic subject indexing research began with the availability of electronic text in the 1950s (Luhn, 1957; Baxendale, 1958; Maron, 1961) and has been a challenging topic ever since. It has the potential to address the exponentially increasing number of digital documents but can also help enrich existing bibliographic records with index terms from other indexing languages (cf. Isaac et al., 2009), establish more connections across and between resources and enhance consistency of bibliographic data.

A variety of factors contribute to the challenge of automatic subject indexing. Texts are a complex cognitive and social phenomenon and cognitive understanding of text engages many knowledge sources, sustains multiple inferences and involves a personal interpretation (Moens, 2000: 7-10). Existing automatic subject indexing tools are far from being able to handle this complexity and in applications it is seldom possible to go much beyond vocabulary and syntax analysis. Therefore, many would argue for machine-aided indexing (e.g., Hagedorn, 2001; Lykke & Eslau, 2010) rather than automatic indexing being able to entirely replace manual/intellectual indexing. For an example of an operating machine-aided indexing system, see the US National Library of Medicine´s Medical Text Indexer (http://ii.nlm.nih.gov/MTI).

Research related to automatic subject indexing includes three major areas: document clustering, text categorisation and controlled-vocabulary-based string matching (Golub, 2006). Document clustering produces clusters (classes) and derives relationships between them. Most challenging are labelling the clusters and deriving relationships like equivalence, relatedness and hierarchical relationships between clusters (Svenonius, 2000: 168). In addition, "automatically-derived structures often result in heterogeneous criteria for category membership and can be difficult to understand" (Chen & Dumais, 2000: 146). Moreover, the labels and the relationships change as new documents are added to the collection; such unstable class names and relationships are not user-friendly. The most common approach to automatic subject indexing is text categorisation using machine learning to assign documents to the appropriate class from an existing classification. The categoriser or classifier learns characteristics of classes from documents to which classes have been manually assigned. However, manually classified documents are often unavailable for the subject areas, document types or collections intended for the user groups of interest. Also, text categorisation algorithms perform well on new documents only if the new documents are similar enough to the training documents. The third approach, string matching, maps from terms (strings) found in the documents to a controlled-vocabulary. A major advantage of this approach is that it does not require training documents, while still maintaining a pre-defined structure of the controlled vocabulary at hand.

Several examples of automatic subject indexing based on DDC exist. OCLC's project Scorpion treated a document to be indexed as a query against the DDC knowledge base (Subramanian & Shafer, 1998). The results of the 'search' were treated as subjects of the document. Clustering was also used, for refining the result set and for further grouping of documents falling in the same DDC class. Wolverhampton Web Library manually maintained a library catalogue of British Web resources, within which experiments on automating its processes were conducted (Jenkins et al., 1998). Each classmark in the DDC captions file was enriched with additional keywords and synonyms. Keywords extracted from the document were weighted on the basis of their position in the document. Recent work (Khoo et al., in press) has investigated the automatic assignment of DDC classes. The algorithm approximates the practice of a human cataloguer, first identifying candidate DDC hierarchies via the relative index table and then selecting the most appropriate hierarchical context for the main subject.

2.3. Evaluation challenges

How well automatic indexing performs in operating information environments cannot be said with confidence because research is usually conducted in laboratory conditions, excluding the complexities of real-life systems and situations. Comparison of different approaches to automatic indexing is also hard without proper evaluation. For example, Hlava (2009) discusses advantages of rule-based versus statistical indexing. In a rule-based system, simple categorisation rules are automatically or manually generated, applying string matching bits of text ('prompt words') to the thesaurus terms. Complex rules (about 10%) are added by editors (these could, for example, involve telling the system what words must be present or absent in the text, or some other specific instructions that point the document to a particular subject). She claims that rule-based indexing offers greater precision and is much more cost-effective than the statistical approach. On the other hand, in the medical domain, Humphrey et al. (2009) compared a rule-based system and statistical system and showed that for their implementations the statistical system was superior. Another example of issues is that even different versions of the same collection have a strong impact on results (Yang, 1999).

Many different approaches to enhancing automatic indexing exist; systems need to be evaluated appropriately to know their true value. There are studies of automatic indexing tools but they use different data collections and different algorithms and apply different evaluation methods, which are often not described in sufficient detail in published papers. This makes it next to impossible to draw conclusions as to how good automatic subject indexing tools truly are.

Furthermore, the problems of aboutness in indexing and issues of relevance in retrieval are often ignored in evaluation. Terms assigned through automatic indexing are often compared with existing subject index terms, referred to as a gold standard. That approach suffers from problems such as different specificity and exhaustivity policies at hand and inter- and intra-indexer inconsistencies, meaning that automatically assigned index terms may be correct but may be left out by manual indexing due to indexing policies, omissions, or errors by human indexers. Because the purpose of indexing is to make relevant documents retrievable, the effect of indexing on retrieval should also be studied. However, although it is dynamic and multidimensional and depending on many factors, the most common approach to evaluating information retrieval is also based on a gold standard of a set of documents, a set of topics and a set of relevance assessments of those documents against the topics.

The problems of gold standards in indexing and retrieval evaluations are discussed in detail in Golub et al. (accepted for publication). Based on a systematic literature review, this paper proposes a framework of three complementary approaches for evaluating automatic indexing: evaluating indexing quality directly through assessment by an evaluator or by comparison with a gold standard; evaluating indexing quality directly in the context of an indexing workflow; and evaluating indexing quality indirectly through retrieval performance.

To better understand the results of the gold-standard methodology, we propose domain analysis. Domain analysis in LIS was first presented by Hjørland and Albrechtsen (1995) in an attempt to provide an alternative to cognitive and system-oriented models of explanation. It has since been integrated in the knowledge formation within LIS and used throughout knowledge organization research. Knowledge organization systems are seen as products of social and intellectual negotiation, corresponding to the division of labour in society. As that changes, so does the construction of and relation between knowledge domains that ultimately are transformed into classes in knowledge organization systems and retrieval practices. As evaluation results need to be understood, not just displayed, dimensions that fall outside the gold standard evaluation practice may be picked up by qualitative domain analysis. Such dimensions may be: 1) terminological convention within various scientific domains; 2) epistemological assumptions in knowledge domains that influence the very prerequisites for classification and retrieval evaluation; and, 3) relations between extra-disciplinary (social) use of terms and uncertainty that arises when different knowledge domains come into play. Using domain theory as one aspect of gold standard analysis not only helps to increase the value of the results themselves, but also provides a framework for problematizing its results in relation to social, epistemological and technological development as well as self-regulated domains of knowledge.

3. Aims and objectives

The aim of the proposed project is to gain a scientifically sound understanding of the level to which it is possible to apply automatic subject indexing to Swedish textual resources, specifically to assign Dewey Decimal Classification (DDC) classes (major focus) and Swedish Subject Headings (SAO) (minor focus), as well as indexing with free keywords derived from the resource at hand itself. Furthermore, the aim is to determine the value of those automatically assigned index terms, in combination and comparison with end-user assigned index terms (DDC, SAO, keywords) as well as cataloguers' assigned index terms in the process of information retrieval by end-users.

Specific objectives of the project are as follows:

- Establish a gold standard of DDC, SAO and free keywords, based on input from cataloguers, subject experts, end-users and reviewed automatic indexing software output;
- Determine the inter-indexer consistency level between cataloguers, end-users, subject experts and automatic output;
- Compare several automatic indexing applications, including one commercial, based on comparison against the established gold standard and in the context of end-user retrieval, for DDC, SAO and free keyword assignment;

- Determine which index terms, or a combination thereof, leads to best end-user retrieval results;
- Analyse differences for the above between the applied sciences and the humanities.

The major research question is to what degree automatic classification can be applied to Swedish textual resources: 1) in assigning DDC and SAO; and 2) in deriving keywords, evaluated based on comparison against the gold standard and in the context of end-user retrieval. The minor research questions are as follows:

- How do automatic indexing tools compare?
- What is the inter-indexer consistency level between cataloguers, end-users, subject experts and automatic indexing tools?
- Which of the five types of index terms achieve best retrieval results, alone or in combination with others: full-text indexing, cataloguers´ index terms, end-user index terms, subject experts´ index terms and automatically assigned index terms?
- How does the above compare in applied sciences versus humanities?

4. Methodology

The methodological approach here follows two of the three suggested approaches in Golub et al. (accepted for publication). The numbers follow guidelines from their framework, although the paper states that the recommended numbers are intuitively derived and that effects of certain numbers on results have not been empirically examined in published research. The approach of testing a tool in an indexing workflow is envisioned for the next step in a new project application.

4.1. Test collection

As test collection we propose a subset of 11,000 full-text Swedish-language documents from SwePub, with half the documents in the humanities and half in the applied sciences. SwePub is the Swedish integrated repository of research works from Swedish universities, comprising over 480,000 documents at the time of writing the paper. We will use the selected 11,000 documents in the information retrieval test comparing automatically assigned index terms from several tools among themselves and with free-text searching. We will select a subset of 180 documents to develop a gold standard for indexing. The 180 documents will be selected as follows: within each of the two broad disciplines (humanities and applied sciences), three distinct subject areas will be chosen that are well-covered by the document collection; for each subject area, thirty random documents will be selected, ideally stratified by type of document.

4.2. Automatic indexing tools

We know of no automatic indexing tools for Swedish that assign DDC classes, probably because DDC has been introduced to Sweden only recently. Therefore, the project will develop *automatic indexing tools* of two types, an automatic classifier for DDC, using a machine-learning tool (SVM – Support Vector Machine) and a string-matching tool. In addition, we will adapt at least one free keyword extractor (for example, KEA (https://code.google.com/p/hive-mrc/wiki/AboutKEA)) for Swedish by applying Swedish-language natural language processing tools like a stop-word list, a stemmer and/or a part-of-speech tagger. Furthermore, a commercial indexing tool, Data Harmony from Access Innovations Inc. (www.dataharmony.com), will be used to assign DDC classes and free keywords. Since Data Harmony as of now does not work with Swedish, the documents will first be translated into English using Google Translate. Data Harmony will use a rule-based classification algorithm for assigning DDC classes and a bag-of-words approach for free keywords. Other commercial companies like Smartlogic and HP claim support for Swedish but do not possess DDC which is the primary focus of our project. OCLC have promised us a DDC research license for the purposes of the project but it does not permit the DDC to be given to commercial partners.

4.3. Gold standard, retrieval test and domain analysis

First, we will create the gold standard as follows: two cataloguers, two subject experts and two end-users who are not subject experts and several automatic indexing tools will independently assign DDC classes, SAO headings and free keywords to the 180 documents using a user-friendly interface that does not require professional DDC knowledge; all assignments will be compiled into one integrated listing for each document. Two senior cataloguers and two end-users will examine all index terms, removing terms assigned erroneously and adding terms missed by all previous processes, resulting in a project gold standard for indexing.

With this gold standard, we can now evaluate an automatic indexing tool by computing for each document

$$\textbf{indexing recall} = \frac{\textbf{\# of correct index terms assigned by the tool}}{\textbf{\# of correct index terms in the gold standard}}$$

$$\textbf{indexing precision} = \frac{\textbf{\# of correct index terms assigned by the tool}}{\textbf{\# of all index terms assigned by the tool}}$$

Soergel (1994) uses the terms completeness of indexing (entity view) for indexing recall and purity of indexing (entity view) for indexing precision.

The second approach to evaluating indexing is through evaluation of retrieval results. Topics to be searched will be selected for each of the six subject areas (three in the humanities and three in the applied sciences as described in Section 4.1). For each of the six subject areas, we will recruit 9 to 12 users (3-4 subject experts, 3-4 end-users who are not subject experts and 3-4 librarians or library science graduates). The users will conduct searches on four topics in their assigned subject area, two topics chosen by the user and two topics assigned by the project researchers. Of the controlled topics, one will be an extensive search for an essay, thesis, or similar, which would require finding an extensive list of documents (such a search would likely benefit from the index terms) and the other would be a minor, factual search for information (this may be less dependent on index terms). Each assigned topic should be selected to have at least 20 relevant documents in the 11,000 test collection so that a reasonable number of documents is retrieved and available for analysis. The order of tasks would be rotated.

We will run users' queries using all available evidence from all indexing sources to produce a 'maximal' retrieved set. From a result list with query terms highlighted, the users will assess the relevance of each document found on a scale from zero to four, not relevant to highly relevant. They will also indicate the type of relevance: direct, providing direct evidence for what the user asks for; indirect, from which one can infer something about the topic; context, which provides background/context for topic; comparison, which provides information on a similar or contrasting situation or in more detail (Huang & Soergel, 2006). In preparation, we will instruct the users on how to assess relevance in order to increase inter-rater consistency.

We can now compute retrieval performance metrics for each individual indexing source (considering the documents found based on indexing from that source alone) and for selected combinations of indexing sources at different degrees of relevance.

For both the first and second parts, we analyse logs. We will observe several users for how they perform their tasks and gain feedback through a pre-study questionnaire, post-task questionnaire and a post-study questionnaire in order to help contextualise the results (following the example of Golub, Tudhope & Lykke, 2014). We will pilot test the entire protocol prior to the actual studies. Most sessions will take place remotely at participants' computers, supported by communication via email (apart from the several that would be observed).

Domain analysis is used as a qualitative complement, primarily to the post-study questionnaire, taking into consideration the social and disciplinary context of: 1) the documents used in the study; and 2) the cataloguers, subject experts and end-users. By doing so we may attain a more complex understanding of the results, relating to not only formal disciplinary context, but also to competing knowledge domains inside and outside of the collection used.

5. Concluding remarks

The major significance of the project is that the value of the professional, the automatic and the end-user ways of creating subject index terms, on their own and in various combinations, would be determined, thereby allowing for informed decisions on ensuring high quality subject access points as part of the Swedish library and information infrastructure, including for resources that are at the moment not being assigned any controlled terms like those in repositories. Provision of (semi-) automatic solutions for assigning DDC in particular would enable:

- cheap assignment of controlled subject terms;
- quicker and more efficient uptake of DDC in Sweden;
- hierarchical browsing by subject;
- retrievability of Swedish resources in multilingual systems and their integration into the Semantic Web (as DDC is used in over 135 countries and available as Linked Data).

Acknowledgements

The Swedish Library Association (Svensk biblioteksförening) provided funding for writing the project proposal.

References

Baxendale, P. B. (1958). Machine-made index for technical literature – an experiment. *IBM Journal of Research and Development*, 2, pp. 354-361.

Chen, H.; Dumais, S. T. (2000). Bringing order to the web: automatically categorizing search results. In: *Human Factors in Computing Systems, Proceedings of the SIGCHI conference, April 01 - 06, 2000, The Hague, Netherlands.* Edited by T. Turner, G. Szwillus. New York: ACM, pp. 145-152.

Golub, K. (2006). Automated subject classification of textual Web documents. *Journal of Documentation*, 62, pp. 350–371.

Golub, K.; Lykke, M.; Tudhope, D. (2014). Enhancing social tagging with automated keywords from the Dewey Decimal Classification. *Journal of Documentation*, 70, pp. 801–828.

Golub, K. et al. (accepted for publication). A framework for evaluating automatic indexing or classification in the context of retrieval. *Journal of the Association for Information Science and Technology.*

Gunnarsson, M. (2011). *Classification along genre dimensions: exploring a multidisciplinary problem*. Borås: University of Borås.

Hjørland, B. (2002). Domain analysis in Information Science: Eleven approaches – traditional as well as innovative. *Journal of Documentation*, 58 (4), pp. 422-462.

Hjørland, B.; Albrechtsen, H. (1995). Towards a new horizon in Information Science: Domain analysis. *Journal of the American Society for Information Science*, 46 (6), pp. 400-425.

Hlava, M. K. (2009). Understanding "rule based" vs. "statistics based" indexing systems: Data Harmony white paper. Available at: http://www.dataharmony.com/library/white Papers/auto_indexing_rule-based_vs_statistics-based.htm.

Huang, X.; Soergel, D. (2006). An evidence perspective on topical relevance types and its implications for exploratory and task-based retrieval. *Information research*, 12 (1). Available at: http://www.informationr.net/ir/12-1/paper281.html.

Humphrey, S. et al. (2009). Comparing a rule-based versus statistical system for automatic categorization of MEDLINE documents according to biomedical specialty. *Journal of the American Society for Information Science*, 60 (12), pp. 2530-2539.

Isaac, A. et al. (2009). Vocabulary matching for book indexing suggestion in linked libraries: A prototype implementation & evaluation. In: *The 8th International Semantic Web Conference, 25-29 October 2009, Chantilly, VA, USA*. Edited by A. Bernstein et al. Berlin, Heidelberg: Springer, pp. 843-859.

Jenkins, C. et al. (1998). Automatic classification of web resources using java and Dewey Decimal Classification. *Computer Networks & ISDN Systems*, 30, pp. 646-648.

Junger, U. (2014). Can indexing be automated?: the example of the Deutsche Nationalbibliothek. *Cataloging & Classification Quarterly*, 52 (1), pp. 102-109.

Khoo, M. et al. (in press). Augmenting Dublin Core digital library metadata with Dewey Decimal Classification. *Journal of Documentation*.

Luhn, H. P. (1957). A statistical approach to mechanized encoding and searching of literary information. *IBM Journal of Research and Development*, 1, pp. 309-317.

Maron, M. (1961). Automatic Indexing: an experimental inquiry. *Journal of the Association for computing Machinery*, 8 (3), pp. 404-417.

Mitchell, J. S.; Zeng, M. L.; Žumer, M. (2014). Modelling classification systems in multicultural and multilingual contexts. *Cataloging & Classification Quarterly*, 52 (1), pp. 90-101.

Moens, M.-F. (2000). *Automatic indexing and abstracting of document texts*. Boston: Kluwer Academic Publishers.

Soergel, D. (1994). Indexing and retrieval performance: The logical evidence. *Journal of the American Society for Information Science*, 8 (45), pp. 589-599.

Subramanian, S.; Shafer, K. (1998). Clustering. In: *Annual Review of OCLC Research (Online)*. Available at: http://worldcat.org/arcviewer/1/OCC/2003/06/03/0000003409/viewer/file1.html.

Svanberg, M. (2013). *Dewey projektet: slutrapport*. Available at: http://www.kb.se/Dokument/Deweyprojektet%20slutrapport%2020130614.pdf

Svenonius, E. (2000). *The intellectual foundation of information organization*. Cambridge, Mass: MIT Press.

Taylor, A. G. (1995). On the subject of subjects. *Journal of Academic Librarianship*, 21 (6), pp. 484-491. Available at: http://www.pitt.edu/~agtaylor/articles/taylor_subjectof subjects.pdf.

Yang, Y. (1999). An evaluation of statistical approaches to text categorization. *Journal of Information Retrieval*, 1 (1/2), pp. 67-88.

KORALJKA GOLUB is a senior lecturer at the Department of Library and Information Science, School of Cultural Sciences, Linnaeus University, Sweden and an adjunct lecturer at the School of Information Studies, Charles Stuart University, Australia. Prior to this she was an information science researcher at UKOLN, University of Bath, United Kingdom. Her research interests are in topics of information retrieval and knowledge organization, integrating existing knowledge organization systems with social tagging and/or automated subject indexing and evaluating resulting end-user information retrieval performance. Three of her major research projects focused on: evaluation of algorithms for automated subject classification and indexing in the context of information retrieval (EASTER); the potential of combining social tagging with Dewey Decimal Classification and Library of Congress Subject Headings (EnTag); and, terminology registries for UK further and higher education needs (TRSS).

JOACIM HANSSON is Professor and Director at the Department of Library and Information Science at the School of Cultural Sciences, Linnaeus University in Växjö, Sweden. His research covers vast range topics within LIS, such as library studies, bibliometrics and critical classification research. He has written on the theoretical and methodological development of LIS. His recent research interests are focused on issues concerning social use of bibliometrics, Open Access in scholarly publication and the new epistemology of documentation and knowledge organization. He authored six books and numerous articles in the field of library and information science.

DAGOBERT SOERGEL is Professor in the Department of Library and Information Studies, Graduate School of Education, University at Buffalo. Prior to this he was Professor in College of Information Studies, University of Maryland and Professore Onorario in Dipartimento di Ingegneria e Scienza dell'Informazione, Univeristy of Trento. He has been working in the area of classification (taxonomy, ontologies) and thesauri for over 50 years. He authored the still-standard text- and handbook *Indexing Languages and Thesauri Construction and Maintenance* (Wiley 1974) and *Organizing Information* (Academic Press 1985), which received the American Society of Information Science Best Book Award. Prof. Soergel is author of over hundred papers and presentations in information retrieval, classification / ontologies, digital libraries, sense-making and relevance. He was the chief architect for the *Alcohol and Other Drug Thesaurus* (http://etoh. niaaa.nih.gov/ AODVol1/Aodthome.htm) and the *Harvard Business Thesaurus*. He received the American Society for Information Science Award of Merit in 1997.

DOUGLAS TUDHOPE is Professor in the Faculty of Computing, Engineering and Science, University of South Wales and leads the Hypermedia Research Unit. His main research interests are the intersecting areas of information science, digital libraries and hypermedia and the Semantic Web. He led the AHRC-funded STAR, STELLAR and SENESCHAL projects (Semantic Tools for Archaeological Resources), investigating semantic interoperability and the EPSRC funded FACET project, investigating thesaurus-based query expansion. He leads the Linking Archaeological Data Work Package for the ARIADNE FP7 Infrastructures Project. He is Editor of the *New Review of Hypermedia and Multimedia* since 1977. He is a reviewer for various journals and international conferences. He is a member of NKOS. He co-authored the JISC State of the Art Review on *Terminology Services and Technology* and the JISC *Terminology Registry Scoping Study*. He served on the ISO TC46/SC9/SC8 (and NISO) working group developing a new thesaurus standard (ISO 25964).

6. Issues and opportunities for classification data

Automatic Interpretation of Complex UDC Numbers: Towards Support for Library Systems

Attila Piros

PhD candidate, University of Debrecen, Hungary

Abstract: Analytico-synthetic and faceted classifications, such as Universal Decimal Classification (UDC) express content of documents with complex, pre-combined classification codes. Without classification authority control that would help manage and access structured notations, the use of UDC codes in searching and browsing is limited. Existing UDC parsing solutions are usually created for a particular database system or a specific task and are not widely applicable. The approach described in this paper provides a solution by which the analysis and interpretation of UDC notations would be stored into an intermediate format (in this case, in XML) by automatic means without any data or information loss. Due to its richness, the output file can be converted into different formats, such as standard mark-up and data exchange formats or simple lists of the recommended entry points of a UDC number. The program can also be used to create authority records containing complex UDC numbers which can be comprehensively analysed in order to be retrieved effectively. The Java program, as well as the corresponding schema definition it employs, is under continuous development. The current version of the interpreter software is now available online for testing purposes at the following web site: http://interpreter-eto.rhcloud.com. The future plan is to implement conversion methods for standard formats and to create standard online interfaces in order to make it possible to use the features of software as a service. This would result in the algorithm being able to be employed both in existing and future library systems to analyse UDC numbers without any significant programming effort.

Keywords: Universal Decimal Classification; UDC; notation parsing; decomposition; XML; UDC interpreter; parsing algorithm; automation

1. The representation of UDC numbers

In an analytico-synthetic and faceted classification, such as Universal Decimal Classification (UDC), the pre-combination of concepts creates a new concept, which not only inherits the semantics of its parts but acquire its own, new meaning. The same UDC number when used in different relationships may represent different subjects. There is a consensus in the literature that the integrity of data elements and UDC semantics depends on better notation management in the process of automation (Slavic & Isaac, 2009; Gödert, 2014; Slavic & Cordeiro, 2005).

Without authority control, handling complex notations is difficult. Tasks such as comparison of different numbers or matching complex numbers to each other automatically taking the relationships into account are hard to implement. This can also restrict subject browsing, which is one of the most important reasons for the use of classification in an information retrieval system (Slavic, 2006). Displaying either the artificial or the natural language terms in different forms may also be problematic without using an authority file as well as mapping the concepts to other knowledge organization systems.

The main advantage of authority control is that an authority record may contain not only the classification number and its metadata, but also additional semantic information. This may include broader, narrower and related classes, mappings to thesauri, subject heading lists or other classifications and access points using either the codes of the classification or keywords in natural languages (Slavic, Cordeiro & Riesthuis, 2007).

Although authority control is often considered to be a costly process, and perhaps the most expensive part of cataloguing, its costs can be reduced by automating parts of the process (cf. Tillet, 2001; O'Neill, Bennett & Kammerer, 2014). This is especially so in the case of UDC in which the correspondence between its hierarchically/syntactically expressive notation and schedule structure is extremely close (Broughton, 2006). For example, in recognizing and maintaining relationships between records if necessary (because of newly added records or changes to the rules) or in identifying the possible entry points or providing suggestions for descriptions and keywords in natural languages. However, human intervention will likely always remain necessary and cannot be eliminated absolutely.

Aiding the construction of authority records in different formats or converting them between formats automatically can also be useful in reducing the effects of the above problem.

1.1. A feasible representation of UDC notation

In the course of this research into improving the ways of storing UDC notations in order to enhance precision during information retrieval, it became clear that almost every UDC number can be represented with the same hierarchical structure. This is determined by the conceptual precedence of the operators and the definitions of common and special auxiliaries (the exceptions are mainly caused by breaking the rules concerning combining numbers) that describe their syntactic structure keeping all relevant information regarding its parts, the way they join to each other, their role in the compound, or perhaps their order if it is relevant.

Hierarchical and other relationships can be extracted automatically from this type of representation, making it useful to determine (and develop) methods to support authority control, as explained in the previous section.

A great advantage to the representation mentioned above is its independence from citation order. If two numbers differ only in the citation order of their parts, they have the same logical structure, which will result in the same representation. However, order can be added as an attribute of the parts of the notation to make a difference if the citation order has a semantic significance[1].

1.1.1. The syntactic structure of complex UDC numbers

The precedence order of the operations is as follows:

+	Coordination
:	Simple relation
::	Order-fixing
[ ]	Subgrouping
`	Synthesis (within special auxiliaries)

The operators above can join numbers or ranges of numbers in the schedules. The top three can also join subgroupings inside which the same hierarchy operates (although it cannot contain additional subgroupings). In addition to the connecting symbols above, there is also synthesis within special auxiliaries which make it possible to join numbers of a given part of a schedule (such as numbers for chemical compounds or political parties). It is also possible to use operators inside common auxiliaries; the rules depend on the type of auxiliary.

The concepts joined by operators can contain zero or one main table number (or a range of main table numbers) with zero or more (or a range of) special auxiliaries and zero or more common auxiliaries (which can also contain numbers, ranges, operands and special auxiliaries).

The special auxiliaries in UDC contain very different solutions in order to describe the most specific subject facets (such as properties, processes, operations, techniques, instruments) which have to be handled in different ways[2].

1.1.2. Using XML to describe the structure of the UDC numbers

A series of UDC numbers (simple and complex) can be represented and possibly stored in a database as a tree. As with every tree, this structure can be described with XML which has the following advantages:

- XML is a standard, widely used format to represent trees with improved and documented support in most programming languages,
- it is possible to establish a schema definition to determine the exact format to describe objects,
- using an intermediate format makes conversion possible to other formats,
- the schema definition can also be used to validate UDC numbers in order to find syntactical errors in them.

---

1 The question of citation order in UDC is discussed in more detail by Robinson (2003).

2 A detailed introduction and overview of facets presented in UDC special auxiliaries are discussed by Gnoli (2011)

This paper will discuss feasible ways of building a UDC-specific XML schema for describing the most detailed and complex UDC numbers (containing not only the common auxiliary signs and numbers, but also the different types of special auxiliaries).

The XML file generated based on the schema definition can be used to describe every possible form of UDC numbers which observe the rules of UDC, and due to its comprehensiveness can be converted into different formats automatically[3].

1.1.3. A feasible XML Schema Definition (XSD)

The intermediate XML uses its own namespace instead of standard namespaces such as Dublin Core, SKOS or UDC's own Master Reference File (UDC MRF) format. Its elements should be replaced with standard types while converting it to standard formats.

The complex types of the XSD (XML Schema Definition) describe the possible elements of UDC numbers: the numbers of the schedules, the auxiliary signs and the UDC number itself.

For example, the following complex type describes the special auxiliary numbers introduced with a hyphen:

```
<xsd:complexType name="special_auxiliary_number_hyphen">
  <xsd:complexContent>
    <xsd:restriction base="udc:special_auxiliary_number">
      <xsd:attribute name="number1"
type="udc:special_auxiliary_number_hyphen_string"
use="required"/>
      <xsd:attribute name="number2"
type="udc:special_auxiliary_number_hyphen_string"
use="optional"/>
    </xsd:restriction>
  </xsd:complexContent>
</xsd:complexType>
```

The following complex type describes the common auxiliaries of human ancestry, ethnic groups and nationality:

```
<xsd:complexType name="common_auxiliary_of_ethnics_number">
  <xsd:complexContent>
    <xsd:restriction
base="udc:common_auxiliary_number_abstract">
      <xsd:sequence>
        <xsd:element name="special_auxiliary"
type="udc:special_auxiliary_number" minOccurs="0"
maxOccurs="unbounded"/>
        <xsd:element name="alphabetical_specification" type=
"udc:alphabetical_specification_ordered" minOccurs="0"
maxOccurs="1"/>
```

3 The XML schema for UDC number descriptions is currently under development and is planned to be made available online under a Creative Commons license. The UDC number interpreter based on this schema is available at: http://interpreter-eto.rhcloud.com/.

```
          <xsd:element name="nonudc_notation"
type="udc:nonudc_notation" minOccurs="0" maxOccurs="1"/>
        </xsd:sequence>
        <xsd:attribute name="number1" type=
"udc:common_auxiliary_of_ethnics_number_string"
use="required"/>
        <xsd:attribute name="number2" type=
"udc:common_auxiliary_of_ethnics_number_string"
use="optional"/>
      </xsd:restriction>
    </xsd:complexContent>
</xsd:complexType>
```

An operator can be described by a complex type containing its possible operands:

```
<xsd:complexType name="main_table_relation">
  <xsd:annotation>
    <xsd:documentation xml:lang="en">
      URI: http://udcdata.info/000005
    </xsd:documentation>
  </xsd:annotation>
  <xsd:sequence>
    <xsd:choice minOccurs="2" maxOccurs="unbounded">
      <xsd:element name="main_table_number"
type="udc:main_table_number" minOccurs="1" maxOccurs="1"/>
      <xsd:element name="main_table_synthesis"
type="udc:main_table_synthesis" minOccurs="1" maxOccurs="1"/>
      <xsd:element name="main_table_subgrouping"
type="udc:main_table_subgrouping" minOccurs="1" maxOccurs="1"/>
      <xsd:element name="main_table_orderfixing"
type="udc:main_table_orderfixing" minOccurs="1" maxOccurs="1"/>
    </xsd:choice>
  </xsd:sequence>
</xsd:complexType>
```

The simple types of the XSD were introduced for validation purposes; the constraints defined for them contain regular expressions to describe the possible formats of the numbers in the different schedules.
For example, the following simple type was created to describe the special auxiliary numbers starting with a hyphen:

```
<xsd:simpleType name="special_auxiliary_number_hyphen_string">
  <xsd:restriction base="xsd:string">
    <xsd:pattern value="-\d(\d{0,1}|(\d{2}(\.[1-9]\d{2})*(\.[1-
9]\d{0,2})?))"/>
    <xsd:minLength value="2"/>
  </xsd:restriction>
</xsd:simpleType>
```

The following type was created for the numbers of common auxiliaries of ethnics:

```
<xsd:simpleType
name="common_auxiliary_of_ethnics_number_string">
  <xsd:restriction base="xsd:string">
    <xsd:pattern value="\(=\d(\d{0,1}|(\d{2}(\.[1-
9]\d{2})*(\.[1-9]\d{0,2})?))\)" />
```

```
    </xsd:restriction>
  </xsd:simpleType>
```

Each of the UDC concepts is described by a complex element. In accordance with the schema XML must contain at least one element to describe a UDC concept:

```
<xsd:element name="udc_concept" type="udc:udc_concept"/>
```

This element contains the other elements as can be seen in the hierarchy above. It also contains the notation of the number as an attribute and the descriptions of the concept in different languages as elements too.

2. The automatic interpretation of complex UDC numbers

Converting UDC numbers manually to a complex format such as that mentioned above is an unrealistic expectation; support to building these representations, as far as possible automatically, is a strong requirement. An additional advantage of this approach is that, in principle, the existing records could also be processed and converted.

Processing UDC numbers directly has the following advantages:

- Although the databases and the formats used in information retrieval systems vary, the UDC number itself is a stable point in all of them.
- In this way the system would not require the indexers and maintainers of the authority files to use special, system-related knowledge; consequently, they can concentrate on building the numbers taking maximum advantage of their skills and competencies related to the classification,
- Future research can be conducted based on the processing of UDC numbers so as to enhance the efficiency of searching and browsing for example by discovering the connections between complex concepts.

The parsing of complex UDC numbers is a topic which has been subject to thorough research and investigation since the 1960s.

The most comprehensive research of this issue was conducted by Gerhard Riesthuis (1998). He explained all questions regarding to parsing complex UDC numbers, in order to create algorithms to recognize their parts and make them retrievable by using even the definitions of these parts in natural languages (using the descriptions contained in UDC MRF). He suggested and explained a set of groups of algorithms in order to parse the numbers in more steps and also provided sample programs written in Pascal[4].

The combination of the algorithms published by Riesthuis can be extended in order to generate the XML representations of UDC. In the course of this research, however, a new algorithm was created which is better suited for the XML schema discussed earlier in Section 1.

4 The summary of the methods mentioned above was also reported in Riesthuis (1997; 1999).

2.1. The underlying principles of the interpreter

The proposed algorithm for UDC notation interpretation has to follow the syntax rules for UDC subject synthesis, as far as possible, with no loss of information. This specifically means the following:

- The algorithm must recognize those numbers and only those numbers which keep to the rules for synthesizing UDC numbers even if they appear very rare in the common practice of indexing or in a particular collection.
- The algorithm must retain all of the information stored in the number. Recognizing only some parts of the number is unsatisfactory, as is recognizing all of its parts but losing the information pertaining to their context and role.
- The parsing method must be fully syntactic as far as possible: processing the numbers must be based on the rules for the composition of concepts and can employ information regarding the meaning of the numbers only if it is unavoidable.
- The process must be fully automated: the program must be able to analyse numbers without requiring the user to act during the parsing process.

The basic requirement for this task is access to the UDC schedules and the online availability is an important consideration[5]. The decomposition of UDC notations for the purpose of information retrieval requires a decomposition program, UDC MRF data in a format compatible with this program and a middleware between the above and the information retrieval system (Slavic-Overfield, 2005). Any development in this area will require some kind of Web services to access and represent classification (Slavic, 2006).

With the evolution of the Internet and related infrastructure, the Software-as-a-Service (SaaS) model has been increasing significantly. Using SaaS delivery model would allow the UDC numbers to be analysed by a remote service and implement only a thin middleware to join its output to the client software. In this way the results could be used for the purposes of managing authority files as well as by systems employing other methods to access UDC numbers.

In order to exploit this possibility to the full, one should implement different interfaces to access the output of the algorithm in as many different formats as are necessary.

Taking into account the above requirements, Java was chosen as the programming language, due to its excellent support for related technologies.

2.2. The basics of how the interpreter works

The rules governing the usage of UDC determine a formal language over an alphabet of decimal digits, dots and the characters of UDC metalanguage symbols. The interpreter is an automata which recognizes this formal language.

---

5 The UDC editions used in this research are Hungarian UDC editions published in 1990 (Egyetemes Tizedes Osztályozás, 1990) and 2005 (Egyetemes Tizedes Osztályozás, 2005), the BSI UDC printed standard edition published in 2005 (UDC, 2005), English UDC Online (2013) and the UDC Summary (Multilingual Universal Decimal Classification Summary, 2011).

The input words are UDC numbers and the states of the automata describe the type and role of that part of the number to which the letter being processed belongs. While processing the number, the automata generates a tree which contains the parts of a number, based on the rules of precedence regarding auxiliary signs and joining auxiliary numbers as explained in the previous sections. It also contains some additional information which may be necessary during a search.

If the automata does not recognize the input word, then the given number is invalid or cannot be interpreted in the given UDC version. This means that, in principle, the language recognized by the automata specified by a year is just the UDC edition for that year.

The inputs of the algorithm are the UDC number and the year of the UDC edition which was used to build it; the output will be the XML representation of the number, or an error message which describes the problem if it cannot be interpreted in the given version.

Using the year is enough for the purposes of syntactical analysis, in so far as it takes the year of introduction of the changes in the rules into account. However, to identify the parts of the numbers and then join them to the MRF using a database ID is a more precise solution (Slavic & Isaac, 2009). Future plans should include the possibility to define these data as well.

The proposition is to construct an algorithm which is able to parse UDC numbers in a syntactic way as far as possible. This would mean that parsing two different numbers having the same structure would result in similar representations, differing only in the numbers themselves. It would also require every UDC number to be parsed without the need for identifying the numbers, based on the punctuation signs and rules only.

However, there are special auxiliaries and various indexing rules which result in complex numbers in which information regarding the exact location of their parts in the schedules determine the structures of the numbers and the access points to them. For example, apostrophes can be used to synthesize numbers in some places in the schedules (e.g., in classes 329 or 547). Recognizing the access points in the parallel division instruction "subdivide as" require information about source and target notation (Riesthuis, 1999).

The interpreter uses a loosely coupled module to make the decisions in the cases mentioned above. The module currently makes decisions employing hardcoded information. However, because of loose coupling it can be replaced with a module employing the MRF.

The interpreter is under continuous development; the algorithm has been improved depending on the current status of the research; standard interfaces and conversion methods have started to be worked out as well. A test version of the software (currently providing html outputs from the generated XMLs) is available on the following web page: http://interpreter-eto.rhcloud.com.

2.3. Examples of parsing UDC numbers

The first example demonstrates the special case of describing literary works:

```
<ns:udc_concept
  xmlns:ns="http://library.inf.unideb.edu/udc/xml"
  xmlns:xsi="http://www.w3.org/2001/XMLSchema-instance"
  udc_edition="2005"
  notation="821.111SHAK7ROM.03=112.2">
  <ns:description xml:lang="EN">
    Shakespeare: Romeo and Juliet (translated to German)
  </ns:description>
  <ns:main_table_number number1="821.111">
    <ns:special_auxiliary
xsi:type="ns:special_auxiliary_number_numerical"
      number1="7"/>
    <ns:special_auxiliary
xsi:type="ns:special_auxiliary_number_pointnought"
      number1=".03"/>
    <ns:alphabetical_specification order="1" text="SHAK"
standard=""/>
    <ns:alphabetical_specification order="2" text="ROM"
standard=""/>
    <ns:common_auxiliary_independent
      xsi:type="ns:common_auxiliary_of_language"   order="1">
      <ns:common_auxiliary_of_language_number
number1="=112.2"/>
    </ns:common_auxiliary_independent>
  </ns:main_table_number>
</ns:udc_concept>
```

The XML above was generated by the software introduced in the previous section.

The concept contains the notation itself, its descriptions (in different languages) and the year of the UDC edition used to build it. Its elements are a main table number and the auxiliaries joining it.

The interpreter is able to recognize not only the alphabetical additions for the name of the author and the title of the work, but also the special auxiliaries for "individual work" and "translation".

The following, more complex example[6] demonstrates the interpretation of extensions i.e. UDC number range (two numbers connected by /):

```
<ns:udc_concept
  xmlns:ns="http://library.inf.unideb.edu/udc/xml"
  xmlns:xsi="http://www.w3.org/2001/XMLSchema-instance"
  udc_edition="2005"
```

6 The example is taken from Riesthuis (1997).

```
  notation="323(47+57)1/.2:81(47+57)'01">
  <ns:description xml:lang="EN">
    Cytology. Diagnosis by methods adopted from of physics:
electrostatics. Cytopatology. Nutrion of infants.
Dissertations.
  </ns:description>
  <ns:main_table_relation>
    <ns:main_table_number number1="323.1" number2="323.2">
      <ns:common_auxiliary_independent
xsi:type="ns:common_auxiliary_of_place">
        <ns:common_auxiliary_of_geography_addition>
          <ns:common_auxiliary_of_geography_number
number1="(47)"/>
          <ns:common_auxiliary_of_geography_number
number1="(57)"/>
        </ns:common_auxiliary_of_geography_addition>
      </ns:common_auxiliary_independent>
    </ns:main_table_number>
    <ns:main_table_number number1="81">
      <ns:special_auxiliary
xsi:type="ns:special_auxiliary_number_apostrophe"
number1="'01"/>
      <ns:common_auxiliary_independent
xsi:type="ns:common_auxiliary_of_place">
        <ns:common_auxiliary_of_geography_addition>
          <ns:common_auxiliary_of_geography_number
number1="(47)"/>
          <ns:common_auxiliary_of_geography_number
number1="(57)"/>
        </ns:common_auxiliary_of_geography_addition>
      </ns:common_auxiliary_independent>
    </ns:main_table_number>
  </ns:main_table_relation>
</ns:udc_concept>
```

The example contains a subject expressed by the number range: 323.1/.2 - which is represented by its beginning and ending numbers. We can use the same method for the ranges either contained in the schedules or combined by the indexer; in this way a range can be retrieved by the range itself, or its elements. It is also possible to break it down into its elements using MRF[7]. The addition inside the geographical auxiliary must be kept in this case, because this combination is contained in the schedules and should be rendered retrievable by both the addition itself and its operands. This example also demonstrates that the interpreter is able to handle intercalation just like special auxiliaries following common auxiliaries.

The last example demonstrates the precedence order of the auxiliary signs:

```
<ns:udc_concept
  xmlns:ns="http://library.inf.unideb.edu/udc/xml"
  xmlns:xsi="http://www.w3.org/2001/XMLSchema-instance"
  udc_edition="2005"
  notation="061.1(100)::[54+66]">
```

7 The method of breaking down a range into its constituent numbers is discussed by Buxton (1992) and explained in detail by Riesthuis (1999).

```xml
  <ns:description xml:lang="EN">
    IUPAC - International Union of Pure and Applied Chemistry
  </ns:description>
  <ns:main_table_orderfixing>
    <ns:main_table_number number1="061.1" order="1">
      <ns:common_auxiliary_independent
xsi:type="ns:common_auxiliary_of_place">
        <ns:common_auxiliary_of_place_number number1="(100)"/>
      </ns:common_auxiliary_independent>
    </ns:main_table_number>
    <ns:main_table_subgrouping order="2">
      <ns:main_table_addition>
        <ns:main_table_number number1="54"/>
        <ns:main_table_number number1="66"/>
      </ns:main_table_addition>
    </ns:main_table_subgrouping>
  </ns:main_table_orderfixing>
</ns:udc_concept>
```

2.4. Recognizing mistakes by the indexer

The analysis of UDC numbers makes it possible to recognize mistakes made during indexing as well. Figure 1 illustrates a few examples of recognized typographical mistakes.

The parsing process failed because of an unexpected error.
There must be a point ('.') after every three digits!
796.332092.2

The parsing process failed because of an unexpected error.
The point ('.') stands in an invalid place.
796.332..092.2

The parsing process failed because of an unexpected error.
The character is invalid in this place.
796.332.092.2.097(100"92"

Figure 1: *Recognizing typographical mistakes*

Assigning an incorrect UDC edition may also result in an invalid number as illustrated in Figure 2.

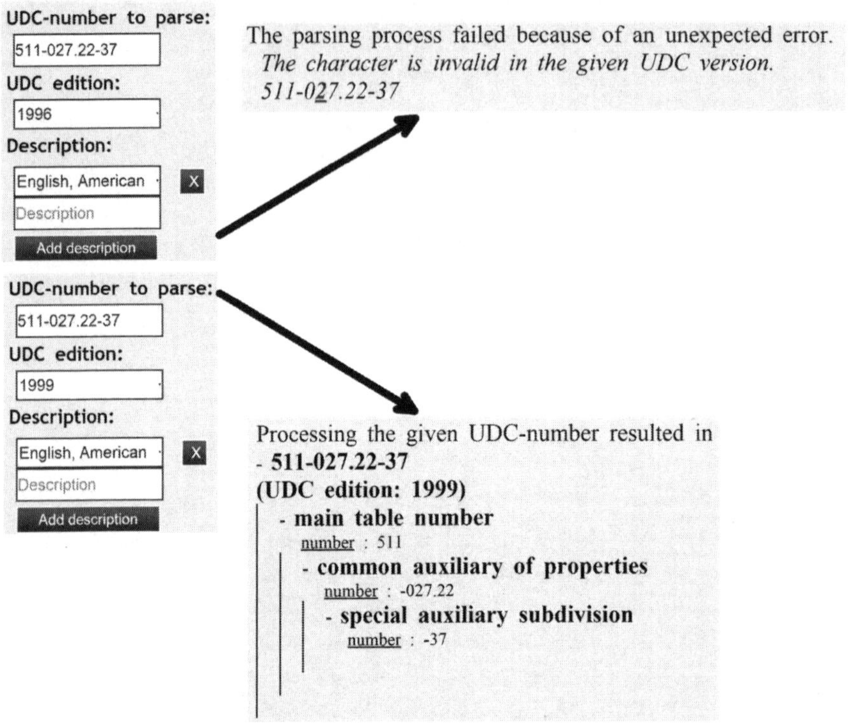

Figure 2: *Recognizing incorrect versions*

3. The conversion of the results

3.1. Conversion to MARC

MARC 21 Format for Authority Data (MARC 21 Format for Authority Data, 2000) defines field 080 for storing the UDC classification data and field 150 for topical term headings. For example:

150 ##$aHistory$vSchoolbook$y19th century$zBaltic states
080 ##$a94$x(474)$x"19"$x(075)$2BIP 0017-1 : 2005

The content of field 080 can be generated automatically from the XML representation of the number:

```
<ns:main_table_number number1="94">
  <ns:common_auxiliary_independent
xsi:type="ns:common_auxiliary_of_place">
    <ns:common_auxiliary_of_place_number number1="(474)"/>
  </ns:common_auxiliary_independent>
  <ns:common_auxiliary_independent
xsi:type="ns:common_auxiliary_of_time">
    <ns:common_auxiliary_of_time_number number1=""19""/>
  </ns:common_auxiliary_independent>
```

```
  <ns:common_auxiliary_independent
xsi:type="ns:common_auxiliary_of_form">
    <ns:common_auxiliary_of_form_number number1="(075)"/>
  </ns:common_auxiliary_independent>
</ns:main_table_number>
```

Field 150 has to be filled in using MRF data and verified by the person creating the record.

Classification formats provide more complex examples[8]. The following example presents the UDC number for the subject "Association and Rugby footballs" described using the MARC 21 Format for Classification Data (MARC 21 Format for Classification Data, 2000):

084 8#$audc$bUniversal Decimal Classification$dBIP 0017-1 : 2005$eeng
153 ##$a796.332$c796.333.4$e796.33$f796.333$hSports. Games. Physical exercises$hBall games$hBall games in which the ball is played with foot and hand$jAssociation and Rugby footballs
353 ##$a796.333.3$iRugby union football

The UDC numbers and their parts can be retrieved from the XML expression shown below. The determination of captions, hierarchical and see also relationships (in this case to the hidden element of the range) requires using MRF data and human interaction as well.

```
<ns:udc_concept
  xmlns:ns="http://library.inf.unideb.edu/udc/xml"
  udc_edition="2005"
  notation="796.332/796.333.4">
  <ns:description xml:lang="EN"/>
  <ns:main_table_number number1="796.332" number2="796.333.4"/>
</ns:udc_concept>
```

The final example is from the UNIMARC Classification Format (Concise UNIMARC Classification Format, 2000):

184 0#$audc$bUniversal Decimal Classification$dBS 1000M : 1993$eeng
250 ##$z $z m$kca78.071-056.45(=411.16)$hCreative and interpretative occupations$Musicians and their functions$hSpecial gifted$jJews
665 0#$a78.071$b-056.45$b(=411.16)

The XML representation of the same number is as follows:

```
<ns:main_table_number number1="78">
  <ns:special_auxiliary
xsi:type="ns:special_auxiliary_number_pointnought"
number1=".071"/>
  <ns:common_auxiliary_independent
xsi:type="ns:common_auxiliary_of_ethnics">
    <ns:common_auxiliary_of_ethnics_number
number1="(=411.16)"/>
  </ns:common_auxiliary_independent>
```

8 The application of MARC classification formats to UDC authority files is discussed by San Segundo (2009).

```
  <ns:common_auxiliary_dependent number1="-056.45"
xsi:type="ns:common_auxiliary_of_persons_number"/>
</ns:main_table_number>
```

The generation of the MARC record above can be similar to that of MARC 21.

3.2. Conversion to SKOS/XML

The following example is taken from the presentation by Slavic & Isaac (2009). The UDC number combination used in the SKOS example was 37:004 ("application of computers in education"). A SKOS/XML form of this number (using UDC Summary Linked Data) may be:

```
<rdf:RDF
  xmlns:rdf="http://www.w3.org/1999/02/22-rdf-syntax-ns#"
  xmlns:skos="http://www.w3.org/2004/02/skos/core#"
  <skos:Concept rdf:about="37:004">
    <skos:broader rdf:resource="http://udcdata.info/024974"/>
    <skos:broader rdf:resource="http://udcdata.info/013566"/>
</skos:Concept>
</rdf:RDF>
```

Broader relationships can be determined from the XML representation automatically. However, phase relationships which were also mentioned in the presentation cited above cannot be recognized automatically.

4. The test set

Online availability and the generation of XML output make it possible to compile an integrity test set, in order to ensure that the software always produces the expected output. The easiest way to achieve the above is to create a small application, which is able to send HTTP requests to the application containing the UDC numbers and compare the responses with previously saved XML files. Test cases usually need to contain valid UDC numbers if more than punctuation marks are required to determine the result of the process (as was mentioned in section 2.2), otherwise test cases should follow the syntax rules.

Compiling a test set as mentioned above helps not only to maintain the integrity of the existing parts of the software during further implementation, but to review the rules of UDC regarding building complex numbers and to facilitate a better comprehension of their meanings. Future plans also involve the release of a test set employed during the implementation.

5. Conclusion

Handling complex concepts is a significant issue which arises during the automation of a faceted, analytico-synthetic classification system.

Authority control provides a satisfactory solution to the issues and questions that have been raised. However, its effectiveness may be enhanced by employing automated methods to analyse numbers, discover their possible entry points, or represent them in different formats.

This paper provides explanations of the principles of representing complex UDC numbers in XML format and introduces a software interpreter made available online which is capable of interpreting UDC numbers in a given format. I hope that that the research described here will advance the application of UDC and the better use of its synthetic features.

Acknowledgements

I would like to express my appreciation to Dr. István Boda for his valuable and constructive suggestions during the planning and development of this research work and to extend my thanks to Jonathan Wild who has been of great help in writing this paper. I would also like to acknowledge the support provided by my family during my work.

References

Broughton, V. (2006). The need for a faceted classification as the basis of all methods of information retrieval. *Aslib proceedings*, 58 (1/2) pp. 49-72. Available at: http://polaris.gseis.ucla.edu/gleazer/260_readings/broughton.pdf.

Buxton, A. (1992). Computer Searching of UDC Numbers. *Encyclopedia of Library and Information Science*, 51 (14), pp. 132-151.

Concise UNIMARC Classification Format. (2000). Concise Edition. International Federation of Library Associations. Available at: http://www.ifla.org/archive/ubcim/p1996-1/concise.htm.

Egyetemes tizedes osztályozás. (1990). Rövidített kiadás. 1. kötet Táblázatok. FID Publ. No. 691. Budapest: OSZK-KMK.

Egyetemes tizedes osztályozás. (2005). 1. kötet Táblázatok 1-2. rész. UDC Publ. No. P057. Budapest: OSZK KI.

Gnoli, C. (2011). Facets in UDC: a review of current situation. *Extensions and Corrections to the UDC*, 33, pp. 19-36. Available at: http://arizona.openrepository.com/arizona/handle/10150/236511.

Gödert, W. (2014). Facets and typed relations as tools for reasoning processes in information retrieval. *The Computing Research Repository (CoRR)*, (abs/1409.0491). Available at: http://arxiv.org/abs/1409.0491

MARC 21 Format for authority data. (2000). 1999 edition. Library of Congress. Available at: http://www.loc.gov/marc/authority/.

MARC 21 Format for classification data. (2000). 2000 edition. Library of Congress. Available at: http://www.loc.gov/marc/classification/.

Multilingual Universal Decimal Classification Summary. (2011). The Hague: UDC Consortium. (UDCC Publication No. 088). Available at: http://www.udcc.org/udcsummary/php/index.php.

O'Neill, E. T.; Bennett, R.; Kammerer, K. (2014). Using authorities to improve subject searches. *Cataloging & Classification Quarterly*, 52 (1), pp. 6-19.

Principles of the Universal Decimal Classification (UDC) and rules for its revision and publication. (1983). FID 603. Budapest: OMIKK.

Riesthuis, G. J. A. (1997). Decomposition of complex UDC notations. *Extensions and Corrections to the UDC*, 19, pp. 13-19.

Riesthuis, G. J. A. (1998). Zoeken met woorden: hergebruik van onderwerpsontsluiting. [doctoral thesis] Amsterdam: Leerstoelgroep Boek-, Archief- en Informatieweten-schap.

Riesthuis, G. J. A. (1999). Searching with words: re-use of subject indexing. *Extensions & Corrections to the UDC*, 21, pp. 24-32.

Robinson, G. (2003). Citation order in UDC. *Extensions and Corrections to the UDC*, 25, pp. 19-27.

San Segundo, R. (2009). Using MARC format classification for UDC and mapping to other KOS systems for an enriched authority file. *Extensions and corrections to the UDC*, 31, pp. 285-291.

Slavic-Overfield, A. (2005). Classification management and use in a networked environment: the case of the Universal Decimal Classification. Doctoral thesis. London: University of London. Available at: http://discovery.ucl.ac.uk/1334914/.

Slavic, A.; Cordeiro, M. I. (2005). Sharing and re-use of classification systems: the need for a common data model. *Signum*, 37 (8), pp. 19-24. Available at: http://hdl.handle.net/10150/105132.

Slavic, A. (2006). Interface to classification some objectives and options. *Extensions and Corrections to the UDC*, 28, pp. 24-45. Available at: http://hdl.handle.net/10150/105459.

Slavic, A.; Cordeiro, M. I.; Riesthuis, G. (2007). Enhancement of UDC data for use and sharing in a networked environment. [Talk presented at The 31st Annual Conference of the German Classification Society on Data Analysis, Machine Learning, and Applications, March 7-9, 2007, Freiburg i. Br., Germany]. Available at: http://arizona.openrepository.com/arizona/handle/10150/106330.

Slavic, A.; Isaac, A. (2009). Identifying management issues in networked KOS: examples from classification schemes. NKOS 2009 workshop, ECDL conference. Corfu, Greece. Available at: https://at-web1.comp.glam.ac.uk/pages/research/hypermedia/nkos/nkos2009/presentations/slavic_isaac_NKOS2009_06.pdf.

Tillett, B. B. (2001). Authority control on the Web. In: *Proceedings of the Bicentennial Conference on Bibliographic Control for the new Millennium: confronting the challenges of networked resources and the Web*. Washington, DC: Library of Congress, Cataloging Distribution Service. Available at http://lcweb.loc.gov/catdir/bibcontrol/tillett_paper.html.

UDC. (2005). Universal Decimal Classification: standard edition: volume 1: systematic tables. London: British Standards Institution.

UDC. (2013). English UDC Online. The Hague: UDC Consortium. Available at: http://www.udc-hub.com/en/login.php.

ATTILA PIROS is a PhD candidate at the Doctoral School of Mathematics and Computer Science at the University of Debrecen. He holds master degree in Teaching Mathematics and Library and Information Sciences from the Faculty of Sciences, University of Debrecen. His doctoral research deals with analysis of the UDC notations and their utilisation in computerized information retrieval. He authored a number of research papers and has reported on his research at conferences. Attila has been working as a software developer and programmer since 2001 and currently works for a company based in the Netherlands on software solutions in market research.

Knowledge maps for libraries and archives - uses and use cases

Andrea Scharnhorst
eHumanities DANS/KNAW, The Hague, Netherlands

Richard P. Smiraglia
University of Wisconsin, Milwaukee (USA)

Christophe Guéret
eHumanities DANS/KNAW, The Hague, Netherlands

Alkim Almila Akdag Salah
eHumanities DANS/KNAW, The Hague, Netherlands

Abstract: At the last Digital Library Conference in London two workshops took place - both (in parallel) devoted to the use of visualization in presenting and navigating large collections. One was entitled "Search is Over!" and the other "Knowledge Maps and Information Retrieval". This anecdotal evidence stands for the growing and accelerating quest for visually enhanced interfaces to collections. Researchers from information visualization, computer human interaction, information retrieval, bibliometrics, digital humanities, art and network theory in parallel, often also in ignorance of each other, sometimes in interdisciplinary alliances are engaged in this quest. This paper reviews the current state-of-the-art, with special emphasis on the work of the COST Action TD1210 Knowescape. We discuss in more depth two examples of the use of visual analytics to create a fingerprint of an archive or a library, a data archive and a national library. We present examples from the micro-level of monitoring activities of users, over the meso-level to visualize features of bibliographic records, to macroscopes (a term coined by Katy Borner) into libraries and archives. We also discuss how different ways to perform visual analytics inform each other, how they are related to questions of data mining and statistical analysis, and which methods need to be combined or which communities need to collaborate. To illustrate some of these points we analysed Universal Decimal Classification (UDC) codes in bibliographic datasets of the National Library of Portugal. This is a potential still awaiting to be fully exploited in improving interfaces to subject access and management of classification data. It should be noted that UDC notation strings stored in bibliographic databases require specialist knowledge in both UDC and programming for any visualization tools to be applied. This UDC Seminar which is devoted to authority control is an opportunity to draw attention to the possibilities in visualization whose wider application depends on the readily structured, richer and more transparent subject metadata.

Keywords: knowledge maps; interfaces; library collections; data archives; visualization; visual analytics; statistical analysis

Invited talk, paper not submitted.
Presentation materials are available on the conference website: http://seminar.udcc.org/2015.

ANDREA SCHARNHORST is Head of research at Data Archiving and Networked Services (DANS) - an institute of the Royal Netherlands Academy of Arts and Sciences (KNAW). She is also scientific coordinator of the computational humanities programme at the e-humanities group of the KNAW. She has published about the transfer of concepts and methods at the interface between physics, information sciences, social sciences and humanities. Her work focuses on modelling and simulating the emergence of innovations (new modes of behaviour and learning, forms of communication, technologies or scientific ideas) in social systems.

RICHARD P. SMIRAGLIA is Professor, Knowledge Organization Research Group, School of Information Studies, at the University of Wisconsin, Milwaukee. He has defined the meaning of "a work" empirically and explored the implications of the phenomenon of instantiation among information objects. Recent work includes domain analytical studies of knowledge organization, the empirical analysis of social classification and epistemological analysis of the role of authorship in bibliographic tradition. An associate researcher of the e-Humanities Group of the Royal Netherlands Academy of Arts and Sciences (KNAW), he is a collaborating member of the Knowledge Space Lab effort to map the evolution of knowledge. He holds a PhD (1992) from the University of Chicago. He is editor-in-chief of the journal Knowledge Organization.

CHRISTOPHE GUÉRET is a postdoctoral researcher in Data Archiving and Networked Services (DANS) at the Dutch Royal Academy of Arts and Sciences (KNAW). Christophe holds a PhD in Computer Science from the Univeristy of Tours (France). His research interest is in the design of decentralised information systems and the study of their societal impact, in particular for less privileged parts of the world (see http://worldwidesemanticweb.wordpress.com/). Between 2007 and 2012, while at the Vrije Universiteit Amsterdam, he worked on the interplay between Computational Intelligence and the Semantic Web (project SOKS), the publication of linked data within the EU funded project LATC and several W3C activities. From 2012 he has been working on the publication of historical data as linked data within the CEDAR project.

ALKIM ALMILA AKDAG SALAH is researcher at the e-Humanities group of the Dutch Royal Academy of Arts and Sceinces (KNAW) and adjunct lecturer at Bogazici University in Istambul where she teaches courses on information visualization. Almila holds a PhD in Arts History from UCLA (USA) and bachelor and master degrees in Industrial Design and Art History from Istanbul Technical University. Her research interest is computational technologies in digital humanities such as social network analysis, image analysis, text analysis, visual analytics and computational analysis of artworks. She was a recipient of the VENI Netherlands Organization for Scientific Research (NWO)and worked as a researcher at the New Media Department of the University of Amsterdam and visiting lecturer at the Utrecht School of the Arts (HKU) and the University of Amsterdam.

A second life for authority records

Shenghui Wang
OCLC, Leiden, The Netherlands

Rob Koopman
OCLC, Leiden, The Netherlands

Abstract: Authority control is a standard practice in the library community that provides consistent, unique, and unambiguous reference to entities such as persons, places, concepts, etc. The ideal way of referring to authority records through unique identifiers is in line with the current linked data principle. When presenting a bibliographic record, the linked authority records are expanded with the authoritative information. This way, any update in the authority records will not affect the indexing of the bibliographic records. The structural information in the authority files can also be leveraged to expand the user's query to retrieve bibliographic records associated with all the variations, narrower terms or related terms. However, in many digital libraries, especially largescale aggregations such as WorldCat and Europeana, name strings are often used instead of authority record identifiers. This is also partly due to the lack of global authority records that are valid across countries and cultural heritage domains. But even when there are global authority systems, they are not applied at scale. For example, in WorldCat, only 15% of the records have DDC and 3% have UDC codes; less than 40% of the records have one or more topical terms catalogued in the 650 MARC field, many of which are too general (such as "sports" or "literature") to be useful for retrieving bibliographic records. Therefore, when a user query is based on a Dewey code, the results usually have high precision but the recall is much lower than it should be; and, a search on a general topical term returns millions of hits without being even complete. All these practices make it difficult to leverage the key benefits of authority files. This is also true for authority files that have been transformed into linked data and enriched with mapping information. There are practical reasons for using name strings instead of identifiers. One is the indexing and query response. The future infrastructure design should take the performance into account while embracing the benefit of linking instead of copying, without introducing extra complexity to users. Notwithstanding all the restrictions, we argue that largescale aggregations also bring new opportunities for better exploiting the benefits of authority records. It is possible to use machine learning techniques to automatically link bibliographic records to authority records based on the manual input of cataloguers. Text mining and visualization techniques can offer a contextual view of authority records, which in return can be used to retrieve missing or mis-catalogued records. In this talk, we will describe such opportunities in more detail.

Keywords: WorldCat; bibliographic records; visualization; digital libraries; largescale aggregation; Dewey Decimal Classification; DDC; library linked data

Invited talk, paper not submitted.
Presentation materials are available on the conference website: http://seminar.udcc.org/2015.

SHENGHUI WANG is a Research Scientist at the OCLC EMEA office in Leiden, The Netherlands. Her current research activities include text and data mining as well as linked data investigations. She holds a PhD. in Computer Science from the University of Manchester. Shenghui has been conducting research in the broad field of Artificial Intelligence with interests in cognitive modelling, knowledge representation and reasoning, natural language semantics and machine learning. Before joining OCLC Research in 2012, Shenghui was a researcher at the Free University of Amsterdam and Wageningen University, exploring Semantic Web and language technologies to improve the semantic interoperability in the domain of cultural heritage and agrifood research.

ROB KOOPMAN is an architect at OCLC innovation and working with OCLC EMEA research. After receiving a BSc (Physics, computer science) at the University of Amsterdam he joined PICA library automation in 1981. For Pica he was team leader and architect within the CBS (central catalogue) group and responsible for the design of the PSI (PICA Searching & Indexing) search engine, the catalogue client and also responsible for the architecture of the CBS cataloguing system. After PICA was taken over by OCLC he became a member of global architecture and later innovation. He is currently working on name disambiguation and data visualization.

Posters – Short papers

Subject information and multilingualism in European bibliographic datasets: experiences with Universal Decimal Classification

Nuno Freire
The European Library, The Hague, The Netherlands

Valentine Charles
Europeana Foundation, The Hague, The Netherlands

Antoine Isaac
Europeana Foundation, The Hague, The Netherlands

Abstract: The Europeana Foundation is a non-profit governmental organization that collects, enriches, innovates and promotes cultural heritage data in Europe. Europeana also oversees The European Library's dataset that has been provided by the National and Research Libraries of Europe. This poster focuses mainly on The European Library's dataset as it is the richest in terms of library's classification systems and subject headings within Europeana. The European Library's dataset is very diverse in the languages it contains and also very rich in classification and subject indexing data. One of the key activities undertaken by The European Library is to support the discoverability of library resources through the cross-language linking of classification and subject indexing data. The Universal Decimal Classification scheme, or UDC, is one of the most widely used classification schemes for all fields of knowledge. UDC is used in libraries, bibliographic, documentation and information services in over 130 countries around the world and is published in over 40 languages. A small subset of UDC has already been published as linked data - the UDC Summary, and the complete UDC scheme will be available shortly. The mechanisms for sharing semantic data nowadays underlie most of the key data distribution channels to users of library data. Examples include the research e-infrastructures and cultural heritage networks in Europe, which construct and maintain their data models under the principles of linked data. Through these mechanisms, the data aggregated by The European Library can reach end-users enriched with multilingual classification and subject indexing information, when linked to the UDC scheme. With this objective in mind, The European Library is currently working on exploring linking possibilities between its aggregated bibliographic dataset, UDC and other ontologies available as linked data (particularly with subject heading systems). UDC has the central attention of The European Library due to its great potential for providing multilingual enrichment of subject data within its bibliographic dataset. This is due to the high-level of language independence of UDC codes, its availability in over 40 languages and by being published as open data under a license that enables its reuse. This poster presents the data linking strategy and methods used at the European Library related to UDC, as well as the experimental results currently available and how they will be distributed across the Europeana network, the research e-infrastructures and publishers. A second experimental use of UDC is also presented in the application area of data mining subject information. An experiment was conducted, in which the potential to use the UDC classification within The European Library Dataset was investigated for its potential to help in locating bibliographic resources, from all Europe and in any language, that could fulfil the very specific information needs of humanities researchers, working within a virtual research environment and addressing specific topics related to the First World War. This work explored co-occurrences of UDC classification codes and subject data within First World War collections for later application in general collections, such as the library catalogues, in locating additional bibliographic resources for researchers. The poster also presents future work, at Europeana and The European Library, towards the establishment of a metadata enrichment service based on UDC RDF data to be available through the Europeana Cloud, addressing the multilingual enrichment of cultural heritage metadata from all domains represented in the Europeana Network.

Keywords: The European Library; Europeana; Universal Decimal Classification; UDC; multilingual subject access; linked data; cross-language searching; controlled vocabulary; cultural heritage; classification; subject indexing

Paper not submitted.
Presentation materials are available on the conference website: http://seminar.udcc.org/2015.

NUNO FREIRE holds a PhD in Informatics and Computer Engineering and is currently the Chief Data Officer at The European Library. During his entire career, he has been involved in data oriented projects in the area of digital libraries. He has been also a member of the programme committees of major international conferences in the area: JCDL (Joint Conference on Digital Libraries) and TPDL (Theory and Practice in Digital Libraries). His areas of interest include information systems, information retrieval, information extraction, data quality and knowledge representation, particularly in their application to digital libraries and bibliographic data. In his recent work, at The European Library, he conducted the governance and utilisation of the aggregated data from European national bibliographies and special library collections via data integration, processing, analysis and data mining.

VALENTINE CHARLES is a Data Research & Development coordinator for Europeana. She is responsible for advising, sharing knowledge and communicating Europeana's scientific coordination and R&D activities. She is also coordinating the further development and adoption of the Europeana Data Model (http://pro.europeana.eu/edm-documentation) (EDM). Valentine is also Co-Chair of the Dublin Core Metadata Initiative (DCMI) Technical Board and Community Specification Committee.

ANTOINE ISAAC is R&D Manager at Europeana. He holds a PhD in Computer Science from University Paris-Sorbonne, where he started to work on applying Semantic Web and Linked Data techniques for cultural heritage (then at the French National Audiovisual Institute, INA). He has contributed to various national and European research projects and has been involved in a number of W3C groups, notably for SKOS and Library Linked Data. He is co-author of the French book "Le Web sémantique en bibliothèque". He is also a guest researcher at the Web & Media group in the Free University Amsterdam.

Enhancing subject authority control at the UK Data Archive: a pilot study using UDC

Suzanne Barbalet
UK Data Archive, University of Essex, Wivenhoe, United Kingdom

Abstract: The UK Data Archive is an internationally acknowledged centre of expertise in data curation and holds the largest collection of digital data in the social sciences and humanities in the United Kingdom. To some degree, the application of subject authority control measures within the Archive has been influenced by the Data Documentation Initiative (DDI). The Archive adopts this standard for describing social science data and contributes to its development. The DDI makes provision not only for the maintenance of a controlled vocabulary of subject categories for classifying the data at data collection level, but also for a controlled vocabulary of keywords to index all topics included in the data at question/variable level. The keyword controlled vocabulary is the Archive's in-house thesaurus HASSET (Humanities and Social Sciences Electronic Thesaurus). What the DDI does not do is provide guidance on the relationships between these separate controlled vocabularies. Here a faceted classification scheme may well provide the answer. A pilot study of an application of the Universal Decimal Classification (UDC) scheme demonstrated how successfully the scheme might ensure quick, controlled and accurate subject access to data collections for its community of data owners, producers, funders and users.

Keywords: Data Documentation Initiative; DDI; HASSET; digital data; classification; Universal Decimal Classification; UDC; thesaurus; controlled vocabulary; subject categories; big data

The preservation and management of digital resources was at first a technical problem for information managers. It was not long before it was also recognized as a knowledge organization problem. The preservation of fragile film, audio and magnetic tape pushed libraries, museums, galleries and archives into programs of digitization which exposed the shortcomings, and especially the cost, of traditional methods of knowledge organization. The arrival of e-documents added insult to injury.

Data archives have been somewhat immune to these particular revolutionary effects of digitization, since a large proportion of the social science data tended to be digitalised at source. Now, however, they need to "future-proof" their knowledge organization systems in preparation for the impact "big data", and the new methodologies that follow in its wake, will have on the way societies collect and store data in the future. UDC has withstood the test of time and proved itself a survivor in an ever changing research environment. This poster presents a pilot study to investigate its suitability as a flexible knowledge organization tool to strengthen the Archive's resources in preparation for future metadata challenges.

1. DDI: the standard for data archive metadata creation

The Data Documentation Initiative (DDI) is an international metadata standard for social science data adopted and contributed to by the UK Data Archive. DDI catalogue records contain mandatory and optional metadata elements which describe the data collection (study), the data file and the variables (Corti et al., 2014: 46-49). Subject and keyword fields are optional in DDI. The current version that the Archive adopts is DDI-Codebook (DDI-C) 2.5 for our collection-level records on our resource discovery system portal Discover[1] and DDI-Lifecycle (DDI-L) version 3.5 for our CLOSER project[2]. DDI-L is more flexible and easier to implement than its predecessors and is the data equivalent of cataloguing-in-publication for books.

Data collections (studies) are not "complete bibliographic items" in the sense described and discussed by Lancaster (2003: 20). They are usually produced in the generic science data life cycle as illustrated in Figure 1.

Figure 1: *The generic science data life cycle (from CEOS Data Life Cycle Models and Concepts, 2011: 25)*

Social science data archives preserve data for a variety of research purposes but their primary research function is preservation for re-use by secondary data analysts. While "study" titles describe the overall content in a similar fashion to book or document titles, the *content* of "studies" is not as easy to index as conventional information objects. The relationship between the dependent variable and the independent variable, that is what is to be measured and its indicators, is not quickly nor easily determined when indexing "studies"; yet capturing this information in sufficient detail is critical for successful information retrieval.

The DDI-L literature has adapted and produced many views of the data life cycle to illustrate the work and requirements of secure data archiving and preservation; one of these will suffice to illustrate the challenge and complexity of data indexing: Figure 2 shows a life cycle diagram with processes of knowledge transfer (KT) according to Humphrey (2006).

1 UK Data Service is available at: http://www.ukdataservice.ac.uk/.

2 The Cohort and Longitudinal Studies Enhancement Resources (CLOSER) is available at: http://ukdataservice.ac.uk/about-us/projects/closer/details.aspx.

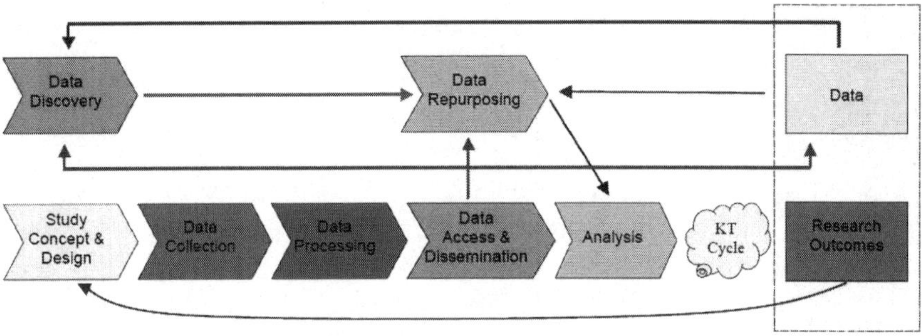

Figure 2: *Knowledge transfer (KT) cycle*
(from CEOS Data Life Cycle Models and Concepts, 2011: 28)

This DDI life cycle model illustrates the complexity of preserving and providing access to data at various stages of its life. Not all data will go through every stage in every case but the critical point for adequate metadata creation is that data collections are, in many cases, "heterogeneous, unstructured or in a variety of different formats" (Corrado & Moulaison, 2014: 180-181); yet, for some research purposes, data collections do need to be treated as a "bibliographic item". Users may require access to either variable and study information as a package ("study") or as variable information from the codebooks and questionnaire schedules depending both on what stage of the data life cycle their project begins and what their research interest is. Some researchers, for instance, are specialists on a particular data series and attend conferences and workshops on these specific data series.

It is not only the fact that data collections are unstructured that make the creation of keyword metadata difficult. Issues of social science measurement also come into play. To ensure the validity and reliability of the survey methodology the concept attached to survey questions and scales, for example, will not always be apparent. Scales may not be described in the documentation nor easily identified in the questionnaire. Even if identified the variables themselves may not appear relevant to the "study" topic until the research design is described in the resulting publications. For example, the range of indicators of ethnicity the UK Office for National Statistics recommends are "Country of birth", "Nationality", "Language spoken at home", "Skin colour", "National/geographical origin", and "Religion". "Studies", on the other hand, are generally quite simple to classify. For example the titles "Family Resources Survey"; "Crime Survey for England and Wales"; or "Health Survey for England" take little time to allocate a classification code.

It is not the purpose here to pursue these issues in any depth. It is sufficient to say that the separate DDI fields of <subject> and <keyword> are complementary and function well to provide quick access to important and relevant "studies", on the one hand, while directing users to key questions and

Variables, on the other, via the Humanities and Social Sciences Electronic Thesaurus (HASSET) index terms.

2. Enhancing Subject Authority Control

The UK Data Archive manages two thesauri: the monolingual HASSET and the multilingual European Language Social Science Thesaurus (ELSST). With respect to DDI development, the Archive shares an interest in the part metadata standards play with its colleagues from the Consortium of European Social Science Data Archives (CESSDA) and the two thesauri are now being developed applying a single management system to ensure standardisation and quality control. These thesauri are post-coordinated products; that is, concepts and terms are added to index UK Data Service[3] data, as well as international virtual data collections. ELSST is similarly developed to facilitate cross-border data retrieval for CESSDA member institutions.

In addition, CESSDA members, including the UK Data Archive, share a pre-coordinated controlled vocabulary of subject categories (SC) and in recent years the labels have begun to be aligned with HASSET and ELSST core terms. To map the products together in their present form, however, raises issues of interoperability that Stella Dextre-Clarke (2009) addressed when introducing the ISO standard 25964. It looks feasible, she argued, to map *from* a pre-coordinated or synthesised class but to map *to* a pre-coordinated class looks more problematic (Dextre-Clarke, 2009).

Two options present themselves:

- Abandon the subject controlled vocabulary and use the thesaurus HASSET in its place as the sole subject retrieval tool;
- Amend the existing SC controlled vocabulary and use UDC to manage not only the content of each category but also the category labels themselves as they change over time.

To date, a pre-coordinated list of subject categories has served Archive users very well. Subjects evolved in line with current research topics funded by the Office for National Statistics or the UK's major economic and social research funder the Economic and Social Research Council (ESRC). Over the past five to six years, however, the range of subjects our "studies" cover has increased. We provided data support for The Rural Economy and Land Use Programme (RELU) and the new Administrative Data Research Network (ADRN). Consequently, we are investigating the feasibility of classifying our data collections so that the existing subject category list can be more chameleon-like in its role of presenting and organizing information in a manner that is ever sensitive to user

3 The UK Data Service is supported by the UK Data Archive to provide a unified point of access to the extensive range of high quality social and economic data, including UK census data, government funded surveys, longitudinal "studies", international macrodata, qualitative data and business microdata.

needs while still allocating "studies" to as many categories as best describe the research topic. Categories then could be expanded or re-labelled, or subdivided, without losing links to the relevant data collections.

3. Applying the classification code

Series and virtual[4] "studies" were excluded from this pilot study sample, as they are easier to classify, so we selected non-series "studies" for classification in order to gain the best estimate of the cost and time the task would take. We organized "studies" for processing by the main subject category they had been allocated in our current system, as illustrated in the worksheet header in Figure 3. Thus, in the main, efficiencies were made in the range of classification numbers required. The entries in the Health Worksheet demonstrate this efficiency with most of the classification codes falling within the range of numbers in UDC main class 6 (Applied sciences. Medicine. Technology).

It was decided to make the codes as specific as possible until we knew how many auxiliary table extensions would be required. In the worksheet example of Figure 3 we can see on the first line of the data the extended number for the health of old people in Telford (an old UDC number allocated before we trialled UDC Online). What is particularly useful about the use of UDC for this project is that we can build numbers to include extra subjects and use either a colon or a plus sign to indicate the relationship between subjects. When required we can retrieve these secondary subjects and allocate the data set accordingly to the extra or new category while still retaining all the required information in the full classification number attached to the study.

We included "form" auxiliaries to explore the use of the notation to link data to resources that may be useful for training and outreach purposes, e.g., case studies, illustrations/photos or bibliographical references. We also added auxiliaries of "place" and "time". The latter, we thought, would be useful for easy identification of our historical data.

We created guides for the most popular UDC numbers and found that by the end of fourteen weeks a part-time employee, working 15 hours a week, completed the classification of 4,289 "studies" (Table 1). Now, with access to UDC Online, the results are even more promising.

---

4 These are data collections curated by other data archives. Permission has been given for our users to access them.

Row Labels	Health services and medical care - Health	Accidents and injuries - Health	Childbearing, family planning and abortion - Health	Drug abuse, alcohol and smoking - Health	General - Health	Health services and medical care - Health	Mental health - Health	Nutrition - Health	Physical fitness and exercise - Health	Specific diseases and medical conditions - Health	Grand Total	
0362 - Survey of Old People in Telford, 1973 (ESDSA)					1	1					2	613 - 0 53 . 9 () 410 . 182
0392 - Trouble with Feet, 1966 (ESDSA)						1				1	2	611 . 986
0393 - Life Before Death, 1969 (ESDSA)						1					1	612 . 0 13
0394 - Patients and Their Doctors, 1964 (ESDSA)						1					1	614 . 255
0396 - Study of Family Size and Family Spacing, 1973 (ESDSA)			1								1	316 . 362 . 4
0399 - Problems of Hospital Communication : An Experimental Study, 1964 (ESDSA)			1			1					2	612 . 21 : 316 . 454 . 5
0401 - Survey of Abortion Patients for the Committee on the Working of the Abortion Act, 1972 (ESDSA)			1								1	173 . 4
0402 - Birth Control Services, 1970 (ESDSA)			1			1					2	613 . 888 . 15
0423 - Survey of Abortion Patients for the Committee on the Working of the Abortion Act, 1972 (ESDSA)			1								1	173 . 4
0424 - Survey of Abortion Patients for the Committee on the Working of the Abortion Act, 1972 (ESDSA)			1								1	173 . 4
0525 - Agency Nurses: a National Survey of Attitudes, Comments and Statistics, 1975 (ESDSA)						1					1	614 . 253 . 5 :614 . 39
0526 - Family Planning in Trinidad : the Problem of Discontinuation, 1975 (ESDSA)			1								1	316 . 362 . 4 () 729 . 87
0704 - Patients and Their Doctors, 1964 (ESDSA)						1					1	614 . 255
0705 - Patients and Their Doctors, 1964 (ESDSA)						1					1	614 . 255
0706 - Patients and Their Doctors, 1964 (ESDSA)						1					1	614 . 255
0707 - Patients and Their Doctors, 1964 (ESDSA)						1					1	614 . 255
0708 - Patients and Their Doctors, 1964 (ESDSA)						1					1	614 . 255
0709 - Patients and Their Doctors, 1964 (ESDSA)						1					1	614 . 255
0710 - Patients and Their Doctors, 1964 (ESDSA)						1					1	614 . 255
0718 - Southampton Health Centre Study, 1973 (ESDSA)						1					1	614 . 212 () 410 . 121
0746 - Community Health Council Members, 1974-1975 (ESDSA)						1					1	316 . 354 . 4 + 364
0835 - Patients and Their Doctors, 1964 (ESDSA)						1					1	614 . 255
0836 - Patients and Their Doctors, 1964 (ESDSA)						1					1	614 . 255
0909 - Birth Control Services, 1970 (ESDSA)			1			1					2	613 . 888 . 15
0910 - Birth Control Services, 1970 (ESDSA)			1			1					2	613 . 888 . 15
0911 - Birth Control Services, 1970 (ESDSA)			1			1					2	613 . 888 . 15
0912 - Birth Control Services, 1970 (ESDSA)			1			1					2	613 . 888 . 15
0954 - Cohort Legitimate Fertility Rates : Canada, 1882-1954 (HDS)			1								1	314 . 116 () 71
0955 - Period Legitimate Fertility Rates : Canada, 1926-1969 (HDS)			1								1	314 . 116 () 71
0961 - School Child Chest Health Survey, 1966 (ESDSA)					1						1	613 . 955 : 351 777 . 6
0962 - Patients and Their Doctors in 1977 (ESDSA)						1					1	614 . 255
0965 - Measurement of Psychological Disturbance in Asian Immigrants, 1975-1976 (ESDSA)					1		1				2	314 . 151 . 3 : 616 . 89 ()
1005 - Transport Services in General Practice, 1968-1969 (ESDSA)						1					1	614 . 255
1086 - Socio-Psychiatric Survey on Distribution and Aetiology of Psychiatric Disorder, 1975-1976 (ESDSA)							1				1	616 . 89 : 616 . 334 . 55
1169 - Life Stress, Symptomatology and First Year Examination Performance in Overseas Students, 1976-1977 (ESDSA)					1		1				2	37 . 0 91 . 27 : 364 . 62
1171 - Studies Using the Nottingham Health Index, 1976-1977 (ESDSA)					1	1					2	614 . 39 - 0 56 () 410
1263 - Experiences of Childbearing, 1975-1976 : the Dignity of Labour? (ESDSA)			1								1	618 . 4
1266 - Psychological Adjustment of Immigrants, 1977 (ESDSA)					1		1				2	314 . 151 . 3 : 616 . 89
1278 - Changes in the Structure of General Practice: the Patient's Viewpoint, 1977 (ESDSA)						1					1	614 . 255
1317 - Young People's Knowledge of Sex and Birth Control, 1974-1975 (ESDSA)			1								1	613 . 88
1387 - Child Development Research Unit Longitudinal Study (ESDSA)			1								1	159 . 992
1410 - Aircraft Noise and Prevalence of Psychiatric Disorders, 1977 (ESDSA)							1				1	331 . 432 . 6 : 616 . 89

Figure 3: *Worksheet example of HEALTH and sub-categories*

The combination of UDC numbers using a colon allowed us to capture multiple subject dimensions of the study and arrange them in an appropriate order. Reviewing the content of one existing subject category via the code label allows for the identification of significant sub-categories which could form a new category in their own right. Within the subject category of "Society and Culture" we can see that "Leisure, Tourism and Sport" is emerging as a significant new category (Figure 4).

Table 1: *Rate of classification of Non-Series "Studies" per week*

SUBJECT FIELD	NUMBER OF STUDIES	NUMBER OF WEEKS
Society and Culture	928	2
Agriculture	182	0.5
Health	473	2
Law, Crime and Legal Systems	131	1
Economics	868	2
Politics	638	2
Education	380	2
Employment and Labour	502	2
Housing	187	0.5

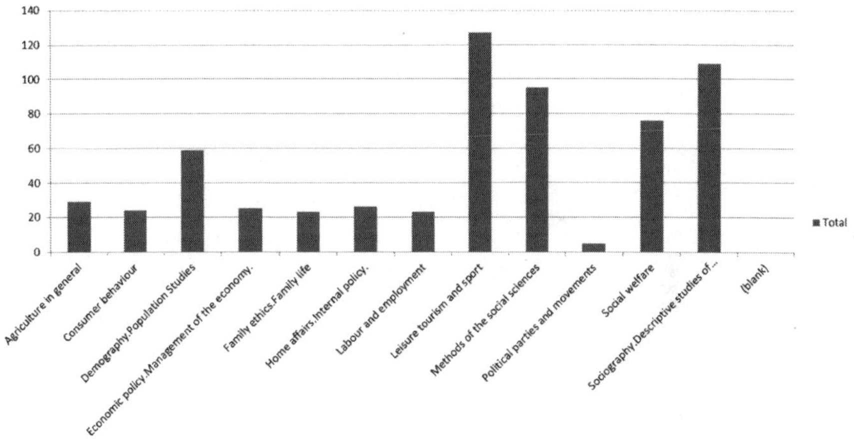

Figure 4: *UDC notations distribution for the subject category "Society and Culture"*

In addition, this granularity of classification, described above, will help us monitor key areas for collection building more accurately, as well as maintain an overview of the distribution of topics across the collection as a whole.

4. The future: linking thesauri and subject categories

User studies on the success of subject retrieval are difficult to model. As Garshol (2004) notes:

> ... the ocean of information rises and leaves what we seek ever more deeply buried in what we do not seek (Garshol, 2004:378)

UK Data Archive user studies have shown that subject faceted searches are preferred by users when presented with the choice of a HASSET search or a subject category search. However, it appears to be the general finding of thesaurus developers that users across the board, not just HASSET users, find thesauri complex and often time consuming to engage. Thus we were interested to learn that the visualization tool (Figure 5) we had added to the new HASSET interface had been received with some acclaim when the British Chapter of the International Society for Knowledge Organization (ISKO) met to debate the topic of the place of the traditional thesaurus in modern information retrieval (See Dextre-Clarke, 2015). It was referred to as an innovation and possibly an example of the way forward for thesauri, making them more attractive and usable for clients.

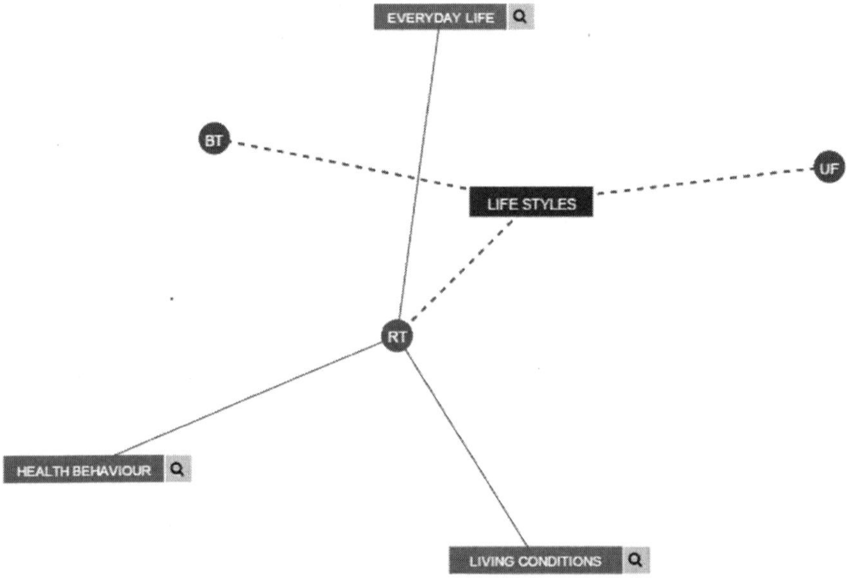

Figure 5: *HASSET Visual Graph for the concept "lifestyles"*

Garshol (2004) also made the argument that topic maps go beyond traditional information retrieval solutions and provide a framework that can be extended to improve retrieval options.

This insight has presented and given weight to the option to link the subject and thesauri controlled vocabularies via the visualization pages. Linking our subject discovery tool with HASSET could at one and the same time preserve the integrity of the DDI <subject> and <keyword> fields, enabling them to perform the separate information retrieval tasks they were designed to perform, as well as providing an attractive "advanced" resource discovery tool for our users.

For most repositories, with large collections developed over many decades, consideration of a project such as this would not be feasible. However, while data collections are complex to index the "studies" themselves tend to be easy to classify. Thus, it is not an insurmountable task to consider formal classification of the data collection.

We have little doubt that social scientists already conducting research using "big data" and "administrative data" will refine research methodologies that will impact on the way data archives curate data in the future. The results of this pilot project suggest that the arrangement of formally classified "studies" under standard, yet current, subject categories, will allow us the flexibility of post co-ordination while at the same time our users will be presented with an interface that is simple, relevant and familiar.

Acknowledgements

My thanks go to my colleagues Anne Etheridge, Lucy Johnson, Lorna Balkan, Alexandra Pop, Sharon Bolton and Herve L'Hours for their contributions.

References

CEOS Data Life Cycle Models and Concepts. (2011). Version 1. [s.l.]: Committee on Earth Observation Satellites (CEOS). (CEOS.WGISS.DSIG.TN01). Available at: http://ceos.org/document_management/Working_Groups/WGISS/Documents/WGISS_DSIG-Data-Lifecycle-Models-and-Concepts-v8_Sep2011.docx.

Corrado, E. M.; Moulaison, H. L. (2014). Digital preservation for libraries, archives and museums. Lanham, MD: Rowman & Littlefield.

Corti, L. et al. (2014). Managing and sharing research data: a guide to good practice. Los Angeles: Sage.

Dextre-Clarke, S. (2009). Providing for interoperability between thesauri and classification schemes in ISO 25964. Presentation at the International UDC Seminar "Classification at a Crossroads: multiple directions to usability", The Hague, 29-30 October 2009. Available at: http://www.udcc.org/seminar2009/presentations/dextreclarke_UDCSeminar2009.pdf.

Dextre-Clarke, S. (2015). Thesaurus debate needs to move on. *ISKO UK: A Blog Space of the British Chapter of ISKO.* 27 February 2015. Available at: http://iskouk.blogspot.co.uk/2015/02/thesaurus-debate-needs-to-move-on.html.

Garshol, L. M. (2004). Metadata? Thesauri? Taxonomies? Topic maps! Making sense of it all. *Journal of information Science*, 30 (4), pp. 378-391.

Humphrey, C. (2006). E-Science and the life cycle of research. Alberta: University of Alberta. Available at: http://datalib.library.ualberta.ca/~humphrey/lifecycle-science060308.doc.

Lancaster, F. W. (2003). Indexing and abstracting in theory and practice. 3rd ed. Champaign, IL: University of Illinois.

SUZANNE BARBALET is responsible for maintaining metadata standards and controlled vocabularies in resource discovery systems at the UK Data Archive. She has day to day responsibility for the thesaurus HASSET. She is a social science librarian and holds a BA (Hons) from the Australian National University, majoring in social science research methods. She has managed data collection for a number of academic social science surveys, including *Rights in Australia, National Household Sample, 1991-1992* and the *Longitudinal Study of the Elderly*, Social Psychiatry Research Unit, Australian National University. She was Sociology Editor for the research gateway *Intute: Social Sciences*.

Towards the creation of integrated authority files in the domain of science and technology: an Italian use case

Elena Cardillo
Institute of Informatics and Telematics, National Research Council, Rende, Italy

Iryna Solodovnik
Institute of Informatics and Telematics, National Research Council, Rende, Italy

Maria Taverniti
Institute of Informatics and Telematics, National Research Council, Rende, Italy

Abstract: Over the years, different organizations have developed and shared a number of authority files with normalized personal names (e.g., Virtual International Authority File - VIAF), inviting others to use these sources as a "common language" and contributing to improved interoperability among resources/systems. Nevertheless, numerous data providers continue to create and to take advantage of locally developed authority lists mined from the resources managed in local repositories and not aligned with external trustworthy sources. These authority lists often remain locked in local databases inhibiting sharing, re-use and interoperability of their data. This poster aims to present a use case on the creation of integrated and dynamic local authority files referring to the personal names of important Italian scientists and academics to be used within a federate Digital Library about Science and Technology. Terminology extraction techniques have been applied to a corpus of 400 documents in the National Centre of Electronic Calculation's archive. This resulted in an authority list of 700 personal names that was further aligned with VIAF and other authorities, such as Library of Congress Classification, via a manual mapping process, thus ensuring its interoperability and retrieval of bibliographic data and topics for each name. Future work will include the creation of CNUCE subject headings based on the list of keywords extracted from the CNUCE corpus and mapping to the Nuovo Soggettario and to LCSH.

Keywords: name authority files; science and technology; University National Centre of Electronic Calculation; CNUCE; VIAF; linked data

1. Introduction

Using shared application profiles such as controlled vocabularies and authorities is fundamental for the efficient knowledge organization and description of bibliographic resources. They provide trustworthy access points to bibliographic information resources driven by authority control which facilitates controlled access points for each entry (e.g., personal and corporate names, subjects etc.). This enables semantic interoperability in bibliographic databases and digital repositories. In addition, different national and international organizations create, maintain and openly share their Knowledge Organization Systems (KOSs) such as subject heading systems, classifications, thesauri, etc. There is an open invitation for these resources to be used which will contribute to high-accuracy retrieval, interoperability and enhanced controlled access points to 'common knowledge'.

Nevertheless, many organizations express the need to create their own (local) authority lists (ALs) and authority files (AFs) for niche knowledge areas which are not completely covered by existing KOSs. Following this perspective, the objective of our project is the creation of a local name AF that integrates ALs in the domain of Science and Technology for their application in the CNR S&TDL project[1], where, together with other KOSs, they will be used as a classification schema organizing information resources at a general level. In our poster presentation we deal only with ALs for persons and organizations (of relevant interest) extracted from a text corpus belonging to the University National Centre of Electronic Calculation (CNUCE), a CNR institute that in the 1970s and 1980s started the spread of Computer Science and the Internet in Italy (Montani, 2009). These ALs provide a control for name variants and name disambiguation, as well as more detailed access to and better retrieval of CNUCE documents in the S&TDL.

2. Background

There are many examples of KOS, various kinds of controlled vocabularies and name authorities which are used for document description and content indexing (e.g., Library of Congress Subject Headings LCSH[2] and LC/NAF, Bibliothèque National de France Authorities[3], VIAF[4], Integrated Authority File - GND[5]). They represent formalized and semantically consistent authorised data which are the foundation of authority control and enhanced resource discovery (Authority control: definition and international experience, 2004; Harper & Tillett, 2007; Hickey, 2009). Many controlled vocabularies and authorities are published as Linked Open Data (LOD)[6] (Isaac et al., 2011; Subirats-Coll, 2014) and shared through open registries (e.g., BARTOC.org[7], CKAN (Comprehensive Knowledge Archive Network) DataHub[8]). This enables their alignment and linking as is often suggested in the controlled vocabulary standards and Semantic Web development literature (ISO 25964-2: 2013; Vatant & Dunsire, 2011; Dunsire et al., 2012). To support vocabulary enrichment, linking, publishing and management,

---

1 Science & Technology Digital Library. Available at: http://stdl.cnr.it/en/.

2 Library of Congress Subject Headings - LC Linked Data Service. Available at: http://id.loc.gov/authorities/subjects.html.

3 Bibliothèque nationale de France: Autorités BnF. Available at: http://www.bnf.fr/fr/professionnels/autorites_bnf/s.autorite_bnf_presentation_statistiques.html

4 VIAF: The Virtual International Authority File. Available at: https://viaf.org/.

5 Deutsche Nationalbibliothek - Integrated Authority File (GND). Available at: http://www.dnb.de/EN/gnd.

6 Library Linked Data Incubator Group Final Report. W3C Incubator Group Report 25 October 201. Available at: http://www.w3.org/2005/Incubator/lld/XGR-lld-20111025/.

7 BARTOC.org: BAsel Register of Thesauri, Ontologies & Classifications. Available at: http://www.bartoc.org/.

8 Datahub. Available at: http://datahub.io/about.

a wide range of tools have already been developed such as EFG Authority File Manager[9], VocBench[10] and Silk[11].

Besides all the advantages that can be achieved in data and information integration through the use of widely-endorsed trustworthy AFs published as LOD (Agenjo, Hernández & Viedma, 2011), in many cases data providers need to create and use locally developed ALs and integrated authority data (mined from the resources managed in their repositories) to represent local names and subject headings. This is the case, for instance, with the BIBFLOW project[12] and NLM Authority Records[13]. Local ALs and AFs are often locked in local databases/systems. In order that they do not remain of limited use and do not proliferate the use of unverified headings and data provided in its default uncontrolled form, it is of great importance to enable searching against similar entities in existing external authorized sources (OCLC, 2012). This also helps in preventing duplicate records but, most of all, it helps unlocking ALs/AFs from local databases through their publication and sharing as LOD sources and/or by establishing reciprocal links (cross-references) between local ALs/AFs and other widely-endorsed authority data published on the Web.

3. Method

In order to create integrated local ALs for personal names and for organizations useful for indexing and retrieving CNUCE related documents, the following phases were executed:

1. CNUCE corpus compilation;
2. Term extraction and named entity recognition;
3. Manual review of the extracted terms;
4. Enrichment of the CNUCE ALs with proper metadata;
5. CNUCE ALs integration with VIAF.

3.1. CNUCE corpus compilation

In the first phase of the study, more than 3,000 pages from a total of 400 CNUCE related documents were collected and digitized (pdf files). These documents were mainly technical reports, constituent acts and memoranda. Documents were then described with the open-source platform xDams 2.0[14], used within the S&TDL-CNR project. In order to allow their automatic

---

9 The European Film Gateway (EFG) Authority File Manager. Available at: http://labs.europeana.eu/apps/EFG-authority-manager/.

10 Agricultural Information Management Standards (AIMS): VocBench. Available at: http://aims.fao.org/vest-registry/tools/vocbench-0.

11 Silk: The Linked Data Integration Framework. Available at: http://silk-framework.com/.

12 BIBFLOW: Personal and Corporate Name Authority Record Creation. Available at: http://www.lib.ucdavis.edu/bibflow/personal-and-corporate-name-authority-record-creation/.

13 U.S. National Library of Medicine: NLM Authority Records Accessible in LocatorPlus. Available at: http://www.nlm.nih.gov/tsd/cataloging/nlmauthrecsfile/nlmauthrec.html#3limit.

14 xDams <http://xdams.org> is a multimedia and document management platform based on EAD, ISAD and ISAAR standards.

processing, documents were further converted into plain text files and then normalized.

3.2. Term extraction and named entity recognition

The CNUCE corpus was processed by using the computational linguistic platform Text2Knowledge (T2K)[15] to allow the automatic extraction of the relevant terms, their indexing and the recognition of Named Entities to be exploited as an access key to documents and/or as subject headings. T2K has been set in terms of linguistic patterns according to the domain of application. This process led to the creation of a glossary (1,250 relevant terms), including term frequency and a list of terms associated with the corresponding named entities (more than 1,400 names categorised as persons, organizations or locations). The main goal of extracting personal names from the analysed corpus was to create a reliable list of authors which would help in resolving identification problems against extremely varied and uncertain forms of names. This represented a solid starting point for the extraction of related biographical, bibliographical and historical cross-reference information.

3.3. Manual review of the extracted terms

The output files from the previous phase underwent a cleaning and normalization process which removed a high percentage of errors and generic terms produced by T2K. This reduced the terms of the two lists respectively to 915 keywords and 805 names. Subsequently, a manual review was performed on a sample of documents selected from the CNUCE corpus in order to identify additional keywords and names, considered important for the document description and not recognized by T2K. After review, the glossary of keywords (to be used for creating a subject headings classification) was improved to a total of 1,110 terms, while the lists for persons and organizations reached a total of 700 and 400 names respectively.

3.4. Enrichment of the CNUCE ALs with proper metadata

In order to be suitable for the description/indexing of CNUCE documents in the S&TDL, ALs persons and organizations were enriched with proper metadata for each name, specifically: name variants, personal data, affiliation, institutional history, role and activity for the former; name variants, location and date of establishment for the latter. This allows for easy compilation of authority records during archival description of the documents. When these data could not be extracted from the CNUCE corpus, they were extracted from different sources on

15 Italian Natural Language Processing Lab - T2K (Text-To-Knowledge). Available at: http://www.italianlp.it/demo/t2k-text-to-knowledge/.

the web (e.g. Wikipedia, Dizionario Biografico Treccani[16] and, when existing, from personal webpages) and assigned to each name on the lists.

3.5. Mapping and integration with VIAF

This last phase was performed to integrate our local ALs Person and Organization with the standardised and integrated authority data in VIAF, in order also to link each name in our list with corresponding bibliographical information. In particular, for each personal name in our lists we attributed a unique persistent URI. Thereafter, we looked for the corresponding VIAF record and if found we manually assigned (according to a 'value-based co-occurrence mapping' method) a VIAF ID to that record in our local AL database. Regarding Organization names, we firstly linked them with the corresponding webpage (in most cases in fact they have a proper URI) and then integrated with VIAF Corporate Names as described for personal names.

4. Results and conclusions

Personal names extracted from the CNUCE corpus revealed, as expected, the presence of different forms of names for the same persons (e.g., Biorgi prof. Giuseppe, Giuseppe Biorgi, Prof. Biorgi, G. Biorgi, etc.). Therefore, significant effort was needed in order to review and match different variants of the same name. Moreover, due to Italian legislation, the investigated CNUCE documents became publically available only a few years ago. This inevitably resulted in: a shortage of historical-literary studies, the absence of large reference works providing extended knowledge about the extracted personal names and insufficient coverage of these names by external AFs. In fact, as shown in Table 1, the percentage of mappings to VIAF found for personal names is about 60%, while for Organizations names it is even less, 27.5%, which means 48.18% only, considering the two lists together.

Table 1: *Statistical results*

	Terms extracted	Terms after review	Mappings to VIAF	Data from Wikipedia	Data from other resources
AL_Persons	237	700	420	280	438
AL_Organizations	295	400	110	205	195
Total	532	1,100	530	485	633

It is worth mentioning that many persons extracted from CNUCE documents and included in our ALs produced only grey literature and many others

16 Treccani. Dizionario Biografico. Available at: http://www.treccani.it/biografie/.

are/were technologists, managers, or administrative staff that did not produce any publication at all. This justifies the limited number of mappings to VIAF.

Benefits derived from the creation of integrated ALs for CNUCE are: (i) the possibility to reuse a consolidated classification, identification and discoverability of people and connected topics; (ii) the possibility to view name records as established by other nations thanks to the links to VIAF, thus making the authorities truly international and facilitating research across languages through interrelated identifiers anywhere in the world.

The described resources have already been used for the indexing of CNUCE documents that are in the process of being ingested within the CNR S&TDL Digital Library, easing the access to data related to CNUCE within the platform. We have also started to create a CNUCE subject headings list based on the list of keywords extracted by T2K (Section 3.2.) and mapping it to the Nuovo Soggettario[17] and to LCSH.

Finally, to make our local data visible, shareable and reusable on the web, we are in the process of formalizing the CNUCE ALs in RDF and publishing them as LOD in a data hub (e.g. CKAN DataHub). This will also allow for the improvement of the mapping methodology by performing semi-automatic/automatic mappings between LODs.

Acknowledgements

This work has been supported by the S&TDL CNR Project, funded by the Agency for Digital Italy (AgID).

References

Agenjo, X.; Hernández, F.; Viedma, A. (2011). Data aggregation and dissemination of authority records through Linked Open Data. In: Proceedings of IFLA 2011. Available at: http://conference.ifla.org/past-wlic/2011/80-agenjo-en.pdf.

Authority control: definition and international experience: Part II: Authority Control for Subjects. (2004). Edited by A. G. Taylor; B. B. Tillett. *Cataloging & Classification Quarterly*, 39 (1-2). Available at: http://www.catalogingandclassificationquarterly.com/ccq39nr1-2.html.

Dunsire, G. et al. (2012). Linked data vocabulary management: infrastructure support, data Integration, and interoperability. *Information Standards Quarterly*, 24 (2/3), pp. 4-13.

Harper, C.; Tillett, B. (2007). Library of Congress controlled vocabularies and their application to the Semantic Web. *Cataloging & Classification Quarterly* 43 (3-4), pp. 47-68. Available at: https://scholarsbank.uoregon.edu/jspui/bitstream/1794/3269/1/ccq_sem_web.pdf.

17 Biblioteca nazionale centrale di Firenze. Nuovo soggettario. Available at: http://thes.bncf.firenze.sbn.it/index_eng.html.

Hickey, T. B. (2009). The Virtual International Authority File: expanding the concept of universal bibliographic control. *NextSpace:* 13, pp. 18-19. Available at: https://www.oclc.org/publications/nextspace/issues/issue013.en.html.

Isaac, A. et al. (2011). Library Linked Data Incubator Group: datasets, value vocabularies, and metadata element sets. W3C Incubator Group Report 25 October 2011. Available at: http://www.w3.org/2005/Incubator/lld/XGR-lld-vocabdataset-20111025/.

ISO 25964-2:2013 Information and Documentation - Thesauri and interoperability with other vocabularies: Part 2, Interoperability with other vocabularies. Available at: http://www.iso.org/iso/catalogue_detail.htm?csnumber=53658.

Montani, C. (2009). Three institutes one soul. *Focus.it*, 4 (15), p. 11.

OCLC - Online Computer Library Center. (2012). Authorities: create name authority records. OCLC Connexion Client Guides. Available at: https://www.oclc.org/content/dam/support/connexion/documentation/client/authorities/create/createauth.pdf.

Subirats-Coll, I. (2014). Seven things you should know about linked data. COAR Repository Observatory, (2). Available at: http://eprints.rclis.org/21139/.

Vatant, B.; Dunsire, G. (2011). Use case vocabulary merging. W3C. Available at: http://www.w3.org/2005/Incubator/lld/wiki/Use_Case_Vocabulary_Merging.

ELENA CARDILLO is researcher at the Institute of Informatics and Telematics of CNR of Rende (IIT-UOS CNR). She holds a PhD in Information and Communication Technologies, specialization "Data and Knowledge Management", from the University of Trento in conjunction with the Fondazione Bruno Kessler (Trento). She worked for three years as researcher in the field of knowledge acquisition, formalization and integration in healthcare at the e-Health research units at the Fondazione Bruno Kessler. In 2010 she was research fellow at the Lister Hill Center for Biomedical Communication, at the National Library of Medicine (NLM – NIH) in Bethesda, USA. Her research interests are focused on knowledge management and representation; terminology integration, classification systems, end-user terminologies, metadata models and on Semantic Web technologies. She has been involved in national and international projects related to data and knowledge management and semantic interoperability and collaborates with several national and international private and public institutions.

IRYNA SOLODOVNIK holds a PhD in Philosophy of Communication (Scientific area Archiving, Library and Librarianship) from the University of Calabria. Her PhD Internship at the University of Vienna focused on research into the conceptual frameworks underpinning Digital Object lifecycle management. She currently works as a research fellow at the Institute of Informatics and Telematics of CNR of Rende (IIT-UOS CNR), where she has been involved in the analysis and development of metadata models, open access institutional repositories, digital library, linked open data and controlled vocabularies. She is a member of the COAR interest group "Controlled Vocabularies for Repository Assets" and a member of the editorial board of the *Journal of the Sciences of Information*.

MARIA TAVERNITI is a technology specialist at the Institute of Informatics and Telematics of CNR of Rende (IIT-UOS CNR), where she is primarily involved in document management activities for digital libraries. From 2009 to 2013 she was visiting professor of Cataloguing and Classification at the University of Salerno. Since 2009, she has been collaborating with the Labdoc (Department of Linguistics of University of Calabria) as research assistant for activities of training and research concerning indexing and classification of archival digital records in general and on the use of automated procedures for digital records appraisal and selection. She also collaborates with the Department of Linguistics at the University of Calabria as educational trainer for the course of Information Science and Documentation. Her research interest is in knowledge and document management.

The Basel Register of Thesauri, Ontologies & Classifications (BARTOC)

Andreas Ledl
University Library of Basel, Switzerland

Abstract: The Basel Register of Thesauri, Ontologies & Classifications (BARTOC) is a bibliographic database of knowledge organization systems, developed by the University Library of Basel, Switzerland. It is the largest database of its kind, multilingual both in content and features and it is still growing. It currently includes more than 1,500 vocabularies in 85 languages from different domains and areas of knowledge. The system is based on the bibliographic tradition, collects metadata and summary descriptions of controlled and structured vocabularies and then applies novel methods, tools and infrastructure to provide an advanced and user-friendly view of its content. BARTOC features a faceted, responsive web design search interface in 20 languages. Data are freely available in the public domain and are connected into a linked open data infrastructure with database dump and SPARQL endpoint. Each record is geo-referenced, so that a special "GeoSearch" function can be offered in addition to basic and advanced searches. What distinguishes BARTOC from other services such as Linked Open Vocabularies (LOV), VEST Directory, BioPortal, etc., is its inclusiveness with respect to vocabulary types (thesauri, ontologies, classifications, glossaries, controlled vocabularies, taxonomies), subject areas, publication formats and accessibility.

Keywords: knowledge organization systems; controlled vocabularies, KOS; KOS metadata; registry; terminology registry; bibliographic database; ontology; classification; thesaurus; linked data; linked open data;

1. Introduction

"Knowledge Organization Systems" (KOS) are generally understood to mean "all types of schemes for organizing information and promoting knowledge management" (Hodge, 2000: 3). This definition encompasses thesauri, ontologies, classifications, taxonomies, glossaries and many more kinds of controlled and structured vocabularies. The Basel Register of Thesauri, Ontologies & Classifications (BARTOC, http://www.bartoc.org/) is a bibliographic database that tries to assemble information about as many KOSs as possible in one convenient place. This effort has a long tradition in library and information science. In the 1970s and 1980s, (to name a few), the following publications marked initial milestones: The *Bibliographie des thesauri et index par matières parus depuis 1960* by Marie-Thérèse Laureilhe; the *International Classification and Indexing Bibliography* (covering a period from 1950-1982) by Ingetraut Dahlberg, the founding president of the International Society of Knowledge Organization (ISKO); the *Tesauros, bibliografia* (covering a period from 1970-1982) by Suly Cambraia Alves et al. and the *Thesaurus Guide* by the Office for Official Publications of the European Communities. Since the beginning of the Internet these attempts continued online by *Thesauri im WWW*[1], the *Thésauro-annuaire*[2], *Knowledge for All*[3], the *TemaTres Vocabulary Server*[4], the *TaxoBank Terminology Registry*[5], the *Taxonomy Warehouse*[6], the *VEST Directory*[7], the *BioPortal*[8], *Ontobee*[9] and *The Open Biological and Biomedical Ontologies*[10]. While these other applications are either presented as link lists or focus on specific KOS types (e.g., ontologies), fields (e.g., agriculture) or software, BARTOC provides an elaborate search interface for all types of KOS from any discipline. At first glance there seem to be large similarities to *Linked Open Vocabularies (LOV)*[11], an "observatory focused on providing an inventory of and analytical metadata about, property-and-class vocabularies used in linked data". Its "openness" allows LOV to let users search for "terms and their interconnections" (Baker, Vandenbussche & Vatant, 2013: 660). BARTOC, on the other hand, deals with vocabulary metadata only, so it can also list "closed" vocabularies - access to which is limited by copyright – as well as vocabularies that are not available online (i.e., which exist in print form only). Clearly, there is overlap and complementarity between the data and services of BARTOC and LOV, so that there are already comprehensive talks about future cooperation.

2. BARTOC's features

BARTOC was launched by the University Library of Basel in November 2013. It is based on the open source content management system Drupal and uses so called *modules* like Entity API, Facet API, Fields, Geofield Map, Internationalization, OpenLayers, Search API, Views etc. to provide the following features:

- BARTOC currently contains more than 1,500 indexed KOS in 85 languages
- BARTOC provides a multilingual search interface in 20 European languages
- BARTOC provides abstracts in the original language (when available).
- BARTOC provides multilingual abstracts from DBpedia via linked open data (when available)
- BARTOC interface design is adapted for handheld and mobile devices
- Metadata are enriched with Dewey Decimal Classification (DDC) numbers down to the third level and subject headings from EuroVoc (European multilingual thesaurus)
- The "DDC Σ" pie chart shows the distribution of vocabularies by subject

---

1 *Thesauri im WWW* is available at: http://www.fbi.fh-koeln.de/institut/labor/bir/thesauri_new/thesauri.htm.

2 *Thésauro-annuaire* is available at: http://www.tard-bourrichon.fr/documents/THESAURUS online/tab/Thesauro-annuaire.html.

3 *Knowledge for All* is available at: http://www.k4all.ca/thesauri.

4 *TemaTres Vocabulary Server* is available at: http://www.vocabularyserver.com/vocabularies/.

5 *TaxoBank Terminology Registry* is available at: http://www.taxobank.org/terminologies.

6 *Taxonomy Warehouse* is available at: http://www.taxonomywarehouse.com/.

7 *VEST Directory* is available at: http://aims.fao.org/vest-registry.

8 *BioPortal* is available at: http://bioportal.bioontology.org/.

9 *Ontobee* is available at: http://www.ontobee.org/.

10 *The Open Biological and Biomedical Ontologies* is available at: http://www.obofoundry.org/.

11 *Linked Open Vocabularies* (LOV) is available at: http://lov.okfn.org/dataset/lov/.

- Search results can be refined intuitively by facets (Topic, DDC, Language, Type, Format, Access)
- In addition to a basic search (with a multilingual autocomplete function) and an advanced search, data can be investigated via a world map (Tab "GeoSearch")
- Users can vote for certain KOS (Tab "Top-rated content"), so that statements can be made about their quality and/or dissemination
- Information about recently added vocabularies is prominently displayed on the interface (Tab "Recent content")

Since its introduction in 2013, BARTOC has had a total of 190,000 visits and 1,500,000 page views (as of July 2015).

3. Semantic Web / Linked Open Data

BARTOC's data is made available under the Public Domain Dedication and License (PDDL) v1.0, which allows the user to "freely share, modify and use this work for any purpose and without any restrictions"[12]. The complete node references link to EuroVoc, ISO639-2 Languages (Library of Congress), VIAF and Wikipedia and more links are being planned, for example to WorldCat or Dewey Web Services. There are mappings to Dublin Core (DC), Schema.org, Friend of a Friend (FOAF) and Semantically-Interlinked Online Communities (SIOC). Each metadata set can be displayed in RDFa (Resource Description Framework in Attributes) "out of the box" by adding ".rdf" to the node URI. The metadata of all vocabularies included in BARTOC can easily be downloaded in XML, CSV, DOC, TXT, XLS and JSON (Tab "Download"). With the help of the SPARQL Views module, BARTOC imports multilingual abstracts from DBpedia[13]. Finally, a SPARQL endpoint with an ARC2 triple store is provided. Nevertheless, there is still a lot of conceptual work to be done. First of all, the RDF module in Drupal 7 core "works in some cases", but "in many cases it outputs unreliable data" (Clarke, 2013). A system upgrade to Drupal 8 may be necessary, once the final release is available. Second, there is no aligned schema/ontology used to describe the KOS in BARTOC at the moment, like for example the Data Catalog Vocabulary (DCAT)[14] or BIBFRAME Vocabulary[15], or, for KOS in particular, NKOS AP[16] or the taxonomy proposed by Souza, Tudhope & Almeida (2012). Third, in light of the cooperation with LOV, a decision has to be taken on including formal (or linked data / Semantic Web) ontologies, e.g., in OWL, together with less formal KOS. This can raise confusion in less technically savvy people, as the two kinds of artefacts are for different usages and with LOV, BioPortal, Ontobee etc., there are already very good inventories for highly formalized structures.

---

12 ODC *Public Domain Dedication and Licence* (PDDL) is available at: http://opendatacommons.org/licenses/pddl/1.0/.

13 *DBpedia* is available at: http://wiki.dbpedia.org/.

14 W3C *Data Catalog Vocabulary* (DCAT) is available at: http://www.w3.org/TR/vocab-dcat/.

15 *BIBFRAME Vocabulary* is available at: http://bibframe.org/vocab/.

16 DCMI *NKOS AP Elements* is available at: http://wiki.dublincore.org/index.php/NKOS_AP_Elements.

4. Conclusion

BARTOC attempts to depict the substantial benefits and many functions KOS can have as outlined by Soergel (2015: 8-11). As a service for the international library and information science scene, it is especially intended for the community working on knowledge organization systems. For the purpose of sharing or merging of classifications (even with other knowledge structures) across the linked data environment, which is the emphasis of the UDC Seminar 2015, BARTOC can hopefully be used as a supportive and rich instrument to identify potential candidates and generally look at classifications from a global perspective.

References

Alves, S. C.; Medeiros, M. B. B.; Bastos, S. (1983). *Tesauros, bibliografia 1970-1982 = Thesauri, bibliography 1970-1982*. Brasilia: Conselho Nacional de Desenvolvimento Científico e Tecnológico; Instituto Brasileiro de Informaçao em Ciéncia e Tecnologia.

Baker, T.; Vandenbussche, P.-Y.; Vatant, B. (2013). Requirements for vocabulary preservation and governance. *Library Hi Tech*, 31 (4), pp. 657-668. Available at: http://dx.doi.org/10.1108/LHT-03-2013-0027.

Clarke, L. (2013). *Why Drupal 8 should drop RDFa (and microdata) in favor of JSON*. Available at: http://lin-clark.com/blog/2013/12/08/drop-rdfa-drupal-8/.

Dahlberg, I. (1982). *International classification and indexing bibliography, ICIB. 1: Classification systems and thesauri, 1950-1982*. Frankfurt a. M.: INDEKS Verlag.

Hodge, G. (2000). *Systems of knowledge organization for digital libraries: beyond traditional authority files*. Washington, DC: The Digital Library Federation. Available at: http://www.clir.org/pubs/reports/pub91.

Laureilhe, M.-T. (1975). *Bibliographie des thesauri et index par matières parus depuis 1960*. Paris: Bibliothèque nationale.

Office for Official Publications of the European Communities. (1993). *Thesaurus guide: analytical directory of selected vocabularies for information retrieval, 1992*. Luxembourg: Office for Official Publications of the European Communities. Available at: http://bookshop.europa.eu/de/thesaurus-guide-pbCDNA14006/.

Soergel, D. (2015). *Knowledge organization systems. Overview*. Available at: http://www.dsoergel.com/UBLIS571DS-08.2a-1Reading4SoergelKOSOverview.pdf.

Souza, R. R.; Tudhope, D.; Almeida, M. B. (2012). Towards a taxonomy of KOS: Dimensions for classifying Knowledge Organization Systems. *Knowledge organization*, 39 (3), pp. 179-192. Available at: http://mba.eci.ufmg.br/downloads/Souza_Tudhope_Almeida_-_KOS_Taxonomy.Submitted.pdf.

ANDREAS LEDL is subject librarian for psychology, philosophy and educational science at the University Library of Basel. He holds a graduate degree in educational science from University of Regensburg, a master degree in library and information science from Humboldt University of Berlin and a PhD from University of Flensburg. He finished his librarianship training at the University and Research Library Erfurt/Gotha. His research interests include information literacy, subject indexing, open data, open access, the Semantic Web and knowledge organization. In recent years, he has focused on developing bibliographical databases / search interfaces with the content management system Drupal. He is the initiator, technical head and manager of the Basel Register of Thesauri, Ontologies & Classifications (BARTOC). Andreas is co-founder and co-editor of the open access publication *027.7 Journal for Library Culture* (http://www.0277.ch).

Experience with UDC updates: the Slovenian perspective

Darija Rozman
The National and University Library, Ljubljana, Slovenia

Abstract: Since the beginning of the nineties a significant part of the Universal Decimal Classification (UDC) scheme has been revised and updated. Every major change in the standard classification scheme causes difficulties which are even more prominent in systems without authority control. In Slovenia, most bibliographic records in the Cooperative Online Bibliographic System and Services (COBISS) contain UDC numbers. Since 1996, a standarised set of the UDC scheme, called "UDC summary", has been implemented as an authority list of UDC notations for Slovenian libraries. Currently, the UDC summary list contains 1,051 UDC codes. In this way a standard and fixed level of the classification scheme is made available to be used for all resources in library collections and represents a useful model of classification authority control. Occasionally, UDC codes in this widely used authority list have been extended and edited following requests from librarians. This was especially the case when the new translations of the UDC into Slovenian were published, based on releases of the UDC Master Reference File (UDC MRF) in 2001, 2006 and 2011. This poster outlines the effects of UDC MRF changes on the content of the authority list of UDC numbers and other Slovenian update experiences.

Keywords: Universal Decimal Classification; UDC; COBISS; COMARC; authority control; classification authority list; UDC summary; changes in UDC; UDC updates; Slovenia

1. The UDC - universal access to contents

At the beginning of the new millennium IFLA initiated the preparation of new international cataloguing principles that can be used in library catalogues accessible through the Web and also in the wider environment. Their main purpose is primarily to meet the needs of the users. The Statement places controlled subject headings and classification numbers for works among the essential elements of access (IFLA, 2009). International cataloguing principles allow the creation of library catalogues by modern principles, which will enable information flow and information exchange in a Semantic Web environment. Traditional library catalogues will be increasingly adapted to the requirements of the Semantic Web. Due to their ability to improve resource discovery, authority data files will become an important part of linked data. A proportion of the UDC scheme is already available and a complete UDC scheme is in preparation to be published as linked data on the open Web. This creates new opportunities for access, processing, linking and mapping of UDC data to other systems (Multilingual Universal Decimal Classification Summary - Linked Data, 2011).

Clearly, not only does authority control of names and subject vocabularies not lose its relevance, but an even more detailed authority control may be needed in the future. Authority control combines two procedures: determination of single elements by which a catalogue is structured and their linking with all the alternative forms of these elements (Dimec, 2002). By assigning class numbers to library materials, new metadata are created. In the online environment of linked data these metadata can be used anywhere, not only in a catalogue. The numeric character of the UDC allows language independent access to contents. contents. Very likely, the adaptation of the conventional catalogue records to the requirements of the Semantic Web will lead to the disaggregation of records, adding URIs, organizing triples, etc.

> "The Working Group on Subject Access by national bibliographic agencies recommends the following levels for subject indexing:
>
> - A full level, providing indexing with enhanced access by authoritative subject terms, as well as classification notations;
> - A minimal level, providing for most of the resources at least one controlled verbal access point and/or classification notations, if necessary shortened"
>
> (Guidelines for subject access in national bibliographies, 2012: 38).

For this reason, the level, the validity and the consistency of classification notations in bibliographic records have an important place.

2. The Slovenian cataloguing environment

The majority of the Slovenian libraries are part of the COBISS.SI bibliographic system with the union catalogue COBIB.SI. Records in the COBIB.SI catalogue follow the COMARC format. Bibliographic records are formed in COMARC format/B (COMARC/B format for bibliographic information, 2008). Authority records are formed in COMARC format/A (COMARC/A format for authority data, 2003). The COMARC format is developed and maintained by the Institute of Information Science (IZUM) in Maribor. Most of the fields in COMARC format/B have been taken from the UNIMARC bibliographic format (UNIMARC manual: bibliographic format, 2008). However, some fields in format/B were added to COMARC. They are treated differently or they have been attributed a different meaning than in the UNIMARC bibliographic format. For example, in the 675 field, subdivisions c, s and u have been added (Rogina, 2014).

A project developing the COBISS.SI General List of Subject Headings (SGC) has been running since 2000. The objectives are twofold: to prepare a uniform bilingual Slovene-English controlled vocabulary for the COBISS.SI system and, at the same time, to set up a corresponding authority database for subject headings (Zalokar, 2006).

2.1 UDC finding scheme – field 675 <c>

At the end of 1995, in order to ensure the consistency of classification codes, the Commission for cataloguing in COBISS.SI proposed the implementation of a controlled list of UDC notations for field 675 <c> that would be mandatory in the process of cataloguing. As a result, in 1996, an authority list of UDC numbers was compiled and implemented in COBISS.SI. The first list included

761 notations. For the classification of serials, a list of shorter notations was created containing only 249 notations. Five years later, the separate list for serial publications was abandoned. Since then, all the library materials as monographs, serials, articles, etc., are classified using the uniform 675<c> list (COMARC/B format for bibliographic information, 2008). With this mandatory authority UDC list, a minimum controlled classification level has been implemented in COBISS.SI.

The UDC authority list contains simple and compound UDC notations. The order in which UDC numbers are listed is the order in which they appear in the Master Reference File. In the authority list, some compound numbers containing the coordination sign +, the extension sign / and the relation sign : are included. The common auxiliaries of place such as (497.4), (4), (100) and the common auxiliaries of human ancestry, ethnic grouping and nationality, such as (=163.6) appear in many combinations with the main UDC numbers in the list.

Table 1: *Number of notations in the individual UDC main classes from 0 to 9 of the authority list in 1996, 2006, 2009 and 2014*

	0	1	2	3	5	6	7	8	9	sum
1991 short. ed.	55	21	15	194	105	178	75	80	38	761
2006 (MRF01)	89	31	42	222	120	207	109	108	46	974
2009 (MRF06)	96	32	45	243	131	214	115	110	40	1026
2014 (MRF11)	98	32	45	244	131	221	116	115	49	1051

So far, seven versions of the UDC summary authority list have been published in Slovenia: May 1996, February 2001, November 2002, December 2006, September 2008, August 2009 and December 2014. Table 1 represents the number of UDC notations appearing in the each of main UDC classes of the UDC authority list for the years 1996, 2005, 2009 and 2014.

The number of UDC notations has increased over the years. The most significant increase took place in 2006, when librarians gained access to the Slovenian translation of the complete UDC Master Reference File containing nearly 50,000 main UDC numbers, rather than 11,000 UDC numbers that were available in the old printed abridged UDC edition. As a result, the list of UDC numbers appearing in the field 675 <c> of the bibliographic record has increased by 28%. Later, due to the further expansion of UDC MRF06 and UDC MRF11 content and following the suggestions of librarians the increase continued. Today, the list includes 38% more UDC numbers than at the beginning.

2.1.1. Updates of the UDC authority scheme for field 675 <c>

Since the beginning of the nineties a significant part of the UDC scheme has been revised and updated. Every such major change in the standard classification scheme causes difficulties which are even more prominent in systems without authority control. Updates to the UDC scheme and informing librarians about the new extensions and corrections of the vocabulary are very important. In Slovenia, we organize regular courses for librarians to inform them about any such changes in the Master Reference File and in the authority code list for field 675<c> as well.. In addition, information about changes can be also found in the newsletter "Library news" ("Knjižničarske novice") where cancelled UDC numbers are published together with the redirections to the new (replacing) classes, as shown in Table 2 (see also COMARC/B format for bibliographic information, 2006).

Table 2: *The UDC authority list (codes for 675 <c>): redirections from cancelled to new UDC numbers*

The Old Entry	References
681.3 Computers. Hardware. Automated data processing	CANCELLED/see: 004.3
681.3.06 Computer programming (theory, languages and logic)	CANCELLED/see: 004.4
681.324 Computer networks	CANCELLED/see: 004.7

Information about related classes are also provided, as shown in Table 3, *see also* (COMARC/B format for bibliographic information, 2006):

Table 3: *The UDC authority list (codes for 675 <c>)*

Entry	See also
786/789 Music for individual instruments	Musical instruments, see: 681.8
81'24 Practical language skills	Textbooks look under the individual languages
811.1 Indo-European languages, with the exception of Oriental	The Oriental languages, Indo-European, see: 811.2/.3

The re-classification of some areas of the UDC scheme was carried out at the end of 2006. These were primarily classes which underwent an overhaul revision with a complete restructuring of hierarchies. The corresponding conversion table was prepared by the National and University Library in Ljubljana in collaboration with IZUM in Maribor (Rogina, 2006).

Table 4: *A part of the conversion table: Class 2 in the UDC authority list (codes for 675<c>)*

Cancelled UDC number	New UDC number
21	2-1
22.0	27-27
22.043	27-23
231	27-1
238	27-47
242/245	27-5
248	27-5
262	27-72
266/268	27-76
276	27-9
29	2
291	29

The conversion table was used to replace all cancelled with new UDC numbers in subfield 675<c> of bibliographic records.

3. Conclusion

The poster shows the development and use of the UDC summary authority List. i.e. codes for field 675<c> of bibliographic records in the COBISS.SI system, over the past 18 years. The authority list of UDC notations had to be expanded following changes in the UDC Master Reference File and subsequent Slovenian translations and editions. Although, outside of these main phases of development, the number of notations in the classification authority list has not increased so dramatically, the management and maintenance of the authority control system had to be set up to cope with continuous changes. The selection and input of UDC notations in the process of cataloguing is well controlled and easy to manage. Most importantly, we expect that it may play an important role in the process of integration of the traditional COMARC data into a linked data environment.

The evolution of knowledge is a continuous process and the classification of knowledge is subject to constant changes. Therefore the tools for maintaining and sharing of classification authority data will continue to demand the attention of both librarians and classification creators and developers.

References

COBISS.SI Virtualna knjižnica Slovenije: vzajemna baza podatkov: COBIB.SI. (2015). Available at: http://www.izum.si/scripts/cobiss?command=CONNECT&base=cobib.

COMARC/A format za normativne podatke. (2003). *Maribor: Institut informacijskih znanosti, IZUM.*

COMARC/B format za bibliografske podatke, priročnik za uporabnike. (2006). *Maribor: Institut informacijskih znanosti, IZUM.*

COMARC/B format za bibliografske podatke: priročnik za uporabnike. (2008). [online] Maribor: Institut informacijskih znanosti. Available at: http://izobrazevanje.izum.si/EntryFormDesktopDefault.aspx?tabid=38&type=manual&manual=Comarc_B_svn (accessed with user name and password).

Dimec, Z. (2002). Normativna kontrola iz preteklosti v prihodnost: ali se sedanjost odloča za mednarodno sodelovanje. *Knjižnica 46 (3),* pp. 91-104.

Guidelines for subject access in national bibliographies. (2012). Edited by Y. Jahns. München: K. G. Saur.

Multilingual Universal Decimal Classification Summary - Linked Data. (2011). The Hague: UDC Consortium. (UDCC Publication No. 088). Available at: http://udcdata.info/.

Rogina, A. (2006). Dopolnitve in popravki bibliografskih zapisov. Available at: http://home.izum.si/cobiss/obvestila_novosti/dokumenti/Konverzija_bibliografskih_baz_podatkov_priloga_20061017.pdf.

Rogina, A. (2014). Cataloging in COMARC format; now what? Some dilemmas as we see them in Maribor library. *Organizacija znanja* 19 (2), pp. 54-59.

IFLA (2009). Statement of International Cataloguing Principles. Available at: http://www.ifla.org/files/assets/cataloguing/icp/icp_2009-en.pdf.

Šauperl, A. et al. (2007). Conclusions from the Conference on the use of the UDC in Slovenia. *Extensions and Corrections to the UDC,* 29, pp. 21-23.

UNIMARC manual: bibliographic format. (2008). 3rd ed. *Edited by A. Hopkinson.* München: K. G. Saur.

Zalokar, M. (2006). Razvoj splošnega geslovnika COBISS.SI. *Organizacija znanja,* 11 (4). Available at: http://splet02.izum.si/cobiss-oz/news.jsp?apl=/2006_4/ar20.jsp.

DARIJA ROZMAN has been working at the National and University Library in Ljubljana since 1996. She was the head of the Subject Cataloguing Department at the National and University Library in Ljubljana from 1998 until 2013. Her main research interests are in cataloguing, especially subject cataloguing and classification (UDC specifically), on which she has published a number of papers. Darija initiated and led a project to publish a Slovenian UDC Manual in 2006. She is active in training for classification experts and in preparing librarians for qualifying examinations and continuing education which is organized by the Library Educational Centre at the National and University Library. Darija is a member of the editorial team of the General Slovenian Subject Headings List Online (Spletni splošni slovenski geslovnik) and a member of the UDC Advisory Board.

Visualization of a library collection based on UDC: research in the Warsaw University of Technology Main Library

Agnieszka Maria Kowalczuk
Main Library of Warsaw University of Technology, Warsaw, Poland

Łukasz Skonieczny
Warsaw University of Technology, Faculty of Electronics and Information Technology, Warsaw, Poland

Małgorzata Wornbard
Main Library of Warsaw University of Technology, Warsaw, Poland

Abstract: The aim of visualization of information is to improve the perception of information and by doing so acquire a better understanding of the knowledge space. Our research project in the Main Library of the Warsaw University of Technology (WUT ML) explores how the visualization of knowledge classes by which the library collection is organized may improve resource discovery and reveal information in primary data that otherwise may remain hidden. The assumption is that this would improve the understanding of information and provide better access to knowledge. The first step was to look into ways in which we can present graphically subject data from our catalogue. The expectation is that through the visualization of the rich catalogue data, it will be easier for users to see the wider context of a sought class and its connections with other knowledge classes. Each document in the WUT ML catalogue contains a UDC notation, keywords in Polish and a symbol from the local classification scheme. The project uses three types of catalogue data: UDC notation, keywords connected with the notation and the number of occurrences of the keyword with the UDC notation. The presentation of classes is based on the data from the current UDC Online English schedules (http://www.udc-hub.com/en/login.php). Research results presented in this poster are prepared using a visualization program - Data Driven Documents (D3), a JavaScript library for handling documents based on data. The visualization shows the knowledge classes in the WUT ML in relation to the knowledge classes from the UDC scheme i.e. the classes of library documents are shown alongside classes taken from UDC Online. At the same time users can view the keywords in Polish and a local classification scheme that are mapped to UDC - which provides flexibility in accessing subject content of the collection. We hope that our research illustrates the potential for providing more user-friendly and effective interfaces and improved subject access in library catalogues.

Keywords: library catalogues; interface; subject access; visualization; mapping; Main Library of the Warsaw University of Technology

Paper not submitted.
Presentation materials are available on the conference website: http://seminar.udcc.org/2015.

AGNIESZKA MARIA KOWALCZUK holds a graduate degree in General Pedagogy and a master degree in Information Science from the University of Warsaw. She has been working in the Main Library of the Warsaw University of Technology since 1995, where she manages the keywords authorities and is involved in the improvement of subject access in the main catalogue of WUT libraries. She works on the maintenance of the local classification system used for the systematic arrangement of open access. She organizes and conducts training for the employees of the WUT Library System.

ŁUKASZ SKONIECZNY has been working in the Institute of Computer Science at Warsaw University of Technology (WUT) since 2010. His research interest is in database systems, data-, text- and web-mining, graph theory and web development. He is the author of ten scientific papers and editor of three books. He is one of the main developers of the WUT Knowledge Base.

MAŁGORZATA WORNBARD holds a graduate degree in Russian Studies, Slavonic Studies and Applied Linguistics and a master degree in Information Science from the University of Warsaw. She is head of the Cataloguing Section of the Main Library of Warsaw University of Technology (WUT). At present, as a system librarian she coordinates collaboration with the National Universal Central Catalogue NUKAT. Wornbard supervises the online catalogue of the Main Library of WUT. Her research interest is in formal cataloguing in traditional and digital libraries, in particular with issues of iconographic documents on which she has presented at national conferences.

UDC as a standardisation method for providing titles of documents

Alenka Šauperl
University of Ljubljana, Ljubljana, Slovenia

Abstract: Some publications, e.g., postcards, have no text. Standards for library and archival description assume that elements of a description may be transcribed. When documents have no text, the description has to be provided by the librarian or archivist. If these specialists follow a different approach to construction of titles and other elements of description, duplicate records may appear in collaborative databases on the national (e.g., Dedi) and international level (e.g., Europeana). Universal Decimal Classification (UDC) syntax rules could be used to guide the construction of title information, which is important for identification. We suggest that construction of a title would follow the syntax of UDC numbers but in the language of the cataloguing agency. Equivalent UDC numbers could be provided in a subject description. For instance, for a Christmas card from 1915 with only a picture and year printed a cataloguer would form a title: Christmas postcard 1915 and subject description: 27-565.3(084.127) "1915".

Keywords: metadata; cultural heritage; postcards; harmonization; Universal Decimal Classification; UDC; libraries; archives; museums

Paper not submitted.
Presentation materials are available on the conference website: http://seminar.udcc.org/2015.

ALENKA ŠAUPERL is a Professor in the Department of Library and Information Science and Book Studies at the Faculty of Arts, University of Ljubljana. Her teaching and research areas are in the organization of information, including descriptive and subject cataloguing, as well as abstracting. She is also interested in aligning the descriptions of cultural heritage objects in libraries, archives and museums. She is the author of several books and many articles in the field of cataloguing, subject indexing and abstracting.

List of contributors

Subject index

A

B

C

D

E

F

G

H

I

J

K

L

V

W

X

Z

Organization: International UDC Seminar 2015

International UDC Seminar 2015 "Classification and Authority Control" took place between 29-30 October 2015 at the National Library of Portugal, Lisbon. This was the fifth biennial conference organized by the UDC Consortium.

Conference Chair

Maria Inês Cordeiro, UDC Consortium Chair, UDC Consortium

Programme Chair

Aida Slavic, UDC Editor-in-Chief, UDC Consortium

Programme Committee

Marie Balíková, Czech National Library, Czech Republic

Pino Buizza, University of Florence, Italy

Andrew Buxton, UDC Editorial Team, UK

Sylvie Davies, Robert Gordon University, UK

Gordon Dunsire, UK

Axel Ermert, Institute for Museum Studies, Berlin, Germany

Wei Fan, Sichuan University, China

Jonathan Furner, University of California, Los Angeles, USA

Claudio Gnoli, University of Pavia, Italy

Winfried Gödert, Cologne University of Applied Sciences, Germany

Rebecca Green, OCLC, USA

Antoine Isaac, Europeana & Vrije Universiteit Amsterdam, The Netherlands

Ulrike Junger, Deutsche Nationalbibliothek, Germany

Kathryn La Barre, University of Illinois at Urbana-Champaign, USA

Organization Committee

UDC
CONSORTIUM

The UDC Consortium is a non-profit association of publishers established to maintain, develop and distribute the Universal Decimal Classification for the benefit of its users.